POL MARTIN

EASY EVERYDAY
Cuisine

POL MARTIN

EASY EVERYDAY Cuisine

BRIMAR

Graphic Design: Zapp

Typesetting: Groupe Data Inc.

Photography: Marc Bruneau
Nathalie Dumouchel
Rodrigo Gutierrez

Food Preparation/Stylist: Josée Robitaille

Assistant Stylists: Marc Maulà
Louis Hudon

Props courtesy of: Arthur Quentin
Pier 1 Imports
Stokes

BRIMAR PUBLISHING INC.

338 St. Antoine St. East
Montreal, Canada
H2Y 1A3

Telephone: (514) 954-1441
Fax: (514) 954-5086

ISBN 2-89433-218-1
Printed in Canada

CONTENTS

◆

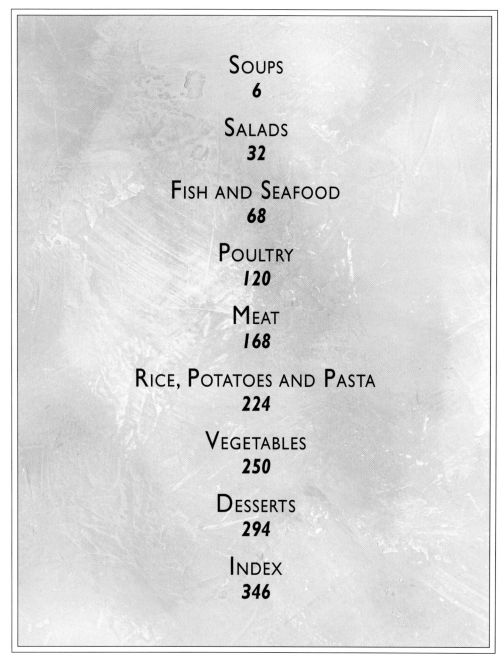

SOUPS
6

SALADS
32

FISH AND SEAFOOD
68

POULTRY
120

MEAT
168

RICE, POTATOES AND PASTA
224

VEGETABLES
250

DESSERTS
294

INDEX
346

SOUPS

Soups are one of the most satisfying categories of food, both to make and to eat. In fact, making soup from scratch is so easy and economical, you need not settle for ready-made varieties.

Most of the recipes in this chapter begin with a good soup stock; included are easy techniques for making flavorful stocks based on chicken, beef and fish. One thrifty suggestion is to save chicken and beef bones from other recipes in a plastic bag in the freezer, until you have enough to make a large batch of stock.

Why not keep a supply of chicken stock, for example, on hand in the refrigerator? It is versatile, keeps for four or five days, and is the basis of a number of tasty soups in this chapter.

From the more traditional *Vichyssoise* or *Minestrone Soup*, to a *Chicken Gumbo and Rice* or *Cream of Fresh Asparagus*, there is no end to the variety of easy yet exquisite soups you can make to suit every occasion and appetite.

Basic Chicken Stock

◆

(8 CUPS – 2 L)

5 lbs	cleaned chicken bones	2.3 kg
16 cups	water	4 L
2	fresh thyme sprigs	2
2	fresh parsley sprigs	2
1 tsp	rosemary	5 mL
1	clove	1
2	bay leaves	2
2	carrots, pared and diced	2
2	celery ribs, diced	2
2	onions, unpeeled, cut in 6	2
	salt and freshly ground pepper	

■ Place chicken bones in large stockpot. Add water and bring to a boil. As soon as liquid boils, skim constantly for 3 minutes.

■ Place fresh herbs, bay leaves and seasonings in piece of cheesecloth; secure with string. Add to stockpot along with remaining ingredients. Bring to a boil again; reduce heat to low and simmer 2 hours uncovered. Correct seasoning.

■ Strain stock through large sieve lined with cheesecloth. Cool; remove solidified fat. Cover and refrigerate. Keeps in the refrigerator 4 to 5 days.

1 SERVING			
Calories	334	Fat	6 g
Carbohydrate	45 g	Fiber	9.3 g
Protein	25 g	Cholesterol	0 mg

Basic Beef Stock

◆

(6 CUPS – 1.5 L)

2½ lbs	cleaned beef bones	1.2 kg
1	leek, pared and chopped	1
1	onion, peeled and chopped	1
1	carrot, peeled and diced	1
1	celery rib, diced	1
2	garlic cloves, peeled and crushed	2
12 cups	water	3 L
2	fresh thyme sprigs	2
2	fresh parsley sprigs	2
1	bay leaf	1
	freshly ground pepper	
	pinch of celery seeds	

■ Place beef bones in large stockpot. Cover with water and bring to a boil. As soon as liquid boils, remove bones from stockpot. Drain bones and rinse under cold water.

■ Return bones to stockpot. Add leek, onion, carrot, celery, garlic and water. Bring to a boil and skim well.

■ Add thyme, parsley, bay leaf, pepper and celery seeds. Simmer 2½ to 3 hours over low heat. Do not cover and skim as needed during cooking. Add water as needed.

■ Strain stock through large sieve lined with cheesecloth. Cool, cover with plastic wrap, ensuring that wrap is touching surface of soup, and refrigerate.

■ Keeps in the refrigerator 3 to 4 days. Remove solidified fat before using.

1 SERVING			
Calories	288	Fat	4 g
Carbohydrate	42 g	Fiber	7.2 g
Protein	21 g	Cholesterol	0 mg

Fish Stock

◆

(3 CUPS – 750 ML)

1 tbsp	butter	15 mL
2	onions, peeled and sliced	2
1	large carrot, pared and sliced	1
1	celery rib with leaves, sliced	1
20	fresh mushrooms, cleaned and sliced	20
2 lbs	fish bones (from white fish)	900 g
1	fresh thyme sprig	1
2	fresh parsley sprigs	2
2	bay leaves	2
½ tsp	fennel	2 mL
12	whole black peppercorns	12
1 cup	dry white wine	250 mL
4 cups	cold water	1 L
	salt	

■ Heat butter in saucepan over medium heat. Add vegetables, cover and cook 6 minutes over low heat.

■ Add fish bones, cover and cook 5 minutes.

■ Stir in remaining ingredients. Bring to a boil, reduce heat to low and simmer 20 minutes. Do not cover.

■ Strain stock into bowl and let cool. Cover with plastic wrap, ensuring that wrap is touching surface of soup, and refrigerate. Keeps in the refrigerator 2 to 3 days.

1 SERVING			
Calories	516	Fat	16 g
Carbohydrate	52 g	Fiber	10.8 g
Protein	21 g	Cholesterol	32 mg

Cabbage Soup

◆

1 tsp	olive oil	5 mL
2 oz	bacon, diced	60 g
1	small head green cabbage, cored and sliced	1
½ cup	fresh basil leaves	125 mL
1	fresh thyme sprig	1
1	garlic clove, peeled and halved	1
2	shallots, peeled and chopped	2
2	large potatoes, peeled and sliced	2
5 cups	chicken stock, heated	1.2 L
	freshly ground pepper	
	pinch of celery seeds	

■ Heat oil in saucepan over medium heat. Add bacon and cook 3 minutes.

■ Add cabbage, season with pepper and mix well. Cook 12 minutes over medium heat to brown cabbage.

■ Place all seasonings, including garlic, in piece of cheesecloth; secure with string. Add to saucepan along with remaining ingredients. Cook 18 minutes or until potatoes are cooked. Correct seasoning.

■ Serve with garlic bread.

1 SERVING			
Calories	230	Fat	10 g
Carbohydrate	23 g	Fiber	3.2 g
Protein	12 g	Cholesterol	12 mg

Potage à la Crécy

◆

(4 to 6 servings)

1 tbsp	olive oil	15 mL
1	onion, peeled and chopped	1
1	shallot, peeled and chopped	1
5	carrots, pared and sliced	5
3	potatoes, peeled and sliced	3
5	fresh basil leaves	5
5 cups	light chicken stock, heated	1.2 L
4	fresh celery leaves	4
	salt and freshly ground pepper	
	a few drops of lemon juice	
	heavy cream (35% MF – optional)	

- Heat oil in saucepan over medium heat. Add onion and shallot; cook 3 minutes over low heat.

- Add carrots and season well; cook 5 minutes.

- Stir in remaining ingredients, except lemon juice and cream. Cook soup until vegetables are well done.

- Pass soup through food mill or purée in food processor; place in clean bowl. Correct seasoning and add lemon juice. Add a little heavy cream, if desired, and serve.

1 SERVING

Calories	139	Fat	3 g
Carbohydrate	23 g	Fiber	3.7 g
Protein	5 g	Cholesterol	0 mg

Napa Broth Soup

◆

(4 SERVINGS)

2	Chinese noodle birds' nests	2
1 tsp	olive oil	5 mL
½	napa*, sliced crosswise ½-in (1-cm) wide	½
6 cups	rich chicken stock, heated	1.5 L
	soy sauce to taste	

■ Cook noodles 3 minutes in salted, boiling water. Drain well and rinse under cold, running water. Drain again and set aside.

■ Heat oil in saucepan over medium heat. Add napa and sauté 3 minutes over high heat.

■ Pour in chicken stock and add noodles. Simmer 3 to 4 minutes and serve with soy sauce.

* Look for birds' nests and napa – a Chinese cabbage – in Oriental specialty stores.

1 SERVING

Calories	175	Fat	3 g
Carbohydrate	29 g	Fiber	3.1 g
Protein	8 g	Cholesterol	0 mg

Soup Savoyarde

◆

(4 SERVINGS)

2	leeks, white part only	2
2 tbsp	butter	30 mL
4	onions, peeled and sliced	4
2	celery ribs, sliced	2
1	white turnip, peeled and sliced	1
2	potatoes, peeled and sliced	2
4 cups	light chicken stock, heated	1 L
1½ cups	scalded milk	375 mL
1 cup	grated Gruyère cheese	250 mL
	salt and freshly ground pepper	

■ Slit leeks from top to bottom twice, leaving 1 in (2.5 cm) intact at base. Wash leeks under cold, running water to remove dirt and sand. Drain and slice.

■ Heat butter in large saucepan over medium heat. Add onions and cook 16 minutes over low heat.

■ Add leeks and celery; mix well. Continue cooking 8 minutes.

■ Add turnip, potatoes and chicken stock. Season and cook soup 20 minutes over low heat.

■ Pour in milk and correct seasoning. Ladle soup into ovenproof soup bowls and top with cheese. Broil in oven until golden brown, about 6 minutes.

1 SERVING

Calories	355	Fat	15 g
Carbohydrate	39 g	Fiber	5.6 g
Protein	16 g	Cholesterol	45 mg

Chicken Gumbo and Rice

◆

(6 SERVINGS)

2	large chicken legs	2
4 tbsp	olive oil	60 mL
3 tbsp	flour	45 mL
2	onions, peeled and chopped	2
2	garlic cloves, peeled and sliced	2
1	celery rib, diced	1
¼ lb	fresh okra, pared and halved	110 g
1	sweet banana pepper, diced	1
4	tomatoes, peeled, seeded and chopped	4
½ tsp	cayenne pepper	2 mL
5 cups	chicken stock, heated	1.2 L
1	fresh thyme sprig	1
1	bay leaf	1
1 cup	long grain rice, rinsed	250 mL
	salt and freshly ground pepper	

■ Cut chicken legs in half at the joint between the thigh and drumstick. Remove skin and season pieces well. Set aside.

■ Heat 3 tbsp (45 mL) of oil in small saucepan over medium heat. Sprinkle in flour and mix well; cook over low heat until golden brown. Remove and set aside.

■ Heat remaining oil in large saucepan over medium heat. Add onions, garlic and celery; cook 4 minutes.

■ Add okra and sweet banana pepper. Stir and cook 6 minutes over low heat.

■ Add chicken pieces and mix well. Cook 8 minutes over medium heat, turning pieces over once.

■ Add remaining ingredients, except rice, and cook 20 minutes over low heat.

■ Add rice and continue cooking 18 to 20 minutes. When rice is cooked, mix browned flour with ½ cup (125 mL) of liquid from soup. Incorporate into soup and simmer 5 minutes. Remove bay leaf and serve.

1 SERVING			
Calories	329	Fat	13 g
Carbohydrate	38 g	Fiber	3.8 g
Protein	15 g	Cholesterol	29 mg

Sprinkle flour into oil and mix well; cook over low heat until golden brown.

Heat remaining oil over medium heat. Add onions, garlic and celery; cook 4 minutes.

Add okra and sweet banana pepper. Stir and cook 6 minutes over low heat.

Add chicken pieces and mix well.
Cook 8 minutes over medium heat,
turning pieces over once.

Add remaining ingredients,
except rice, and cook 20 minutes
over low heat.

Add rice and continue cooking
18 to 20 minutes.

17

Purée of Brussels Sprouts

◆

(4 TO 6 SERVINGS)

1 lb	Brussels sprouts	450 g
3 tbsp	butter	45 mL
2	shallots, peeled and sliced	2
1 tbsp	chopped fresh chives	15 mL
1 tbsp	chopped fresh tarragon	15 mL
2	potatoes, peeled and sliced	2
4½ cups	chicken stock, heated	1.1 L
¼ cup	heavy cream (35% MF – optional)	50 mL
	salt and pepper	

■ Remove outer leaves from Brussels sprouts and discard. Wash Brussels sprouts well. Using a paring knife, score an "X" on stems. This technique promotes even cooking.

■ Place Brussels sprouts in a pot of salted, boiling water. Cook 12 minutes; drain well.

■ Heat butter in saucepan over medium heat. Add Brussels sprouts, shallots, chives and tarragon. Season well, cover and cook 6 minutes over low heat.

■ Add potatoes and chicken stock. Season and cook soup 20 minutes over low heat. Do not cover.

■ Pass soup through food mill or purée in food processor; place in clean bowl. Incorporate cream, if desired, and correct seasoning. Serve.

1 SERVING			
Calories	142	Fat	6 g
Carbohydrate	17 g	Fiber	4.5 g
Protein	5 g	Cholesterol	16 mg

Vegetable and Lentil Soup

◆

(4 SERVINGS)

1 tbsp	olive oil	15 mL
1	onion, peeled and chopped	1
1	garlic clove, peeled, crushed and chopped	1
1	celery rib, diced finely	1
1 cup	dried lentils, rinsed	250 mL
6 cups	light chicken stock, heated	1.5 L
1	fresh thyme sprig	1
2	fresh parsley sprigs	2
1	bay leaf	1
2	small potatoes, peeled and diced	2
1	green bell pepper, diced	1
1	red bell pepper, diced	1
	salt and freshly ground pepper	

■ Heat oil in saucepan over medium heat. Add onion, garlic and celery. Cook 3 minutes over low heat. Add lentils and chicken stock.

■ Tie fresh herbs and bay leaf together. Add to liquid, season well and bring to a boil. Cook 1 hour, partly covered.

■ Add remaining ingredients and continue cooking 30 minutes.

■ Remove herbs, sprinkle with fresh chopped herbs and serve.

1 SERVING

Calories	229	Fat	5 g
Carbohydrate	35 g	Fiber	6.0 g
Protein	11 g	Cholesterol	0 mg

Stir in turnip, bell pepper, potatoes and cabbage.

Pour in chicken stock and season well.

Tie thyme, parsley and bay leaf together; add to soup. Bring to a boil.

Minestrone Soup

◆

(4 TO 6 SERVINGS)

2 tbsp	olive oil	30 mL
1	onion, peeled and chopped	1
1	celery rib, diced	1
2	carrots, pared and diced	2
1	small turnip, peeled and diced	1
1	green bell pepper, diced	1
2	potatoes, peeled and diced	2
¼	small head green cabbage, sliced	¼
5 cups	chicken stock, heated	1.2 L
1	fresh thyme sprig	1
2	fresh parsley sprigs	2
1	bay leaf	1
4	large tomatoes, peeled, seeded and chopped	4
2	large garlic cloves, peeled, crushed and chopped	2
1 tbsp	chopped fresh basil	15 mL
½ cup	small dry pasta	125 mL
½ cup	cooked white beans	125 mL
	salt and freshly ground pepper	
	grated Parmesan cheese	

■ Heat half of oil in large saucepan over medium heat. Add onion, celery and carrots; cook 4 minutes over low heat.

■ Stir in turnip, bell pepper, potatoes and cabbage. Pour in chicken stock and season well.

■ Tie thyme, parsley and bay leaf together; add to soup. Bring to a boil and cook until vegetables are tender.

■ Heat remaining oil in frying pan over medium heat. Add tomatoes, garlic and basil; season well. Cook 5 minutes over high heat and add to soup.

■ Add pasta and beans. Correct seasoning and cook 10 minutes over low heat. Remove herbs and serve with grated Parmesan.

1 SERVING			
Calories	235	Fat	7 g
Carbohydrate	34 g	Fiber	5.4 g
Protein	9 g	Cholesterol	4 mg

Heat remaining oil in frying pan; add tomatoes, garlic and basil. Season well and cook 5 minutes.

Add pasta and beans. Correct seasoning and cook 10 minutes over low heat.

Garden Bounty Soup

◆

(4 TO 6 SERVINGS)

1	leek, white part only	1
1 tbsp	olive oil	15 mL
2	onions, peeled and diced	2
1	celery rib, diced	1
2	carrots, pared and diced	2
2	potatoes, peeled and diced	2
1	small white turnip, peeled and diced	1
¼	head green cabbage, sliced	¼
6 cups	light chicken stock, heated	1.5 L
2	fresh parsley sprigs	2
1	fresh tarragon sprig	1
1	bay leaf	1
1	green bell pepper, diced	1
	salt and freshly ground pepper	
	grated Swiss cheese	

■ Slit leek from top to bottom twice, leaving 1 in (2.5 cm) intact at base. Wash leek under cold, running water to remove dirt and sand. Drain and slice.

■ Heat oil in saucepan over medium heat. Add leek, onions, celery and carrots; cook 4 minutes.

■ Add potatoes, turnip and cabbage. Pour in chicken stock and season generously.

■ Tie herbs together, add to soup and cook 18 minutes over low heat.

■ Add bell pepper and cook 3 minutes. Remove herbs, correct seasoning and serve with grated Swiss cheese.

1 SERVING			
Calories	156	Fat	4 g
Carbohydrate	24 g	Fiber	4.2 g
Protein	6 g	Cholesterol	4 mg

Vichyssoise

◆

(4 TO 6 SERVINGS)

2	leeks, white part only	2
2 tbsp	butter	30 mL
1	onion, peeled and sliced	1
1	fresh thyme sprig	1
2	fresh parsley sprigs	2
4	fresh basil leaves	4
1	bay leaf	1
4	large potatoes, peeled and sliced	4
5 cups	light chicken stock, heated	1.2 L
½ cup	heavy cream (35% MF)	125 mL
	salt and freshly ground pepper	
	chopped fresh chives	

■ Slit leeks from top to bottom twice, leaving 1 in (2.5 cm) intact at base. Wash leeks under cold, running water to remove dirt and sand. Drain and slice.

■ Heat butter in saucepan over medium heat. Add leeks and onion. Cover and cook 6 minutes over low heat.

■ Tie herbs together and add to soup along with potatoes and chicken stock. Season well and cook 30 minutes over low heat.

■ Remove herbs and pass soup through food mill or purée in food processor. Cool and stir in heavy cream. Cover with plastic wrap and refrigerate 3 hours before serving. Garnish with chopped chives.

1 SERVING			
Calories	224	Fat	12 g
Carbohydrate	24 g	Fiber	2.8 g
Protein	5 g	Cholesterol	37 mg

Scallop and Mushroom Soup

◆

(4 TO 6 SERVINGS)

1	shallot, peeled and chopped finely	1
1 lb	fresh scallops, cleaned	450 g
½ lb	fresh mushrooms, cleaned and cut in 3	225 g
2	green onions, chopped	2
2	potatoes, peeled and diced small	2
1 cup	dry white wine	250 mL
5 cups	water	1.2 L
½ tsp	fennel seeds	2 mL
1 tsp	chopped fresh parsley	5 mL
4 tbsp	butter	60 mL
4 tbsp	flour	60 mL
	salt and pepper	
	cayenne pepper to taste	
	chopped fresh parsley	

■ Place shallot, scallops, mushrooms, green onions and potatoes in saucepan. Pour in wine and water. Add fennel seeds, 1 tsp (5 mL) chopped parsley, and season well.

■ Bring to a slow boil over medium heat. Scallops will become opaque when cooked. Using slotted spoon, remove cooked scallops and set aside.

■ Continue cooking liquid and vegetables 15 minutes over medium heat, or until potatoes are cooked.

■ Heat butter in sauté pan over medium heat. Sprinkle in flour and mix well; cook 1 minute. Add 2 cups (500 mL) of cooking liquid from scallops and whisk to incorporate.

■ Pour contents of sauté pan into saucepan. Whisk liquids to incorporate and cook 3 minutes.

■ Return scallops to soup and simmer 1 minute over low heat. Add chopped fresh parsley and cayenne pepper and serve.

1 SERVING

Calories	197	Fat	8 g
Carbohydrate	14 g	Fiber	1.8 g
Protein	14 g	Cholesterol	46 mg

Fresh Clam Chowder

◆

(4 SERVINGS)

36	fresh clams	36
3	potatoes, peeled and diced	3
2 tbsp	butter	30 mL
1	onion, peeled and diced	1
1	green bell pepper, diced	1
2 tbsp	flour	30 mL
1½ cups	water	375 mL
1½ cups	clam juice	375 mL
2	green onions, chopped	2
1 cup	light cream, scalded	250 mL
1 tbsp	chopped fresh parsley	15 mL
	salt and freshly ground pepper	
	a few drops of Tabasco sauce	

■ Steam fresh clams and reserve ½ cup (125 mL) of steaming liquid. Chop clams and set aside.

■ Pour reserved steaming liquid into saucepan. Add potatoes and cover with water. Season and bring to a boil. Cook until potatoes are done. Drain and set aside.

■ Heat butter in saucepan over medium heat. Add onion and bell pepper; cook 2 minutes. Sprinkle in flour, mix well and cook 1 minute.

■ Incorporate water and clam juice; mix well. Bring to a boil, season and cook 4 minutes over medium heat.

■ Add potatoes, chopped clams, green onions and cream. Simmer soup 3 minutes.

■ Add Tabasco sauce and correct seasoning. Sprinkle with parsley and serve.

1 SERVING			
Calories	297	Fat	13 g
Carbohydrate	27 g	Fiber	2.3 g
Protein	18 g	Cholesterol	72 mg

Cold Lettuce Soup

◆

(4 TO 6 SERVINGS)

2 tbsp	butter	30 mL
3	large shallots, peeled and sliced	3
1	garlic clove, peeled and sliced	1
1	head Boston lettuce, washed and sliced	1
10	fresh celery leaves	10
10	fresh basil leaves	10
3	large potatoes, peeled and sliced	3
4 cups	light chicken stock, heated	1 L
	salt and freshly ground pepper	
	grated rind of 1 small lemon	
	a few drops of Tabasco sauce	

■ Heat butter in saucepan over medium heat. Add shallots and garlic; cook 3 minutes over low heat.

■ Add lettuce, celery and basil leaves. Season well, cover and cook 10 minutes over low heat.

■ Add remaining ingredients except lemon rind and mix well. Cook uncovered over low heat until potatoes are done. Correct seasoning.

■ Force soup through sieve or pass through food mill into clean bowl. Refrigerate before serving. Top with dollops of sour cream, if desired, and garnish with lemon rind.

1 SERVING			
Calories	112	Fat	4 g
Carbohydrate	15 g	Fiber	2.0 g
Protein	4 g	Cholesterol	10 mg

Old-Fashioned Beef Soup

◆

(4 SERVINGS)

1 tbsp	olive oil	15 mL
2	onions, peeled and diced large	2
2	garlic cloves, peeled and sliced	2
1½ lbs	beef chuck, cut into 1½-in (3.5-cm) cubes	675 g
5 cups	water	1.2 L
2	fresh parsley sprigs	2
1	fresh thyme sprig	1
1	bay leaf	1
4	potatoes, peeled and diced large	4
1 cup	large, dry macaroni shells	250 mL
1 cup	canned baby corn, drained	250 mL
1 cup	tomato juice	250 mL
	salt and freshly ground pepper	

■ Heat oil in large saucepan over medium heat. Add onions and garlic; cook 3 minutes over low heat.

■ Add beef, season well with pepper and cook 5 minutes.

■ Pour in water and bring to a boil. Skim and season well.

■ Tie herbs together and add to soup. Season well and cook 2 hours over low heat. Skim as needed during cooking.

■ Add potatoes and cook 6 minutes.

■ Add macaroni, corn and tomato juice. Cook 10 minutes. Remove herbs, correct seasoning and serve.

1 SERVING			
Calories	544	Fat	12 g
Carbohydrate	60 g	Fiber	5.5 g
Protein	49 g	Cholesterol	102 mg

Pare asparagus and trim stem ends.
Cut stalks into 1-in (2.5-cm) pieces.

Place asparagus, onion and
chicken stock in large saucepan.
Season well and bring to a boil.

Drain vegetables, reserving
stock and several asparagus
tips for garnishing.

Cream of Fresh Asparagus

◆

(4 SERVINGS)

1 lb	fresh asparagus	450 g
1	onion, peeled and quartered	1
5 cups	light chicken stock, heated	1.2 L
3 tbsp	butter	45 mL
3 tbsp	flour	45 mL
4 tbsp	heavy cream (35% MF – optional)	60 mL
1 cup	croûtons	250 mL
	salt and freshly ground pepper	

■ Pare asparagus and trim stem ends. Cut stalks into 1-in (2.5-cm) pieces.

■ Place asparagus, onion and chicken stock in large saucepan. Season well and bring to a boil. Cook 8 minutes over medium heat or until tender.

■ Drain vegetables, reserving stock and several asparagus tips for garnishing.

■ Purée vegetables in food processor.

■ Heat butter in clean saucepan over medium heat. Sprinkle in flour and mix well. Cook 1 minute.

■ Incorporate reserved stock and puréed vegetables. Correct seasoning.

■ Add cream, if desired, and simmer 5 minutes over low heat.

■ Garnish servings with croûtons and asparagus tips, and serve.

1 SERVING			
Calories	252	Fat	12 g
Carbohydrate	27 g	Fiber	3.9 g
Protein	9 g	Cholesterol	24 mg

Heat butter over medium heat. Sprinkle in flour and mix well.

Incorporate reserved stock and puréed vegetables.

Add cream, if desired, and simmer 5 minutes over low heat.

Gazpacho

♦

(6 SERVINGS)

2-3	garlic cloves, peeled, crushed and chopped	2-3
1 cup	cubed soft French bread, crust trimmed	250 mL
3-4 tbsp	wine vinegar	45-60 mL
4	tomatoes, peeled and seeded	4
1 tbsp	tomato paste	15 mL
2	small cucumbers, peeled and seeded	2
1	green bell pepper, diced	1
½ cup	olive oil	125 mL
2 cups	cold water	500 mL
1½ cups	spicy tomato juice	375 mL
2 tbsp	chopped fresh chives	30 mL
	salt and freshly ground pepper	
	a few drops of Tabasco sauce	
	a few drops of lime juice	

■ Place garlic in large mortar and purée. Add bread and vinegar; grind into paste with pestle.

■ Place garlic paste, tomatoes, tomato paste, cucumber and bell pepper in food processor. Blend to desired consistency. Transfer mixture to bowl, cover and chill 30 minutes.

■ Whisk oil into blended vegetables until well-incorporated. Add all remaining ingredients and season well.

■ Cover and refrigerate soup at least 1 hour. Garnish servings with a slice of lime, if desired.

1 SERVING			
Calories	253	Fat	21 g
Carbohydrate	14 g	Fiber	2.6 g
Protein	2 g	Cholesterol	0 mg

SALADS

Not so many years ago, salad was considered primarily a summertime food. Not any more. Salads are a refreshing and nutritious addition to any meal, any time of the year.

Of course, one of the advantages nowadays is the wonderful variety of salad ingredients that are readily available all year round. In addition to old standards such as Romaine and Boston lettuce, we can now find Belgian endive, watercress, radicchio and arugula to add color and zing to salad combinations.

But salads made without greens can be just as interesting. Some favorite winter salads included in this chapter are based on old-fashioned vegetables such as beets, leeks and cabbage. Along with pasta, cold meat and seafood salads, these salads make hearty main course meals in themselves.

But whichever type of salad you prepare, presentation is important. It takes only a few extra seconds to arrange ingredients as creatively as professional food stylists, and the results speak for themselves.

Belgian Endive Salad

◆

(4 SERVINGS)

SALAD:

5	large Belgian endives	5
1	red onion, peeled and sliced in rings	1
1	large apple, cored, peeled and sliced	1
1 tbsp	chopped fresh parsley	15 mL
	salt and freshly ground pepper	
	lemon juice	

■ Core endives and separate into leaves. Rinse under cold water and dry thoroughly. Slice leaves in half and place in large bowl.

■ Add onion, apple and parsley. Season generously and sprinkle with lemon juice. Toss gently.

VINAIGRETTE:

2	shallots, peeled and chopped finely	2
2	blanched garlic cloves, puréed	2
3 tbsp	balsamic vinegar	45 mL
9 tbsp	olive oil	135 mL
3 tbsp	sour cream	45 mL
1 tbsp	chopped fresh parsley	15 mL
	salt and pepper	

■ Place shallots and garlic in bowl. Add vinegar, salt and pepper; whisk together.

■ Add oil and whisk to incorporate. Mix in sour cream, correct seasoning and pour over salad. Add parsley and serve.

1 SERVING

Calories	362	Fat	34 g
Carbohydrate	12 g	Fiber	1.1 g
Protein	2 g	Cholesterol	4 mg

Cold Julienne of Vegetables with Apples

◆

(4 SERVINGS)

½ lb	green beans, pared	225 g
1	celery rib, in julienne	1
2	carrots, pared and in julienne	2
1	yellow bell pepper, in julienne	1
1	orange bell pepper, in julienne	1
1	small cucumber, peeled, seeded and in thick julienne	1
14	mushrooms, cleaned and sliced	14
2	apples, cored, peeled and sliced	2
1 tsp	Dijon mustard	5 mL
⅓ cup	mayonnaise	75 mL
1 tbsp	sour cream	15 mL
¼ cup	toasted slivered almonds	50 mL
	salt and freshly ground pepper	
	lemon juice	
	a few drops of Worcestershire sauce	
	cleaned mixed greens	
	chopped fresh parsley	

■ Cook beans 5 minutes in salted, boiling water. Remove beans with slotted spoon and transfer to bowl of cold water. Add celery and carrots to boiling water; cook 4 minutes. Transfer to bowl of cold water.

■ Drain cooked vegetables and pat dry with paper towels.

■ Place cooked and raw vegetables in large bowl. Add apples and season generously.

■ In separate bowl, mix mustard with mayonnaise and sour cream. Pour dressing over salad and mix well.

■ Season with salt, pepper, lemon juice and Worcestershire sauce. Mix well.

■ Line serving plates with mixed greens and top with vegetables. Sprinkle with toasted almonds and parsley. Serve.

1 SERVING			
Calories	303	Fat	19 g
Carbohydrate	27 g	Fiber	5.9 g
Protein	6 g	Cholesterol	11 mg

Marinated Mushrooms

◆

(4 SERVINGS)

½ cup	olive oil	125 mL
¾ cup	wine vinegar	175 mL
¾ cup	dry white wine	175 mL
2	garlic cloves, peeled, crushed and chopped	2
1	fresh parsley sprig	1
1	fresh thyme sprig	1
1	bay leaf	1
12	whole black peppercorns	12
1½ lbs	fresh mushrooms, cleaned	675 g
	pinch of coriander and fennel seeds	
	salt and freshly ground pepper	
	lemon juice	

■ Place all ingredients, except mushrooms and 3 tbsp (45 mL) of oil, in large saucepan. Bring to a boil and simmer marinade 12 minutes.

■ Heat remaining oil in large frying pan. Add mushrooms and season well; cook 4 minutes.

■ Transfer mushrooms to saucepan containing marinade. Mix well and let cool on counter. Cover with plastic wrap, ensuring that wrap touches surface of marinade, and refrigerate before serving.

1 SERVING			
Calories	171	Fat	13 g
Carbohydrate	7 g	Fiber	1.5 g
Protein	2 g	Cholesterol	0 mg

Charred Garlic Peppers

◆

(4 SERVINGS)

2	red bell peppers	2
2	green bell peppers	2
2	yellow bell peppers	2
4 tbsp	balsamic vinegar	60 mL
6 tbsp	olive oil	90 mL
3	garlic cloves, peeled, crushed and chopped	3
1 tbsp	chopped fresh parsley	15 mL
	salt and freshly ground pepper	
	lemon juice	

■ Cut bell peppers in half and remove seeds. Oil skin and place cut-side-down on cookie sheet; broil 6 to 10 minutes. When peppers are charred, remove from oven and let cool. Peel off skin, slice each half into three and set aside.

■ Mix vinegar, oil, garlic, parsley, salt and pepper in small bowl. Pour over peppers.

■ Sprinkle with lemon juice and season with freshly ground pepper. Marinate peppers 2 hours at room temperature. Turn peppers over several times during process.

■ Serve at room temperature.

1 SERVING			
Calories	220	Fat	20 g
Carbohydrate	9 g	Fiber	1.7 g
Protein	1 g	Cholesterol	0 mg

Cut off tips and stems
from artichokes.

Rub lemon over cut edges.

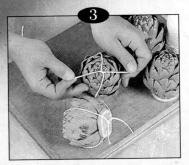

Secure lemon slices to base
with kitchen string.

38

Fresh Artichokes

◆

(4 SERVINGS)

4	large artichokes	4
4	slices of lemon	4
2	shallots, peeled and chopped	2
1 tbsp	Dijon mustard	15 mL
1 tbsp	chopped fresh parsley	15 mL
4 tbsp	balsamic vinegar	60 mL
¾ cup	olive oil	175 mL
	salt and freshly ground pepper	
	lemon juice to taste	

■ Cut off tips and stems from artichokes. Rub lemon over cut edges and secure lemon slices to base with kitchen string.

■ Place artichokes in salted, boiling water. Cook 30 to 40 minutes or according to size. Center leaves should detach easily when cooked.

■ Meanwhile, prepare vinaigrette. Place shallots, mustard, parsley, vinegar and oil in bowl. Season generously and whisk thoroughly. Add lemon juice and set aside.

■ When artichokes are done, place pot under cold, running water to stop cooking process. Drain very well and arrange artichokes on serving dishes.

■ Whisk vinaigrette and serve with artichokes.

■ To eat artichokes, detach leaves with fingers and dip meaty ends in vinaigrette. Only the soft part of the leaf is eaten. Once all the leaves are detached, the inedible choke is exposed. Cut away and discard this part. The remaining heart and bottom can be eaten.

1 SERVING			
Calories	463	Fat	43 g
Carbohydrate	15 g	Fiber	0 g
Protein	4 g	Cholesterol	0 mg

Place artichokes in salted, boiling water.

Salade Niçoise

◆

(4 TO 6 SERVINGS)

8	anchovy fillets	8
2 lbs	tomatoes, cored and quartered	900 g
1	cucumber, peeled, seeded and sliced	1
½ lb	green beans, pared and blanched	225 g
1	green bell pepper, sliced	1
1	yellow bell pepper, sliced	1
1 cup	pitted green olives	250 mL
1 tbsp	chopped fresh parsley	15 mL
4	blanched garlic cloves, puréed	4
6-8 tbsp	olive oil	90-120 mL
2 tbsp	chopped fresh basil	30 mL
3	hard-boiled eggs, quartered	3
	cleaned mixed greens for presentation	
	salt and freshly ground pepper	
	juice of 1½ lemons	

■ Soak anchovy fillets in cold water. Drain well and pat dry with paper towels. Chop coarsely.

■ Line serving platter with mixed greens. Set aside.

■ Place vegetables, olives, anchovies and parsley in bowl. Season generously and mix well.

■ In separate bowl, mix garlic with lemon juice, salt and pepper. Whisk in oil and basil. Pour dressing over salad ingredients and mix well.

■ Spoon salad onto serving platter. Stud with wedges of hard-boiled egg and season with freshly ground pepper.

1 SERVING			
Calories	291	Fat	23 g
Carbohydrate	14 g	Fiber	3.3 g
Protein	7 g	Cholesterol	112 mg

Tomato Bacon Salad

◆

(4 SERVINGS)

VINAIGRETTE:

3 tbsp	balsamic vinegar	45 mL
9 tbsp	olive oil	135 mL
2	garlic cloves, peeled, crushed and chopped	2
2 tbsp	chopped fresh basil	30 mL
	salt and freshly ground pepper	

■ Combine all ingredients together in small bowl and set aside.

SALAD:

5	tomatoes, cored, halved and sliced	5
3	shallots, peeled and chopped	3
2	avocados, pitted, peeled and sliced	2
6	bacon slices, cooked crisp and chopped	6
½ lb	Feta cheese, diced	225 g
4	canned hearts of palm, drained and diced	4
	freshly ground pepper	

■ Combine tomatoes, shallots, avocados and bacon in large bowl. Add cheese and hearts of palm. Season generously with freshly ground pepper.

■ Pour in vinaigrette and mix well. Correct seasoning and serve.

1 SERVING			
Calories	743	Fat	63 g
Carbohydrate	27 g	Fiber	4.4 g
Protein	17 g	Cholesterol	59 mg

Mixed Greens
with Avocado Dressing

◆

(4 SERVINGS)

1	head Boston lettuce	1
1	head Romaine lettuce	1
1	head radicchio lettuce, cored	1
1	large ripe avocado	1
3	blanched garlic cloves, puréed	3
4 tbsp	lemon juice	60 mL
4 tbsp	olive oil	60 mL
3 tbsp	sour cream	45 mL
	salt and pepper	
	a few drops of Tabasco sauce	

■ Separate lettuce into leaves and wash well in cold water. Drain and dry thoroughly. Tear leaves into smaller pieces and set aside in large salad bowl.

■ Cut avocado in half, lengthwise. Twist halves apart and remove pit. Peel and cut flesh into pieces. Purée in mortar.

■ Place puréed avocado and garlic in bowl; mix well. Add lemon juice and olive oil; mix until well-incorporated. Season to taste, then mix in sour cream. Stir in a few drops of Tabasco sauce.

■ Pour dressing over lettuce, toss and serve.

1 SERVING

Calories	258	Fat	22 g
Carbohydrate	11 g	Fiber	2.8 g
Protein	4 g	Cholesterol	4 mg

German-Style Potato Salad

◆

(4 SERVINGS)

6	potatoes, cleaned	6
3 tbsp	lemon juice	45 mL
½ cup	olive oil	125 mL
1	red onion, peeled and chopped	1
1 tsp	horseradish	5 mL
⅓ cup	sour cream	75 mL
1 tbsp	chopped fresh dill	15 mL
	salt and freshly ground pepper	
	pinch of granulated sugar	

■ Boil unpeeled potatoes until cooked. Peel potatoes while still warm, dice and place in large bowl.

■ Pour lemon juice into separate bowl. Add oil and mix well.

■ Season well and stir in remaining ingredients. Pour dressing over potatoes and mix thoroughly.

1 SERVING			
Calories	453	Fat	33 g
Carbohydrate	35 g	Fiber	3.1 g
Protein	4 g	Cholesterol	7 mg

Marinated Apple Slaw

◆

(6 SERVINGS)

1	small green cabbage	1
3	apples, cored and sliced	3
1	carrot, pared and in fine julienne	1
1	onion, peeled and grated	1
½ cup	mayonnaise	125 mL
½ cup	buttermilk	125 mL
1 tsp	horseradish	5 mL
2 tbsp	chopped fresh dill	30 mL
	salt and freshly ground pepper	
	lemon juice to taste	

■ Core cabbage and remove outer leaves. Cut cabbage into quarters and slice in fine julienne. Place in large bowl. Add apples, carrot and onion.

■ Mix remaining ingredients together in separate bowl. Pour over cabbage and mix until well-combined. Season generously.

■ Cover with waxed paper, ensuring that cover is touching surface of salad, and marinate 3 hours in refrigerator before serving.

1 SERVING			
Calories	219	Fat	15 g
Carbohydrate	19 g	Fiber	2.7 g
Protein	2 g	Cholesterol	11 mg

Watercress and Radicchio Salad

◆

(4 SERVINGS)

VINAIGRETTE:

3	blanched garlic cloves, puréed	3
3	anchovy fillets, rinsed and chopped	3
2	shallots, peeled and chopped	2
1 tbsp	Dijon mustard	15 mL
3 tbsp	balsamic vinegar	45 mL
9 tbsp	olive oil	135 mL
	salt and freshly ground pepper	
	lemon juice to taste	

SALAD:

1	red bell pepper	1
1	yellow bell pepper	1
3	bunches watercress	3
1	small radicchio lettuce, cored	1
12	cherry tomatoes, halved	12
12	pitted marinated olives	12
	salt and pepper	

■ Mix all vinaigrette ingredients, except lemon juice, in bowl. Whisk in lemon juice and set aside.

■ Cut bell peppers in half and remove seeds. Oil skin and place cut-side-down on cookie sheet; broil 6 minutes. Remove from oven and let cool. Peel off skin, slice peppers and set aside.

■ Trim stem ends of watercress. Separate radicchio into leaves and wash with watercress in cold water. Drain and dry thoroughly.

■ Place greens in large bowl. Add remaining ingredients and mix. Pour in dressing and toss until well-combined. Season well and serve.

1 SERVING

Calories	367	Fat	35 g
Carbohydrate	10 g	Fiber	2.2 g
Protein	3 g	Cholesterol	2 mg

Salade Drolet

◆

(4 SERVINGS)

VINAIGRETTE:

2 tbsp	green peppercorns, mashed	30 mL
1 tbsp	Dijon mustard	15 mL
2	blanched garlic cloves, puréed	2
¼ cup	balsamic vinegar	50 mL
¾ cup	olive oil	175 mL
	salt and freshly ground pepper	
	lemon juice to taste	

SALAD:

8	cooked ham slices	8
1	head Romaine lettuce	1
1	bunch asparagus	1
2	avocados	2
4	bacon slices, cooked crisp and chopped	4
4	hard-boiled eggs, quartered	4
1 cup	Garlic Croûtons (see page 65)	250 mL
	salt and freshly ground pepper	

■ Combine all vinaigrette ingredients, except lemon juice, in small bowl. Whisk in lemon juice and set aside.

■ Roll slices of ham and cut each roll in half; set aside. Separate lettuce into leaves and wash well in cold water. Drain and dry thoroughly. Tear leaves into smaller pieces and set aside in large salad bowl.

■ Pare asparagus if necessary and trim stem ends. Cook stalks in salted, boiling water until tender. Drain well and pat dry with paper towels. Cut stalks into 3 pieces and add to salad bowl.

■ Cut avocados in half, lengthwise. Twist halves apart and remove pit. Peel, slice flesh and add to bowl along with bacon, eggs and croûtons.

■ Season generously and pour in dressing. Mix well and arrange on serving platter. Top with ham rolls and serve.

1 SERVING

Calories	862	Fat	74 g
Carbohydrate	22 g	Fiber	4.2 g
Protein	27 g	Cholesterol	249 mg

Hearty Sliced Beef and Rice Salad

◆

(4 SERVINGS)

VINAIGRETTE:

1 tbsp	Dijon mustard	15 mL
2	shallots, peeled and chopped	2
2	garlic cloves, peeled, crushed and chopped	2
¼ cup	wine vinegar	50 mL
¾ cup	olive oil	175 mL
	salt and freshly ground pepper	
	lemon juice to taste	

■ Place mustard in bowl. Add shallots, garlic and vinegar; whisk together. Season generously and mix again.

■ Add oil in thin stream, whisking constantly. Add few drops of lemon juice and correct seasoning.

SALAD:

1 lb	leftover boiled beef, sliced	450 g
2 cups	cooked rice	500 mL
¼ cup	toasted pine nuts	50 mL
2	hard-boiled eggs, chopped	2
12	cherry tomatoes, halved	12
1	large avocado, peeled, halved, pitted and sliced	1

■ Line serving platter with lettuce leaves.

■ Place remaining ingredients, except avocado, in bowl. Add some of vinaigrette and mix well.

■ Spoon mixture over lettuce leaves and decorate with avocado slices. Add vinaigrette to taste and serve.

1 SERVING			
Calories	877	Fat	65 g
Carbohydrate	27 g	Fiber	2.6 g
Protein	46 g	Cholesterol	189 mg

Leeks Vinaigrette

◆

(4 SERVINGS)

4	large leeks, white part only	4
1 tbsp	Dijon mustard	15 mL
2	shallots, peeled and chopped	2
1 tbsp	chopped fresh parsley	15 mL
3 tbsp	red wine vinegar	45 mL
9 tbsp	olive oil	135 mL
	salt and freshly ground pepper	
	lemon juice to taste	

■ Slit leeks from top to bottom twice, leaving 1 in (2.5 cm) intact at base. Wash leeks under cold, running water to remove dirt and sand.

■ Cook leeks in salted, boiling water about 30 to 35 minutes, or according to size. Leeks should be tender when done.

■ Place leeks under cold, running water to stop cooking process. Drain well and transfer to large colander. Using wide spoon, press out excess water from leeks. Drain on paper towels if necessary.

■ Place mustard, shallots, parsley, vinegar, salt and pepper in bowl. Whisk together.

■ Add oil in thin stream, whisking constantly. Season well and add lemon juice.

■ Serve leeks with vinaigrette.

1 SERVING			
Calories	349	Fat	33 g
Carbohydrate	12 g	Fiber	1.3 g
Protein	1 g	Cholesterol	0 mg

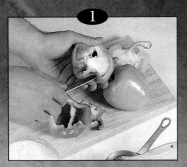

1. Cut bell peppers in half and remove seeds.

2. Oil skin and place cut-side-down on cookie sheet; broil 6 minutes.

3. Remove from oven and let cool in large bowl covered with plastic wrap.

Seafood Salad with Roasted Bell Peppers

♦

(4 SERVINGS)

VINAIGRETTE:

1 tbsp	Dijon mustard	15 mL
1	egg yolk	1
1 tbsp	chopped fresh chives	15 mL
1 tsp	chopped fresh parsley	5 mL
2	blanched garlic cloves, puréed	2
3 tbsp	white wine vinegar	45 mL
½ cup	olive oil	125 mL
2 tbsp	sour cream	30 mL
	salt and freshly ground pepper	

- Place mustard, egg yolk, chives, parsley and garlic in bowl. Whisk together.

- Add vinegar and season well; whisk again. Add oil and whisk to incorporate. Mix in sour cream and set aside.

SALAD:

1	green bell pepper	1
1	yellow bell pepper	1
3	halibut steaks, cooked	3
12	shrimp, cooked, peeled and deveined	12
1	large apple, cored, peeled and sliced	1
2	celery ribs, sliced thinly	2
	salt and freshly ground pepper	
	lemon juice to taste	

- Cut bell peppers in half and remove seeds. Oil skin and place cut-side-down on cookie sheet; broil 6 minutes. Remove from oven and let cool in large bowl covered with plastic wrap. Peel off skin, slice peppers and return to bowl.

- Remove skin and bones from halibut. Flake fish and add to large bowl.

- Cut shrimp in half. Add to bowl along with remaining ingredients.

- Pour in vinaigrette and toss well. Season generously with salt and pepper. Serve on bed of lettuce.

1 SERVING			
Calories	447	Fat	35 g
Carbohydrate	10 g	Fiber	1.5 g
Protein	23 g	Cholesterol	117 mg

Peel off skin, slice peppers
and place in large bowl.

Shrimp and Artichoke Bottoms

◆

(4 SERVINGS)

VINAIGRETTE:

½ cup	mayonnaise	125 mL
2 tbsp	ketchup	30 mL
2 tbsp	chili sauce	30 mL
1 tsp	horseradish	5 mL
2 tbsp	sour cream	30 mL
	salt and freshly ground pepper	
	a few drops of Tabasco sauce	

SALAD:

1 lb	fresh shrimp	450 g
4	artichoke bottoms, cooked and sliced	4
1	red onion, peeled and sliced in rings	1
1	apple, cored, peeled and sliced	1
1	celery rib, sliced thinly	1
	salt, pepper and lemon juice to taste	
	cleaned lettuce and lemon slices	

■ Mix all vinaigrette ingredients together in small bowl. Correct seasoning and set aside.

■ Place shrimp in saucepan and cover with cold water. Add salt and lemon juice; bring to a boil. As soon as water boils, remove pan from heat. Stir shrimp and let stand 2 minutes. Place pan under cold, running water until shrimp cool. Remove from water, peel and devein.

■ Place shrimp in large bowl. Add artichoke bottoms, onion, apple and celery. Season with salt and pepper. Pour in vinaigrette and mix well. Sprinkle with lemon juice.

■ Line serving plates with lettuce. Top with shrimp salad and garnish with lemon slices. Serve.

1 SERVING			
Calories	404	Fat	24 g
Carbohydrate	20 g	Fiber	1.9 g
Protein	27 g	Cholesterol	238 mg

Curried Vegetable Salad

◆

(4 TO 6 SERVINGS)

CURRY VINAIGRETTE:

2	garlic cloves	2
1 tbsp	Dijon mustard	15 mL
2	shallots, peeled and chopped	2
1 tbsp	chopped fresh parsley	15 mL
1 tbsp	curry powder	15 mL
¼ cup	balsamic vinegar	50 mL
¾ cup	olive oil	175 mL
	salt and freshly ground pepper	
	lemon juice to taste	

■ Place garlic cloves in salted, boiling water. Blanch 4 minutes, peel and purée; place in bowl.

■ Add remaining ingredients, except lemon juice, and whisk until thickened.

■ Whisk in lemon juice and set aside.

SALAD:

1	head broccoli, in florets	1
1	small head cauliflower, in florets	1
12	pearl onions, cooked	12
12	cherry tomatoes, halved	12
1	celery rib, diced small	1

■ Blanch broccoli and cauliflower separately in salted, boiling water until slightly tender, about 2 to 3 minutes. Place briefly under cold, running water to stop cooking process. Drain well on paper towels.

■ Place all vegetables in bowl. Add curry dressing and mix well. Season generously and mix again. Serve salad on bed of lettuce.

1 SERVING			
Calories	290	Fat	26 g
Carbohydrate	11 g	Fiber	2.5 g
Protein	3 g	Cholesterol	0 mg

Roast Turkey Pasta Salad

◆

(4 SERVINGS)

VINAIGRETTE:

1 tbsp	Dijon mustard	15 mL
1	egg yolk	1
3	garlic cloves, blanched and puréed	3
1	shallot, peeled and chopped	1
4 tbsp	white wine vinegar	60 mL
9 tbsp	olive oil	135 mL
2 tbsp	sour cream	30 mL
	salt and freshly ground pepper	
	lemon juice to taste	

■ Place all ingredients, except sour cream and lemon juice, in small bowl. Whisk together until thick. Add lemon juice to taste and whisk in sour cream. Set aside.

SALAD:

1	large head Romaine lettuce, washed and dried	1
2 cups	cooked rotini pasta	500 mL
1	small head broccoli, florets blanched	1
12	pitted green olives	12
12	cherry tomatoes, halved	12
5	slices roast turkey, in julienne	5
½ cup	toasted pine nuts	125 mL
	salt and freshly ground pepper	

■ Tear lettuce leaves into smaller pieces. Place in bowl with remaining salad ingredients, except turkey and nuts. Season generously.

■ Pour in some of vinaigrette and toss well.

■ Divide salad between serving plates and top with julienne of turkey and pine nuts. Drizzle with more vinaigrette, if desired.

1 SERVING

Calories	695	Fat	51 g
Carbohydrate	33 g	Fiber	4.4 g
Protein	26 g	Cholesterol	82 mg

Fresh Beet Salad with Red Onion

♦

(4 SERVINGS)

6	medium fresh beets, cleaned	6
1	red onion, peeled and sliced in rings	1
1 tbsp	chopped fresh basil	15 mL
4 tbsp	wine vinegar	60 mL
½ cup	olive oil	125 mL
	salt and freshly ground pepper	

■ Cook beets in salted, boiling water about 40 minutes or according to size. Beets should be tender when done. Remove beets and cool slightly. Peel and slice while still warm; place in bowl.

■ Add red onion, basil, vinegar and oil. Mix well, season and set aside to cool. Serve.

1 SERVING			
Calories	315	Fat	31 g
Carbohydrate	8 g	Fiber	2.1 g
Protein	1 g	Cholesterol	0 mg

Celeriac Rémoulade with Shrimp

♦

(4 SERVINGS)

1	celeriac	1
½ cup	mayonnaise	125 mL
2 tsp	Dijon mustard	10 mL
1 tbsp	chopped fresh parsley	15 mL
20	shrimp, cooked, peeled, deveined and cut in three	20
	salt and freshly ground pepper	
	juice of 1 lemon	
	a few drops of Tabasco sauce	

■ Peel celeriac and cut into fine julienne. Place in large bowl.

■ Mix remaining ingredients, except shrimp, in separate bowl. Season to taste and add to celeriac. Mix well.

■ Add shrimp, mix and correct seasoning. Serve on lettuce leaves.

1 SERVING			
Calories	259	Fat	23 g
Carbohydrate	6 g	Fiber	0 g
Protein	7 g	Cholesterol	68 mg

Fresh Mussels in Salad

◆

4 SERVINGS)

3 lbs	fresh mussels, washed, bearded and scrubbed	1.4 kg
1	head Boston lettuce, washed and dried	1
1 tbsp	olive oil	15 mL
2	shallots, peeled and chopped	2
1	garlic clove, peeled, crushed and chopped	1
1	celery rib, sliced	1
12	cherry tomatoes, halved	12
1 tbsp	chopped fresh basil	15 mL
1 cup	heavy cream (35% MF)	250 mL
2 tbsp	buttermilk	30 mL
3 tbsp	fresh lime juice	45 mL
	salt and freshly ground pepper	

■ Place mussels in large saucepan; cover and bring to a boil. Cook over low heat until shells open, about 5 minutes. Shake pan several times during cooking to mix mussels.

■ Remove mussels from pan, discarding the shells and any unopened mussels. Strain cooking liquid through sieve lined with cheesecloth, reserving ¼ cup (50 mL) of liquid.

■ Tear lettuce leaves into smaller pieces. Place in large bowl with mussels. Set aside.

■ Heat oil in frying pan over medium heat. Add shallots, garlic, celery, tomatoes and basil. Season well and cook 2 minutes. Pour over salad and toss gently.

■ Mix reserved cooking liquid with heavy cream in small bowl. Add buttermilk and lime juice. Mix well and season to taste. Pour mixture over salad, toss and serve.

1 SERVING			
Calories	557	Fat	33 g
Carbohydrate	21 g	Fiber	1.3 g
Protein	44 g	Cholesterol	179 mg

Caesar Asparagus

◆

(4 SERVINGS)

VINAIGRETTE:

4	anchovy fillets	4
1 tbsp	Dijon mustard	15 mL
2	garlic cloves, peeled, crushed and chopped	2
1	egg yolk	1
¼ cup	wine vinegar	50 mL
¾ cup	olive oil	175 mL
	salt and freshly ground pepper	
	lemon juice to taste	

■ Soak anchovy fillets in cold water. Drain well and pat dry with paper towels. Purée and place in bowl.

■ Add remaining ingredients and whisk until thick. Correct seasoning and set aside.

SALAD:

1	head Romaine lettuce, washed and dried	1
2	bunches asparagus	2
4	bacon slices, cooked crisp and chopped	4
1 cup	Garlic Croûtons (see page 65)	250 mL
	freshly ground pepper	

■ Pare asparagus if necessary and trim stem ends. Cook stalks in salted, boiling water until tender. Drain well and pat dry with paper towels.

■ Arrange asparagus on lettuce-lined plates. Top with bacon and croûtons. Season with pepper, drizzle vinaigrette over asparagus and serve.

1 SERVING			
Calories	551	Fat	51 g
Carbohydrate	15 g	Fiber	2.5 g
Protein	8 g	Cholesterol	60 mg

Seasonal Fruit Salad

◆

(4 SERVINGS)

VINAIGRETTE:

¾ cup	light sour cream	175 mL
1 tbsp	Dijon mustard	15 mL
	salt and pepper	
	lemon juice to taste	

■ Mix all ingredients together in small bowl. Correct seasoning and set aside.

SALAD:

½ lb	cottage cheese	225 g
3	oranges	3
¼ lb	seedless green grapes	125 g
3	apples, cored, peeled and sliced	3
4	kiwis, peeled and sliced	4
2	large bananas, peeled and sliced	2
4	wedges cantaloupe	4
12	small pieces watermelon, seeded	12
	cleaned Boston lettuce for presentation	
	lemon juice	

■ Line serving plates with lettuce leaves. Spoon cottage cheese on each plate and set aside.

■ Cut thin slice from top and bottom of each orange. Use sharp knife to remove rind and white pith. Hold fruit in one hand and cut between membranes to release sections of fruit.

■ Divide grapes into 4 small bunches. Arrange grapes and remaining fruit on serving plates around cottage cheese. Drizzle fruit with lemon juice.

■ Accompany with vinaigrette and serve.

1 SERVING			
Calories	403	Fat	7 g
Carbohydrate	72 g	Fiber	8.3 g
Protein	13 g	Cholesterol	17 mg

Cut thin slice from top
and bottom of each orange.

Use sharp knife to remove rind
and white pith.

Hold fruit in one hand and cut
between membranes to release
sections of fruit.

Roquefort Salad

◆

(4 SERVINGS)

VINAIGRETTE:

2 oz	Roquefort cheese, crumbled	60 g
½ cup	heavy cream (35% MF)	125 mL
1 tbsp	cognac	15 mL
2	garlic cloves, blanched and puréed	2
1 tbsp	wine vinegar	15 mL
	salt and freshly ground pepper	

■ Combine all ingredients and mix well. Set aside.

SALAD:

2	small heads Romaine lettuce	2
1 cup	croûtons	250 mL
2 oz	Roquefort cheese, crumbled	60 g
	salt and freshly ground pepper	
	lemon juice to taste	

■ Separate lettuce into leaves and wash well in cold water. Drain and dry thoroughly. Tear leaves into smaller pieces and set aside in large salad bowl.

■ Season lettuce generously with salt and pepper. Pour in dressing and toss well. Sprinkle in lemon juice and add croûtons. Toss, garnish portions with crumbled Roquefort cheese and serve.

1 SERVING			
Calories	307	Fat	23 g
Carbohydrate	13 g	Fiber	1.9 g
Protein	10 g	Cholesterol	67 mg

Mixed Vegetable Salad

◆

(4 SERVINGS)

2	carrots, cooked and diced	2
10	asparagus stalks, cooked and diced	10
2	potatoes, boiled and diced	2
¼ lb	cooked green beans, diced	110 g
½	celery rib, diced	½
1	green bell pepper, diced	1
1	red bell pepper, diced	1
1 tbsp	Dijon mustard	15 mL
2	shallots, peeled and chopped	2
½ cup	mayonnaise	125 mL
1 lb	seedless green grapes	450 g
	salt and freshly ground pepper	
	lemon juice to taste	
	a few drops Tabasco sauce	

■ Place all vegetables in large bowl. Season generously with salt and pepper.

■ Mix mustard with shallots, mayonnaise and lemon juice. Season generously. Mix in a few drops of Tabasco sauce.

■ Add dressing to salad and mix thoroughly. Serve on bed of lettuce and garnish with small bunches of grapes.

1 SERVING			
Calories	374	Fat	22 g
Carbohydrate	40 g	Fiber	4.6 g
Protein	4 g	Cholesterol	16 mg

Basic Oil & Vinegar Vinaigrette

◆

1 tbsp	Dijon mustard	15 mL
2	shallots, peeled and chopped	2
1 tbsp	chopped fresh parsley	15 mL
¼ cup	wine or balsamic vinegar	50 mL
¾ cup	olive oil	175 mL
	salt and freshly ground pepper	
	lemon or lime juice to taste	

■ Place all ingredients, except lemon juice, in bo
Whisk together until thick.

■ Add lemon juice and correct seasoning. Whisk again before using.

1 SERVING			
Calories	1485	Fat	161 g
Carbohydrate	8 g	Fiber	0 g
Protein	1 g	Cholesterol	0 mg

Yogurt Vinaigrette

◆

½ cup	plain yogurt	125 mL
1 tsp	honey	5 mL
¼ cup	lemon juice	50 mL
1 tsp	chopped fresh chives	5 mL
	salt and freshly ground pepper	

■ Place all ingredients in bowl. Whisk together until well-incorporated. Correct seasoning. Whisk again before using.

1 SERVING			
Calories	122	Fat	2 g
Carbohydrate	19 g	Fiber	0 g
Protein	7 g	Cholesterol	8 mg

Garlic Croûtons

◆

1	loaf stale French bread	1
¼ cup	olive oil	50 mL
4	large garlic cloves, peeled, crushed and chopped	4

■ Trim crusts off bread. Cut into wide slices and dice. Toast pieces on all sides in oven.

■ Heat oil in large frying pan over high heat. Add toasted bread and garlic. Cook 3 minutes, stirring frequently.

■ Drain croûtons on paper towels. Cool before using and store in airtight container to preserve crispness.

1 SERVING			
Calories	1128	Fat	52 g
Carbohydrate	142 g	Fiber	4.0 g
Protein	23 g	Cholesterol	0 mg

Homemade Herb Mayonnaise

◆

2	egg yolks	2
1 tbsp	Dijon mustard	15 mL
1¼ cups	olive oil	300 mL
2 tsp	wine vinegar	10 mL
1 tsp	chopped fresh parsley	5 mL
1 tsp	chopped fresh tarragon	5 mL
1 tsp	chopped fresh chives	5 mL
	lemon juice to taste	
	salt and freshly ground pepper	

■ Place egg yolks and mustard in bowl; whisk together.

■ Add oil in thin stream, whisking constantly. Increase flow as mixture thickens. When mixture is very thick and before all of oil is incorporated, whisk in vinegar and lemon juice.

■ Incorporate remaining oil, adding more if necessary.

■ Stir in fresh herbs and season generously. Use immediately in a variety of fresh salads.

* To keep mayonnaise in refrigerator, stir in 1 tsp (5 mL) of boiling water. Cover with plastic, ensuring that wrap touches surface of mayonnaise, and use within 24 hours.

Calories	2791	Fat	307 g
Carbohydrate	1 g	Fiber	0 g
Protein	6 g	Cholesterol	430 mg

Garlic Vinaigrette

◆

4	garlic cloves	4
1 tbsp	Dijon mustard	15 mL
2	shallots, peeled and chopped	2
¼ cup	wine or balsamic vinegar	50 mL
¾ cup	olive oil	175 mL
	salt and freshly ground pepper	
	lemon juice to taste	

■ Place garlic cloves in salted, boiling water. Blanch 4 minutes, peel and purée.

■ Place all ingredients, except lemon juice, in bowl. Whisk together until thick.

■ Add lemon juice and correct seasoning. Whisk again before using.

Calories	1706	Fat	186 g
Carbohydrate	7 g	Fiber	0 g
Protein	1 g	Cholesterol	0 mg

Lemon Vinaigrette

◆

1 tbsp	Dijon mustard	15 mL
6 tbsp	lemon juice	90 mL
½ cup	olive oil	125 mL
2 tbsp	sour cream	30 mL
	salt and freshly ground pepper	
	a few drops of Tabasco sauce	

■ Place all ingredients, except sour cream, in bowl. Whisk together until well-incorporated.

■ Add sour cream and correct seasoning. Whisk again before using.

Calories	1196	Fat	128 g
Carbohydrate	9 g	Fiber	0 g
Protein	2 g	Cholesterol	12 mg

FISH AND SEAFOOD

Many home cooks are reluctant to prepare fish, even though they will happily attempt far more complicated dishes. In reality, fish and seafood are among the quickest, easiest and most nutritious foods to prepare, as long as you follow a few basic rules.

First and foremost, start with the freshest possible ingredients. If at all possible, find a good fish supplier who knows how to handle fish and seafood, and doesn't just treat them as varieties of meat. A good fish merchant will be happy to recommend the best and freshest buys, and will even share cooking advice if you ask for it.

When you select whole fish, look for those with clear, bright, bulging eyes. Cut fish pieces should have firm, resilient flesh. Above all, use your nose. Fresh fish should never smell "fishy", but instead it should have a pleasant, seawater smell.

Once you get your fish home, cook it within a day or two. The most common mistake made with fish is to overcook it, so follow the timing instructions carefully to get the full benefits of flavor and goodness that fish has to offer.

Grilled Whole Mackerel with Herb Butter Sauce

◆

(4 SERVINGS)

FISH:

2	2 lb (900 g) fresh whole mackerel, prepared for cooking	2
2 tbsp	butter	30 mL
1	bunch fresh fennel	1
1	bunch fresh Italian parsley	1
2	bay leaves	2
2	garlic cloves, chopped	2
¼ cup	olive oil	50 mL
	salt and freshly ground pepper	
	juice of 1 lemon	

■ Season fish inside and out. Divide butter, lemon juice, herbs, bay leaves and garlic between cavities. Truss fish and baste skins with oil. Season well.

■ Grill fish 7 to 8 minutes over hot coals. Baste with olive oil during cooking. Adjust time according to size; do not overcook. When done, flesh will feel firm to the touch and central bone will turn white.

■ Serve with Herb Butter Sauce.

HERB BUTTER SAUCE:

3 tbsp	butter	45 mL
2	shallots, peeled and chopped	2
1 tbsp	chopped fresh parsley	15 mL
1 tsp	chopped fresh tarragon	5 mL
	freshly ground pepper	
	juice of 1½ lemons	

■ Heat butter in small saucepan over medium heat. Add shallots, herbs and freshly ground pepper. Cook 20 seconds.

■ Add lemon juice and pour over fish.

* Choosing and handling fresh fish requires attention. When buying whole fish, look for clear, bright eyes and firm flesh. Cook fresh fish within 1 day of purchase. Pack on ice and rinse well before cooking.

1 SERVING			
Calories	581	Fat	45 g
Carbohydrate	3 g	Fiber	0.6 g
Protein	41 g	Cholesterol	166 mg

71

Red Snapper Cooked in Foil

◆

(4 SERVINGS)

2	2 lb (900 g) whole red snapper, prepared for cooking	2
4 tbsp	butter	60 mL
1	bunch fresh fennel	1
1	bunch fresh parsley	1
2	bay leaves	2
2	garlic cloves, chopped	2
2 tbsp	olive oil	30 mL
½ cup	dry white wine	125 mL
	salt and freshly ground pepper	
	lime juice to taste	
	lemon juice to taste	

■ Preheat oven to 450°F (230°C).

■ Season fish inside and out. Divide butter, lime juice, herbs, bay leaves and garlic between cavities. Truss fish and baste skins with oil. Season well.

■ Place each fish in a large piece of doubled foil. Add wine and fold package to secure juices. Place in roasting pan and cook in oven.*

■ Fillet fish and serve with cooking juices and lemon juice.

* Fish is easily overcooked. A good rule of thumb to follow is to cook the fish 10 minutes per inch (2.5 cm) of thickness, measured at the thickest part of the whole fish, steak or fillet. When properly cooked, the flesh will become opaque and firm to the touch. The backbone will turn white.

1 SERVING

Calories	377	Fat	20 g
Carbohydrate	10 g	Fiber	0.6 g
Protein	35 g	Cholesterol	94 mg

Steamed Mussels with Cream Sauce

◆

(4 SERVINGS)

5 lbs	fresh mussels, bearded and scrubbed	2.3 kg
5 tbsp	butter	75 mL
3	shallots, peeled and chopped	3
2 cups	dry white wine	500 mL
1 cup	heavy cream (35% MF)	250 mL
1 tbsp	chopped fresh parsley	15 mL
	salt and freshly ground pepper	

■ Place mussels in large saucepan. Add 3 tbsp (45 mL) of butter, shallots, wine and freshly ground pepper.

■ Cover and bring to a boil. Cook mussels over low heat until shells open, about 5 minutes. Shake pan several times during cooking to mix mussels.

■ Remove mussels from pan, discarding any unopened shells; keep warm. Strain liquid through sieve lined with cheesecloth into saucepan. Cook liquid over medium heat until reduced by ⅓.

■ Add cream and remaining butter. Cook 4 minutes over low heat. Stir in parsley and correct seasoning.

■ Return mussels to large saucepan and pour in cream sauce. Simmer several minutes and serve.

1 SERVING			
Calories	844	Fat	49 g
Carbohydrate	24 g	Fiber	0 g
Protein	67 g	Cholesterol	274 mg

Tropical Scampi

◆

(4 SERVINGS)

24	large scampi	24
½ cup	mayonnaise	125 mL
1 tsp	curry powder	5 mL
1 tbsp	chopped fresh parsley	15 mL
⅓ cup	mango chutney	75 mL
1 tsp	Dijon mustard	5 mL
1 tbsp	chopped fresh fennel	15 mL
¼ cup	toasted slivered almonds	50 mL
	juice of 1 lemon	
	salt and freshly ground pepper	
	lettuce leaves for garnishing	

▬ Place scampi in saucepan and cover with water. Add lemon juice, season and bring to a boil. Remove immediately from heat and let stand 3 minutes.

▬ Place pan under cold, running water to stop cooking process. Using scissors, peel scampi and devein. Rinse under cold water and pat dry with paper towels.

▬ Place whole scampi in bowl and season well. Add lemon juice to taste.

▬ Mix mayonnaise with curry powder, parsley, chutney, Dijon mustard and fennel. Season and mix well.

▬ Line scallop shells or small dishes with lettuce leaves, and top with scampi. Sprinkle with lemon juice and almonds. Serve with curry dressing.

1 SERVING

Calories	417	Fat	29 g
Carbohydrate	11 g	Fiber	0.8 g
Protein	28 g	Cholesterol	103 mg

Deep-Fried Smelts

◆

(4 SERVINGS)

1½ lbs	fresh smelts, rinsed and dried	675 g
2 cups	all-purpose flour	500 mL
1 tsp	paprika	5 mL
3	eggs, beaten with a few drops of oil	3
2 cups	breadcrumbs	500 mL
	salt and freshly ground pepper	
	peanut oil for deep-frying	
	lemon wedges	

■ Season smelts generously with salt and pepper. Dredge in flour seasoned with paprika. Dip smelts in beaten eggs and coat with breadcrumbs.

■ Preheat peanut oil to 350°F (180°C). Deep-fry smelts until golden brown. Drain on paper towels.

■ Accompany with lemon wedges and serve.

1 SERVING

Calories	764	Fat	16 g
Carbohydrate	64 g	Fiber	1.2 g
Protein	91 g	Cholesterol	467 mg

Halibut Steaks with Bell Peppers and Red Onion

◆

(4 SERVINGS)

4	halibut steaks, rinsed and dried	4
½ cup	all-purpose flour	125 mL
3 tbsp	olive oil	45 mL
1	small red onion, peeled and sliced thinly	1
1	red bell pepper, sliced thinly	1
1	yellow bell pepper, sliced thinly	1
2	garlic cloves, peeled and sliced	2
1 tbsp	chopped fresh ginger	15 mL
1 tbsp	soy sauce	15 mL
	salt and freshly ground pepper	
	lemon juice to taste	

■ Season halibut generously with salt and pepper. Dredge in flour.

■ Heat 2 tbsp (30 mL) of oil in large frying pan over high heat. Add fish and reduce heat to medium. Cook 3 minutes. Turn halibut over and cook 3 minutes.

■ Turn fish over again and cook 2 minutes, or according to size. When cooked, remove from pan and keep warm in oven.

■ Add remaining oil to hot pan. Add all remaining ingredients, except soy sauce and lemon juice, and cook 5 minutes over high heat. Stir occasionally.

■ Sprinkle in soy sauce and lemon juice. Mix, pour over fish and serve.

1 SERVING

Calories	371	Fat	15 g
Carbohydrate	17 g	Fiber	1.4 g
Protein	42 g	Cholesterol	61 mg

Steamed Mussels with Curry

◆

(4 SERVINGS)

5 lbs	large mussels, bearded and scrubbed	2.3 kg
5 tbsp	butter	75 mL
2	shallots, peeled and chopped	2
2	fresh fennel sprigs	2
2	fresh parsley sprigs	2
1 cup	dry white wine	250 mL
1	onion, peeled and chopped	1
1 tbsp	curry powder	15 mL
1 cup	heavy cream (35% MF)	250 mL
2 tbsp	chopped fresh parsley	30 mL
	lemon juice to taste	
	salt and freshly ground pepper	

■ Place mussels, 4 tbsp (60 mL) of butter, shallots, herb sprigs, wine and lemon juice in large saucepan. Season with freshly ground pepper.

■ Cover and cook over low heat until shells open, about 5 minutes. Shake pan several times during cooking to mix mussels.

■ Remove mussels from pan, discarding any unopened shells, and keep warm. Strain liquid through sieve lined with cheesecloth; set aside.

■ Heat remaining butter in saucepan, add onion and curry; cook 5 minutes over medium heat. Add reserved liquid, increase heat to high and bring to a boil.

■ Add cream and parsley; season well and cook 4 minutes.

■ Return mussels to saucepan, simmer 2 minutes and serve immediately.

1 SERVING

Calories	833	Fat	49 g
Carbohydrate	26 g	Fiber	0.5 g
Protein	67 g	Cholesterol	274 mg

Sautéed Pickerel Fillets
with Anchovy Butter

◆

(4 SERVINGS)

FILLETS:

2 tbsp	olive oil	30 mL
4	pickerel fillets, rinsed and dried	4
	salt and freshly ground pepper	

■ Heat oil in frying pan over medium heat. Season fillets generously and add to pan. Cook 3 minutes. Turn fish over and cook 3 to 4 minutes, or according to size.

■ Transfer cooked fish to ovenproof platter and keep warm in oven. Serve with Anchovy Butter.

ANCHOVY BUTTER:

2½ oz	anchovy fillets	70 g
½ lb	unsalted butter, at room temperature	225 g
1 tsp	chopped chervil	5 mL
	juice of ¼ lemon	
	pinch of cayenne pepper	
	a few drops Tabasco sauce	
	salt and freshly ground pepper	

■ Purée anchovy fillets in mortar and push through fine-meshed sieve into clean bowl.*

■ Add remaining ingredients to anchovy purée. Mix well and correct seasoning.

■ Roll anchovy butter in foil and seal ends tightly. Keeps up to 3 months in the freezer.

If you don't have a mortar, chop the anchovies twice and push through fine-meshed sieve.

1 SERVING			
Calories	367	Fat	31 g
Carbohydrate	0 g	Fiber	0 g
Protein	22 g	Cholesterol	63 mg

Ginger Fried Shrimp

◆

(4 SERVINGS)

1½ lbs	fresh shrimp, peeled and deveined	675 g
3 tbsp	cornstarch	45 mL
1	large egg white, beaten lightly	1
2 tbsp	sherry	30 mL
4 tbsp	peanut oil	60 mL
2	green onions, sliced	2
1 oz	sliced fresh ginger	30 g
1½ cups	fish stock or light chicken stock, heated	375 mL
1 cup	frozen green peas	250 mL
3 tbsp	cold water	45 mL
	salt and freshly ground pepper	

■ Place shrimp in large bowl. Sprinkle in 2 tbsp (30 mL) of cornstarch and mix well. Stir in egg white and sherry; season well.

■ Heat oil in large cast iron skillet over high heat. Add green onions and sliced ginger. Cook 30 seconds, remove from pan and set aside in bowl.

■ Divide shrimp in two batches. Cook each batch 3 minutes in saucepan over high heat, stirring once. Season during cooking. Add shrimp to bowl with green onions and ginger.

■ Add fish stock and peas to hot pan. Dilute remaining cornstarch with cold water and add to liquid in pan. Mix well and cook 20 seconds. Pour over shrimp and serve.

1 SERVING

Calories	414	Fat	18 g
Carbohydrate	20 g	Fiber	3.0 g
Protein	41 g	Cholesterol	387 mg

Crêpes for Seafood

◆

(4 SERVINGS)

1 cup	all-purpose flour	250 mL
3	large eggs	3
1 cup	milk	250 mL
½ cup	water	125 mL
2 tbsp	vegetable oil	30 mL
	pinch salt	
	butter	

- Place flour and salt in large bowl. Add eggs and mix well with wooden spoon.

- Whisk in milk and water. If batter is too thick, add more water. Whisk in oil and strain batter into clean bowl.

- Cover with plastic wrap, ensuring that wrap touches surface of batter. Refrigerate 1 hour.

- Bring batter to room temperature before using. If too thick, add more milk.

- Place crêpe pan over medium heat. When hot, use a paper towel to wipe pan with butter. Pour out excess butter.

- Add ladle of crêpe batter and, holding pan above stove, rotate to spread batter evenly. Turn pan on a 90 degree angle and let excess batter drip back into bowl.

- Return pan to stove and cook crêpe over medium-high heat until underside is golden brown. Using long metal spatula, turn crêpe over carefully and cook other side.

- Remove pan from heat and let crêpe slide out onto large dinner plate.

- Add more butter to pan, heat and repeat process. Stack crêpes on plate.

1 SERVING

Calories	278	Fat	14 g
Carbohydrate	28 g	Fiber	1.0 g
Protein	10 g	Cholesterol	172 mg

Shrimp and White Sauce Crêpes

◆

(4 SERVINGS)

3 tbsp	butter	45 mL
2	shallots, peeled and chopped	2
1 lb	fresh shrimp, peeled, deveined and halved	450 g
½ lb	fresh mushrooms, cleaned and sliced	225 g
3 tbsp	all-purpose flour	45 mL
2 cups	milk, heated	500 mL
1 tbsp	chopped fresh chives	15 mL
8	crêpes	8
¼ cup	grated Parmesan cheese	50 mL
	salt and freshly ground pepper	
	paprika and nutmeg to taste	

■ Heat butter in frying pan over medium heat. Add shallots and shrimp. Season well and cook 2 to 3 minutes. Remove shrimp and set aside.

■ Add mushrooms to pan and increase heat to high. Cook 4 minutes.

■ Sprinkle in flour and mix well. Pour in milk and add all seasonings. Whisk thoroughly and cook 6 minutes over low heat.

■ Remove pan from heat and incorporate shrimp. Divide half of mixture between crêpes, roll and place in baking dish. Top with remaining sauce and cheese; broil 4 minutes in oven. Serve.

1 SERVING			
Calories	429	Fat	21 g
Carbohydrate	27 g	Fiber	2.3 g
Protein	33 g	Cholesterol	320 mg

Fresh Fillet of Sole with Mushrooms

◆

(4 SERVINGS)

4	fresh sole fillets, rinsed and dried	4
½ cup	all-purpose flour	125 mL
2 tbsp	olive oil	30 mL
1 tbsp	butter	15 mL
½ lb	fresh mushrooms, cleaned and sliced	225 g
1 tbsp	chopped fresh parsley	15 mL
	salt and freshly ground pepper	
	juice of 1 lemon	

■ Season fillets generously with salt and pepper, and dredge in flour.

■ Heat oil in frying pan over high heat. Add sole and cook 2 minutes. Turn fillets over and cook 1 minute.

■ Transfer fillets to ovenproof platter and keep warm in oven.

■ Add butter to hot frying pan. Add mushrooms and season well; cook 4 minutes over high heat. Add parsley and lemon juice, mix and pour over fillets. Serve immediately.

1 SERVING			
Calories	315	Fat	11 g
Carbohydrate	16 g	Fiber	2.0 g
Protein	38 g	Cholesterol	116 mg

Shrimp Cocktail

◆

(4 SERVINGS)

¾ cup	mayonnaise	175 mL
2 tbsp	chili sauce	30 mL
1 tsp	Worcestershire sauce	5 mL
1 tbsp	whisky	15 mL
24	large shrimp, cooked, peeled and deveined	24
	salt and freshly ground pepper	
	lemon juice to taste	
	lemon wedges	

■ Mix mayonnaise with remaining ingredients, except shrimp and lemon wedges. Correct seasoning.

■ Serve shrimp with cocktail sauce and lemon wedges.

1 SERVING

Calories	360	Fat	32 g
Carbohydrate	3 g	Fiber	0.5 g
Protein	7 g	Cholesterol	87 mg

Baked Swordfish with Almonds

◆

(4 SERVINGS)

4	small swordfish steaks, rinsed and dried	4
2 tbsp	olive oil	30 mL
1 tbsp	butter	15 mL
¼ cup	slivered almonds	50 mL
2 tbsp	capers	30 mL
1 tbsp	chopped fresh parsley	15 mL
	salt and freshly ground pepper	
	juice of 2 limes	

- Preheat oven to 375°F (190°C). Season fish with salt and pepper.

- Heat oil in large, ovenproof frying pan over medium heat. Add fish and cook 2 minutes. Turn fish over and cook 1 minute.

- Transfer pan to oven and cook 6 to 7 minutes, or according to size. When cooked, transfer fish to serving platter and keep warm in oven.

- Return frying pan with juices from fish to stove set at medium heat. Add butter, almonds, capers and parsley; cook 2 minutes.

- Add lime juice, pour over fish and serve.

1 SERVING

Calories	283	Fat	19 g
Carbohydrate	3 g	Fiber	0.6 g
Protein	25 g	Cholesterol	53 mg

Marinated Scallops and Vegetable Brochettes

◆

(4 SERVINGS)

MARINADE:

1 cup	dry white wine	250 mL
1	shallot, peeled and chopped	1
2 tbsp	olive oil	30 mL
2	garlic cloves, peeled and sliced	2
1 tsp	*each* chopped fresh parsley, tarragon, basil and oregano	5 mL
1½ lbs	fresh scallops, rinsed	675 g
	salt and freshly ground pepper	
	lemon juice to taste	

■ Place all ingredients, except scallops, in bowl and mix well. Add scallops and cover with plastic wrap, ensuring that wrap touches surface of marinade. Refrigerate 1 hour. Remove scallops and reserve marinade.

BROCHETTES:

2	large carrots, pared and sliced ½-in (1-cm) thick	2
¼	head broccoli, cut in bite-size pieces	¼
½ lb	fresh mushroom caps, cleaned	225 g
	salt and freshly ground pepper	

■ Blanch carrots and broccoli separately in salted, boiling water. Drain well and pat dry with paper towels.

■ Alternate scallops, mushroom caps, carrots and broccoli on metal skewers. Baste with marinade and season generously. Broil 4 to 5 minutes in oven, rotating 2 or 3 times during cooking. Baste frequently with marinade.

■ Sprinkle with lemon juice and serve on a bed of rice.

1 SERVING			
Calories	211	Fat	3 g
Carbohydrate	14 g	Fiber	3.5 g
Protein	32 g	Cholesterol	57 mg

Lobster Newburg

◆

(4 SERVINGS)

1½ cups	dry white wine	375 mL
½ cup	clam juice or fish stock	125 mL
2	1½ lb (675 g) boiled lobsters, split in half	2
4 tbsp	butter	60 mL
4	shallots, peeled and chopped	4
¾ lb	fresh mushrooms, cleaned and diced	350 g
2 tbsp	all-purpose flour	30 mL
1 cup	light cream, heated	250 mL
¼ cup	Madeira wine	50 mL
	salt and freshly ground pepper	
	paprika to taste	
	chopped fresh parsley	

■ Bring white wine to a boil in saucepan and cook 3 minutes. Add clam juice and reduce heat to low. Simmer until ready to use.

■ Split lobsters in half. Discard intestinal sac. Scoop out any tomalley and coral and reserve in small bowl. Remove lobster meat from shells and dice large; set aside.

■ Clean shells and dry in warm oven.

■ Heat butter in frying pan over medium heat. Add lobster, shallots, pepper and paprika. Cook 2 minutes over high heat. Remove lobster from pan and set aside.

■ Add mushrooms to pan and season well. Cook 4 minutes over medium heat. Sprinkle in flour and mix well; cook 2 minutes.

■ Incorporate simmering wine mixture to mushrooms. Mix well and pour in cream. Season, mix and cook sauce 6 minutes over low heat.

■ Stir in reserved tomalley and coral. Return lobster to pan and stir in Madeira wine. Season well and simmer 4 minutes.

■ Fill lobster shells with mixture and sprinkle with parsley. Serve.

1 SERVING			
Calories	557	Fat	21 g
Carbohydrate	18 g	Fiber	1.6 g
Protein	72 g	Cholesterol	287 mg

Stuffed Fresh Clams

◆

(4 SERVINGS)

32	fresh clams, cleaned	32
1 cup	water	250 mL
3 tbsp	butter	45 mL
2	onions, peeled and chopped	2
2 tbsp	chopped fresh parsley	30 mL
4	garlic cloves, peeled, crushed and chopped	4
¾ lb	fresh mushrooms, cleaned and chopped	350 g
1 cup	coarse white breadcrumbs	250 mL
½ cup	heavy cream (35% MF)	125 mL
	salt and freshly ground pepper	
	a few drops of Tabasco sauce	

■ Place clams and water in saucepan. Cover and cook over medium heat until shells open.

■ Remove clams from pan and detach from shells. Chop clams and set aside. Twist off lower shells and dry well; arrange in single layer in roasting pan. Strain cooking liquid through sieve lined with cheesecloth; set aside.

■ Heat butter in frying pan over medium heat. Add onions and cook 4 minutes. Add parsley, garlic and mushrooms; season well. Cook 5 minutes over high heat.

■ Add chopped clams and breadcrumbs. Mix well and incorporate some of strained cooking liquid. Add cream and Tabasco sauce; season well. Mixture should not be too loose.

■ Fill lower shells with stuffing and broil 8 minutes or until lightly browned. Serve.

1 SERVING

Calories	454	Fat	22 g
Carbohydrate	33 g	Fiber	3.4 g
Protein	31 g	Cholesterol	128 mg

Cod with Mashed Potatoes and Swiss Cheese

◆

(4 SERVINGS)

1 tbsp	butter	15 mL
1½ lbs	fresh cod fillets, rinsed	675 g
3	shallots, peeled and chopped	3
1	fresh thyme sprig	1
2	fresh parsley sprigs	2
4	potatoes, peeled and sliced thinly	4
¼ cup	grated Swiss cheese	50 mL
	salt and freshly ground pepper	

■ Grease baking dish with butter. Place cod in dish and season generously. Add shallots, fresh herbs and potatoes.

■ Cover with cold water. Place dish on stove over medium heat; bring to a boil. Reduce heat to low and simmer fish 3 minutes.

■ Remove fish and set aside; discard herbs. Continue cooking potatoes until tender.

■ Remove potatoes from dish, drain well and pass through food mill.

■ Place cod in clean baking dish and top with puréed potatoes. Season well with pepper and sprinkle with grated Swiss cheese. Broil 5 minutes or until lightly browned. Serve.

1 SERVING			
Calories	289	Fat	5 g
Carbohydrate	20 g	Fiber	1.8 g
Protein	41 g	Cholesterol	103 mg

Scampi au Gratin

◆

(4 SERVINGS)

GARLIC BUTTER:

½ lb	soft butter	225 g
1	shallot, peeled, crushed and chopped	1
2	garlic cloves, peeled and chopped	2
1 tsp	chopped fresh parsley	5 mL
	freshly ground pepper	
	lemon juice to taste	

■ Mix all ingredients together in bowl and set aside.

SCAMPI:

16	large scampi	16
⅔ cup	white breadcrumbs	150 mL
	freshly ground pepper	
	lemon wedges	

■ Preheat oven to 425°F (220°C).

■ Place scampi shell-side-up on cutting board. Using sharp knife, cut lengthwise through shell, leaving enough flesh intact to open butterfly-style. Devein.

■ Wash under cold water, drain and pat dry with paper towels.

■ Place scampi, flesh-side up, on ovenproof tray. Season with pepper and spread with garlic butter to taste.

■ Top with breadcrumbs. Cook 4 minutes in oven. Change oven setting to broil and brown several minutes.

■ Serve with lemon wedges.

1 SERVING

Calories	543	Fat	47 g
Carbohydrate	13 g	Fiber	0 g
Protein	17 g	Cholesterol	175 mg

Seafood in Pastry

◆

(4 SERVINGS)

2	sole fillets	2
1 lb	small scallops, rinsed	450 g
½ lb	fresh mushrooms, cleaned and sliced	225 g
2	shallots, peeled and chopped	2
1½	red bell peppers, sliced thinly	1½
1	fresh fennel sprig	1
2	fresh parsley sprigs	2
1 cup	dry white wine	250 mL
3 tbsp	butter	45 mL
3 tbsp	all-purpose flour	45 mL
4	small vol-au-vent pastry shells	4
	salt and freshly ground pepper	
	lemon juice to taste	

■ Place fillets in large frying pan. Add scallops, mushrooms, shallots, bell peppers, herbs and wine. Cover with cold water and season well.

■ Cover pan with sheet of waxed paper, ensuring that cover touches surface. Bring to a boil over medium heat. Remove immediately from heat and let stand 2 minutes.

■ Using slotted spoon, remove seafood and set aside. Reserve cooking liquid with vegetables; discard herb sprigs.

■ Heat butter in saucepan over medium heat. Sprinkle in flour and mix well; cook 20 seconds. Incorporate reserved cooking liquid and vegetables. Season and cook 4 minutes.

■ Meanwhile, heat pastry shells in warm oven.

■ Add seafood to sauce and simmer 2 minutes over low heat. Sprinkle with lemon juice and fill vol-au-vent with mixture. Serve.

1 SERVING			
Calories	362	Fat	14 g
Carbohydrate	18 g	Fiber	2.3 g
Protein	31 g	Cholesterol	90 mg

93

Salmon Steaks Poached in White Wine

◆

(4 SERVINGS)

1	celery rib with leaves, sliced	1
2	shallots, peeled and sliced	2
1	carrot, pared and sliced	1
1	fresh thyme sprig	1
2	fresh parsley sprigs	2
1	bay leaf	1
12	whole black peppercorns	12
1 cup	dry white wine	250 mL
4 cups	cold water	1 L
4	¾-in (2-cm) thick salmon steaks, rinsed	4
	salt and freshly ground pepper	
	lemon juice to taste	

- Place all ingredients, except fish, in sauté pan. Bring to a boil and cook 16 minutes over low heat.

- Place salmon steaks in liquid; simmer 6 to 7 minutes over very low heat.

- Fish is cooked when flesh is firm to the touch. Serve with a julienne of fresh vegetables and lemon juice.

1 SERVING

Calories	236	Fat	8 g
Carbohydrate	3 g	Fiber	0.7 g
Protein	36 g	Cholesterol	97 mg

Trout with Capers

◆

(4 SERVINGS)

4	small whole trout, prepared for cooking	4
½ cup	all-purpose flour	125 mL
2 tbsp	olive oil	30 mL
1 tbsp	butter	15 mL
2 tbsp	capers	30 mL
1 tbsp	chopped fresh fennel	15 mL
1 tbsp	chopped fresh tarragon	15 mL
	salt and freshly ground pepper	
	juice of 2 large limes	

- Preheat oven to 400°F (200°C). Season cavities of fish with salt and pepper. Dredge in flour.

- Heat oil in large ovenproof frying pan over medium heat. Add fish and cook 2 minutes on each side.

- Transfer frying pan to oven and cook fish 8 minutes, or according to size. When done, transfer fish to serving platter and tent with foil.

- Return pan with juices from fish to stove set at medium heat. Add butter and cook 30 seconds.

- Add remaining ingredients, except lime juice, and cook 1 minute. Squeeze in lime juice and pour sauce over fish. Season with freshly ground pepper. Serve with fresh sautéed summer squashes, if desired.

1 SERVING

Calories	405	Fat	21 g
Carbohydrate	15 g	Fiber	0.5 g
Protein	39 g	Cholesterol	112 mg

Scampi with Julienne of Vegetables

◆

(4 SERVINGS)

3 tbsp	olive oil	45 mL
24	large scampi, peeled, deveined and halved	24
8	green onions, cut in 1-in (2.5-cm) lengths	8
2	large carrots, pared and in short julienne	2
½ lb	fresh mushroom caps, cleaned	225 g
½ lb	green beans, pared, cooked and halved	225 g
3	garlic cloves, peeled and sliced	3
2 tbsp	chopped fresh basil	30 mL
1 tbsp	chopped fresh parsley	15 mL
	salt and freshly ground pepper	
	lemon juice to taste	

- Heat 2 tbsp (30 mL) of oil in frying pan over high heat. Add scampi and sauté 2 minutes. Remove from pan and set aside.

- Add remaining oil to pan. Cook remaining ingredients 5 minutes over high heat.

- Return scampi to pan, mix well and cook 2 minutes.

- Sprinkle with more lemon juice and serve over white rice.

1 SERVING			
Calories	292	Fat	12 g
Carbohydrate	17 g	Fiber	3.8 g
Protein	29 g	Cholesterol	87 mg

Whole Snapper with Spring Vegetables

◆

(4 SERVINGS)

¼ tsp	oregano	1 mL
¼ tsp	cumin	1 mL
2	garlic cloves, peeled, crushed and chopped	2
1	4-5 lb (1.8-2.3 kg) whole red snapper, prepared for cooking	1
5	fresh fennel sprigs	5
4 tbsp	olive oil	60 mL
12	baby carrots	12
2	bunches green onions, cut in 1-in (2.5-cm) lengths	2
½ cup	dry white wine	125 mL
	salt and freshly ground pepper	
	juice of 4 limes	

- Preheat oven to 400°F (200°C). Mix oregano, cumin, garlic, salt and pepper together. Sprinkle in cavity of fish. Stuff fennel sprigs inside and add half of lime juice.

- Place fish in baking dish. Drizzle with half of oil and remaining lime juice. Season generously, cover with plastic wrap and chill 30 minutes.

- Pour remaining oil over snapper and surround with baby carrots. Cook 35 minutes in oven.

- Add green onions and cook 6 more minutes in oven, or until fish is cooked.

- Transfer fish to serving platter.

- Place baking dish on stove over medium heat. Add wine and cook 3 minutes. Pour over fish and serve.

1 SERVING			
Calories	578	Fat	20 g
Carbohydrate	7 g	Fiber	1.2 g
Protein	90 g	Cholesterol	160 mg

Seafood and Rice

◆

(4 SERVINGS)

4 tbsp	olive oil	60 mL
1	onion, peeled and chopped	1
½	celery rib, diced small	½
1 cup	long grain white rice, rinsed and drained	250 mL
1½ cups	light chicken or vegetable stock, heated	375 mL
½ lb	fresh shrimp, peeled and deveined	225 g
1 lb	fresh scallops, rinsed and dried	450 g
2	garlic cloves, peeled and sliced	2
1	zucchini, halved lengthwise and sliced	1
½ lb	fresh mushrooms, cleaned and sliced	225 g
	salt and freshly ground pepper	
	soy sauce	
	lemon juice to taste	

■ Preheat oven to 350°F (180°C).

■ Heat 1 tbsp (15 mL) of oil in ovenproof casserole over medium heat. Add onion and celery; cook 2 minutes.

■ Add rice, mix well and cook 2 minutes over high heat. Season generously.

■ Pour in chicken stock, cover and cook 18 minutes in oven.

■ About 6 minutes before end of cooking, heat remaining oil in frying pan over high heat. Add seafood and sauté 2 minutes, or according to size. Remove seafood from pan and set aside.

■ Add garlic, zucchini and mushrooms to pan. Season well and cook 4 minutes over high heat.

■ Return seafood to pan. Add soy sauce and lemon juice; mix well and season generously. Cook 1 minute, or according to size, and incorporate to rice. Mix with fork and serve.

1 SERVING

Calories	412	Fat	16 g
Carbohydrate	35 g	Fiber	4.0 g
Protein	32 g	Cholesterol	130 mg

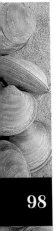

Cold Shrimp with Curry Dressing and Fruit

◆

(4 SERVINGS)

1½ lbs	fresh shrimp	675 g
1 tbsp	olive oil	15 mL
1	onion, peeled and chopped	1
2	shallots, peeled and chopped	2
2	garlic cloves, peeled, crushed and chopped	2
1 tbsp	curry powder	15 mL
½ cup	mayonnaise	125 mL
2 tbsp	chili sauce	30 mL
2 tbsp	sour cream	30 mL
1 cup	canned mandarin segments, drained	250 mL
2	apples, cored, peeled and sliced	2
	salt and freshly ground pepper	
	a few drops of Tabasco sauce	

■ Place shrimp in saucepan filled with cold, salted water. Place over medium heat and bring to a boil. Remove pan from heat and let stand 2 minutes.

■ Place pan under cold, running water to stop cooking process. Peel and devein shrimp.

■ Heat oil in frying pan over medium heat. Add onion, shallots and garlic; cook 4 minutes over low heat. Season well.

■ Sprinkle in curry powder and mix well. Cook 3 minutes.

■ Transfer vegetable mixture to bowl. Incorporate mayonnaise, chili sauce and sour cream. Add a few drops of Tabasco sauce. Mix well and season to taste.

■ Add fruit and combine gently.

■ Arrange shrimp on serving plates and top with dressing. Accompany with nuts, grapes and greens.

1 SERVING

Calories	521	Fat	29 g
Carbohydrate	28 g	Fiber	2.5 g
Protein	37 g	Cholesterol	348 mg

Oysters au Gratin on the Half Shell

♦

(4 SERVINGS)

32	fresh oysters, shucked, reserving lower shells	32
½ cup	dry white wine	125 mL
2 tbsp	olive oil	30 mL
2	onions, peeled and chopped	2
3	garlic cloves, peeled, crushed and chopped	3
½ lb	fresh mushrooms, cleaned and chopped finely	225 g
2 tbsp	chopped fresh basil	30 mL
2 tbsp	chopped fresh parsley	30 mL
1 cup	coarse white breadcrumbs	250 mL
¼ cup	heavy cream (35% MF)	50 mL
	salt and freshly ground pepper	

■ Place oysters and wine in frying pan; season well. Cover with sheet of waxed paper and bring to a boil. Remove immediately from heat, cool slightly and chop oysters.

■ Heat oil in separate frying pan over medium heat. Add onions and garlic; cook 3 minutes.

■ Add mushrooms and all seasonings; cook 6 minutes over high heat. Mix in chopped oysters and breadcrumbs. Pour in cream, mix well and cook 1 minute over medium heat.

■ Fill shells with stuffing and broil 3 minutes or until lightly browned. Serve.

1 SERVING			
Calories	339	Fat	15 g
Carbohydrate	34 g	Fiber	3.0 g
Protein	12 g	Cholesterol	72 mg

Fresh Sea Scallops au Gratin

◆

(4 SERVINGS)

1½ lbs	fresh scallops, rinsed	675 g
½ cup	dry white wine	125 mL
2	shallots, peeled and chopped	2
½ lb	fresh mushrooms, cleaned and sliced	225 g
1	fresh thyme sprig	1
2 cups	cold water	500 mL
3 tbsp	butter	45 mL
3 tbsp	all-purpose flour	45 mL
½ cup	heavy cream (35% MF)	125 mL
1 cup	grated Gruyère cheese	250 mL
	salt and freshly ground pepper	
	lemon juice to taste	

■ Place scallops in sauté pan. Add wine, shallots, mushrooms and all seasonings. Pour in 2 cups (500 mL) of water. Cover with sheet of waxed paper, ensuring that cover touches surface. Bring to boiling point over medium heat.

■ Remove pan from heat, turn scallops over and let stand in hot liquid for 2 minutes. Remove scallop shells and reserve; transfer scallops to bowl and set aside. Continue cooking liquid in pan 4 minutes over high heat. Discard thyme sprig.

■ Meanwhile, heat butter in saucepan over medium heat. Sprinkle in flour and mix well; cook 20 seconds.

■ Incorporate reduced cooking liquid and stir in cream. Cook sauce 3 minutes over low heat.

■ Season well and add reserved scallops. Add lemon juice; mix well. Divide mixture between scallop shells and top with cheese. Broil 2 minutes in oven or until lightly browned, and serve.

1 SERVING

Calories	437	Fat	27 g
Carbohydrate	12 g	Fiber	1.7 g
Protein	34 g	Cholesterol	138 mg

Tossed Vegetables with Sea Scallops

◆

(4 SERVINGS)

3 tbsp	olive oil	45 mL
1½ lbs	scallops, rinsed, drained and dried	675 g
1	onion, peeled and sliced	1
2 cups	cooked spinach, drained and chopped	500 mL
2	carrots, pared and sliced	2
1	yellow bell pepper, sliced	1
1 cup	frozen green peas	250 mL
1½ cups	fish stock or clam juice	375 mL
¼ tsp	fennel seeds	1 mL
2 tsp	cornstarch	10 mL
3 tbsp	cold water	45 mL
	salt and freshly ground pepper	
	cayenne pepper to taste	

■ Heat 2 tbsp (30 mL) of oil in large frying pan over high heat. Add scallops and cook 2 to 3 minutes, browning both sides. Season well, remove with slotted spoon and set aside.

■ Add vegetables, except peas, to pan. Season well and cook 5 minutes over high heat. Add peas, fish stock or clam juice, and fennel seeds. Simmer 3 minutes and season with cayenne pepper.

■ Dilute cornstarch in cold water; incorporate to mixture. Return scallops to pan, season well and simmer 2 minutes. Serve.

1 SERVING			
Calories	378	Fat	14 g
Carbohydrate	28 g	Fiber	7.4 g
Protein	35 g	Cholesterol	56 mg

103

Tomato Halibut Steaks

◆

(4 SERVINGS)

4	halibut steaks, rinsed	4
2 tbsp	butter	30 mL
2	onions, peeled and sliced thinly	2
2	garlic cloves, peeled, crushed and chopped	2
4	tomatoes, peeled, seeded and chopped	4
1 tbsp	chopped fresh basil	15 mL
1 tsp	chopped fresh parsley	5 mL
1½ cups	dry white wine	375 mL
½ cup	water	125 mL
	salt and freshly ground pepper	

■ Season fish with salt and pepper.

■ Heat butter in sauté pan over medium heat. Add onions and cook 12 minutes over low heat, stirring occasionally.

■ Add garlic, tomatoes and herbs; season well. Increase heat to high and cook 6 minutes.

■ Arrange halibut steaks on top of vegetables in pan. Pour in wine and water; season well. Cover with sheet of waxed paper, ensuring that cover touches surface. Bring to a boil over medium heat.

■ Reduce heat to low and turn steaks over. Cover and simmer 5 minutes, or until done.

■ Transfer cooked halibut to serving platter. Remove and discard middle bone.

■ Cook remaining liquid 3 minutes over high heat, pour over fish and serve.

1 SERVING

Calories	346	Fat	10 g
Carbohydrate	12 g	Fiber	2.5 g
Protein	42 g	Cholesterol	77 mg

Turbot au Gratin

◆

(4 SERVINGS)

4	turbot fillets, rinsed	4
2	shallots, peeled and chopped	2
½ lb	fresh mushrooms, cleaned and quartered	225 g
1 cup	dry white wine	250 mL
1 cup	cold water	250 mL
1	fresh fennel sprig	1
2 tbsp	butter	30 mL
2 tbsp	all-purpose flour	30 mL
1 tbsp	chopped fresh parsley	15 mL
1 cup	grated Gruyère cheese	250 mL
	salt and freshly ground pepper	

■ Season fillets generously on both sides. Place in sauté pan with shallots, mushrooms, wine, water and fennel sprig. Season well and cover with sheet of waxed paper, ensuring that cover touches surface. Bring to a boil over medium heat.

■ Reduce heat to low and simmer 2 minutes. Remove fillets from pan and keep warm in oven. Continue cooking liquid in pan 6 minutes over high heat.

■ Heat butter in separate saucepan over medium heat. Sprinkle in flour, mix well and cook 30 seconds. Incorporate reduced cooking liquid with mushrooms. Simmer 8 minutes over low heat and correct seasoning.

■ Arrange fish in baking dish and cover with sauce. Sprinkle with parsley and top with cheese. Broil 3 minutes or until golden brown, and serve.

1 SERVING			
Calories	532	Fat	24 g
Carbohydrate	70 g	Fiber	1.6 g
Protein	7 g	Cholesterol	228 mg

Whole Trout with Green Grapes

◆

(4 SERVINGS)

4	small whole trout, prepared for cooking	4
1 cup	all-purpose flour	250 mL
2 tbsp	olive oil	30 mL
2 tbsp	butter	30 mL
2	shallots, peeled and chopped	2
1½ lbs	seedless green grapes	675 g
1	lemon, peeled, seeded and diced	1
1 tbsp	chopped fresh parsley	15 mL
	salt and freshly ground pepper	

■ Preheat oven to 400°F (200°C). Season cavities of fish and dredge in flour.

■ Heat oil in large ovenproof frying pan over medium heat. Add fish and cook 2 minutes on each side.

■ Transfer frying pan to oven and cook fish 8 minutes, or according to size. When done, transfer fish to serving platter and tent with foil.

■ Return pan with juices from fish to stove set at medium heat. Add butter and remaining ingredients; sauté 2 minutes. Correct seasoning and pour over trout. Serve.

1 SERVING			
Calories	617	Fat	25 g
Carbohydrate	56 g	Fiber	2.8 g
Protein	42 g	Cholesterol	120 mg

Stuffed Egg Roll Skins

◆

(4 SERVINGS)

2 tbsp	olive oil	30 mL
½ lb	fresh mushrooms, cleaned and in julienne	225 g
8	green onions, cut in ¾-in (2-cm) lengths	8
1	celery rib, in julienne	1
3	garlic cloves, peeled, crushed and chopped	3
1	Chinese cabbage leaf, sliced thinly	1
1½ cups	bean sprouts	375 mL
1 tbsp	soy sauce	15 mL
12	shrimp, cooked, peeled, deveined and sliced thinly	12
1 tbsp	cornstarch	15 mL
2 tbsp	cold water	30 mL
	salt and freshly ground pepper	
	a few drops of Tabasco sauce	
	egg roll skins	
	peanut oil for deep-frying	

■ Heat olive oil in frying pan over medium heat. Add mushrooms, green onions, celery, garlic and cabbage. Cook 3 minutes over high heat.

■ Add bean sprouts and soy sauce. Season well, cover and cook 3 to 4 minutes over low heat. Add few drops of Tabasco sauce.

■ Stir in shrimp and season well. If mixture is too dry, add a little water.

■ Dilute cornstarch in cold water, incorporate to mixture and cook 1 minute over low heat.

■ Remove pan from heat and let cool. Preheat peanut oil to 375°F (190°C).

■ Place small amount of shrimp stuffing in middle of egg roll skin. Fold one side over stuffing and cover with opposite side. Wet ends with a little water to seal; press together gently. Deep-fry in peanut oil until golden brown.

■ Drain on paper towels and serve.

1 SERVING

Calories	174	Fat	10 g
Carbohydrate	14 g	Fiber	2.1 g
Protein	7 g	Cholesterol	35 mg

Place small amount of shrimp stuffing in middle of egg roll skin.

Fold one side over stuffing and cover with opposite side.

Wet ends with a little water to seal; press together gently.

Crab Patties

◆

(4 SERVINGS)

8 oz	cream cheese	225 g
1	egg, beaten	1
1 tbsp	Dijon mustard	15 mL
1 tbsp	chopped fresh parsley	15 mL
1 tbsp	chopped fresh chives	15 mL
2 tbsp	all-purpose flour	30 mL
1 tsp	lemon juice	5 mL
1 lb	crab meat, drained and flaked	450 g
½ cup	all-purpose flour	125 mL
2	eggs, beaten	2
1 cup	seasoned breadcrumbs	250 mL
4 tbsp	peanut oil	60 mL
	salt and freshly ground pepper	

■ Combine cream cheese, 1 beaten egg and mustard together. Add parsley, chives, 2 tbsp (30 mL) of flour and lemon juice; season to taste. Combine thoroughly and mix in crab meat.

■ Form mixture into small patties using palm of your hand. Refrigerate patties 30 minutes.

■ Dredge patties in flour, dip in beaten egg and coat with breadcrumbs. Heat oil in frying pan over medium heat and cook patties 3 minutes per side.

■ Serve with salad.

1 SERVING			
Calories	653	Fat	41 g
Carbohydrate	39 g	Fiber	1.0 g
Protein	32 g	Cholesterol	289 mg

Cold Lobster and Shrimp

◆

(4 SERVINGS)

4	1½ lb (675 g) live lobsters	4
½ cup	mayonnaise	125 mL
2 tbsp	capers	30 mL
2 tbsp	chili sauce	30 mL
4	hard-boiled eggs, halved	4
⅓ lb	shrimp, cooked, peeled and deveined	150 g
	salt and freshly ground pepper	
	a few drops of Tabasco sauce	
	lemon juice to taste	

■ Fill large pot with salted water. Bring to a boil over high heat. Plunge live lobsters into water. Cover until water resumes boil and cook 15 minutes over medium heat. Shells will turn bright red in color when cooked.

■ Remove lobsters from water and let cool on counter.

■ Split lobsters in half. Discard intestinal sac. Remove meat from body and claws. Slice and set aside. Clean shells and dry in warm oven.

■ Mix mayonnaise with capers, chili sauce, salt, pepper and Tabasco sauce. Force hand-boiled egg yolks through wire sieve; incorporate to mixture. Season well and add lemon juice.

■ Serve lobster meat in shells with mayonnaise mixture. Place two hard-boiled egg white shells on each serving and fill with shrimp. Top with more mayonnaise. Garnish with lemon wedges and serve.

1 SERVING			
Calories	763	Fat	31 g
Carbohydrate	9 g	Fiber	0 g
Protein	112 g	Cholesterol	639 mg

Tuna Spinach Pâté

◆

(6 SERVINGS)

2	tins solid Albacore tuna, drained	2
1 tbsp	chopped fresh parsley	15 mL
1½ cups	cooked spinach, chopped	375 mL
2 tbsp	capers	30 mL
⅓ cup	whipped cream	75 mL
2 tbsp	sour cream	30 mL
	salt and freshly ground pepper	
	Tabasco sauce to taste	

■ Place tuna, parsley, spinach and capers in food processor and purée. Season generously, add Tabasco sauce and blend to incorporate.

■ Transfer mixture to bowl and fold in whipped cream and sour cream. Fill buttered custard or terrine mold with mixture. Cover with plastic wrap, ensuring that wrap touches surface. Refrigerate 8 hours.

■ Remove from mold and place on serving platter, if desired. Accompany with chutney, assorted crackers and crudités.

1 SERVING			
Calories	114	Fat	6 g
Carbohydrate	2 g	Fiber	1.2 g
Protein	13 g	Cholesterol	25 mg

Hearty Cod Stew

◆

(4 SERVINGS)

4	bacon slices, diced	4
½	red onion, peeled and chopped	½
2	garlic cloves, peeled, crushed and chopped	2
4	potatoes, peeled and diced	4
4 cups	vegetable stock, heated	1 L
2	fresh fennel sprigs	2
1½ lbs	fresh cod, rinsed and cubed	675 g
2 tbsp	butter	30 mL
2 tbsp	all-purpose flour	30 mL
1 tbsp	chopped fresh parsley	15 mL
	salt and freshly ground pepper	

■ Cook bacon 6 minutes in large saucepan over medium heat. Add onion and garlic. Reduce heat to low and cook 4 minutes.

■ Stir in potatoes, vegetable stock and fresh fennel. Season well and cook 12 minutes over low heat.

■ Add fish and cook 6 minutes. Discard fennel sprigs. Remove 1 cup (250 mL) of cooking liquid and set aside.

■ Heat butter in separate saucepan over medium heat. Sprinkle in flour and mix well. Cook 15 seconds. Incorporate reserved cooking liquid. Pour mixture into pan containing fish and vegetables; mix gently. Add parsley and serve.

1 SERVING

Calories	403	Fat	11 g
Carbohydrate	30 g	Fiber	3.2 g
Protein	46 g	Cholesterol	113 mg

Turbot with Sun-Dried Tomatoes

◆

(4 SERVINGS)

2	large turbot fillets, rinsed and halved	2
2	shallots, peeled and chopped	2
1	celery rib with leaves, sliced	1
1 cup	dry white wine	250 mL
1½ cups	water	375 mL
2	fresh fennel sprigs	2
1	fresh thyme sprig	1
2	fresh parsley sprigs	2
1 tbsp	olive oil	15 mL
3	garlic cloves, peeled, crushed and chopped	3
3	tomatoes, peeled, seeded and chopped	3
2 tbsp	chopped sun-dried tomatoes	30 mL
1 tbsp	chopped fresh basil	15 mL
	salt and freshly ground pepper	
	lemon juice	

■ Arrange fillets in large frying pan. Add shallots, celery, wine, water and fresh herb sprigs. Season well and cover with sheet of waxed paper, ensuring that cover touches surface. Bring to a boil over medium heat.

■ Reduce heat to low and turn fillets over. Simmer 2 minutes. Remove fish and set aside.

■ Heat cooking liquid over high heat until reduced by one third; set aside.

■ Heat oil in separate frying pan over high heat. Add garlic and cook 1 minute. Add fresh and sun-dried tomatoes. Sprinkle in basil and season well. Cook 6 minutes over high heat.

■ Add fish and some of reserved cooking liquid to tomato mixture. Simmer 3 minutes to reheat turbot. Sprinkle with lemon juice and serve.

1 SERVING			
Calories	261	Fat	9 g
Carbohydrate	7 g	Fiber	1.4 g
Protein	33 g	Cholesterol	95 mg

Arrange fillets in large frying pan. Add shallots, celery, wine, water and fresh herb sprigs.

Season well and cover with sheet of waxed paper, ensuring that cover touches surface.

Turn fillets over and simmer 2 minutes. Remove fish and set aside.

Heat oil in separate frying pan over high heat. Add garlic and fresh and sun-dried tomatoes.

Sprinkle in basil and season well. Cook 6 minutes over high heat.

Add fish and some of reserved cooking liquid to tomato mixture.

Fresh Cod with Tomato Curry

♦

(4 SERVINGS)

2 tbsp	olive oil	30 mL
1	Spanish onion, peeled and sliced thinly	1
2 tbsp	curry powder	30 mL
12	cherry tomatoes, halved	12
2 lbs	fresh cod fillets, rinsed	900 g
1 cup	clam juice	250 mL
1 cup	water	250 mL
1	fresh thyme sprig	1
1	fresh fennel sprig	1
1	fresh parsley sprig	1
1 tbsp	cornstarch	15 mL
2 tbsp	cold water	30 mL
	salt and freshly ground pepper	
	juice of 1 lemon	

■ Heat oil in sauté pan over medium heat. Add onion and cook 6 minutes over low heat, stirring occasionally.

■ Sprinkle in curry powder and mix well. Continue cooking 3 minutes.

■ Stir in cherry tomatoes and season well. Cook 4 minutes.

■ Add fish, clam juice, water and fresh herbs. Season well and bring to a boil over medium heat.

■ As soon as liquid boils, reduce heat to low. Turn fish over and simmer 3 minutes or until done. Remove fish from pan and keep warm in oven.

■ Dilute cornstarch in cold water. Incorporate to sauce and cook 4 minutes over high heat. Pour over fish, sprinkle with lemon juice and serve.

1 SERVING			
Calories	349	Fat	9 g
Carbohydrate	19 g	Fiber	1.6 g
Protein	48 g	Cholesterol	111 mg

Pickerel with Fresh Herbs

♦

(4 SERVINGS)

4	pickerel fillets, rinsed and dried	4
2 tbsp	olive oil	30 mL
2 tbsp	butter	30 mL
1 tbsp	chopped fresh parsley	15 mL
1 tbsp	chopped fresh chives	15 mL
1 tbsp	chopped fresh tarragon	15 mL
	salt and freshly ground pepper	
	juice of 1 lemon	

■ Season fillets generously with salt and pepper. Heat oil in frying pan over high heat. Add fish and reduce heat to medium. Cook 3 minutes.

■ Turn fillets over and continue cooking 2 minutes. Fish is cooked when flesh feels firm to the touch. Do not overcook. Transfer fillets to serving platter.

■ Add butter to pan and increase heat to high. Add herbs and lemon juice. Mix and cook 10 seconds.

■ Pour over fish and serve immediately.

1 SERVING			
Calories	197	Fat	13 g
Carbohydrate	1 g	Fiber	0 g
Protein	19 g	Cholesterol	16 mg

Halibut and Potato Casserole

◆

(4 SERVINGS)

3	halibut steaks, rinsed	3
½ cup	dry white wine	125 mL
2	shallots, peeled and chopped	2
1	fresh thyme sprig	1
2	fresh fennel sprigs	2
2	fresh parsley sprigs	2
2½ cups	water	625 mL
32	raw parisienne potatoes	32
32	fresh mushroom caps, cleaned	32
2	carrots, pared and cut in small sticks	2
3 tbsp	butter	45 mL
3 tbsp	all-purpose flour	45 mL
	salt and freshly ground pepper	

■ Place fish in large sauté pan. Add wine, shallots and herbs. Cover with water and season well. Bring to a boil over medium heat.

■ As soon as water boils, reduce heat to low. Turn fish over and simmer 3 minutes. Remove fish from pan and set aside.

■ Add potatoes, mushrooms and carrots to liquid remaining in pan. Cover and cook until tender. Remove vegetables and set aside. Discard herbs and reserve cooking liquid.

■ Heat butter in saucepan over medium heat. Sprinkle in flour and mix well. Cook 1 minute.

■ Incorporate 2 cups (500 mL) of cooking liquid from fish. Season generously and cook sauce 6 minutes to thicken.

■ Bone and flake fish. Arrange in bottom of baking dish and cover with vegetables. Pour sauce over and broil in oven until heated through. Serve.

1 SERVING			
Calories	386	Fat	12 g
Carbohydrate	32 g	Fiber	3.6 g
Protein	35 g	Cholesterol	70 mg

POULTRY

Turkey, duck and some of the more exotic birds all lend themselves well to some wonderful recipe treatments, but for sheer versatility, nothing compares with chicken. No wonder it plays a starring role in favorite recipes all around the world.

The poultry recipes in this chapter reflect its international appeal; you will find dishes with a tropical twist, and others with an Asian flair, as well as some with a decidedly French or European pedigree.

But however complicated these succulent dishes may look at your favorite restaurant, they can all be successfully prepared in your own kitchen. Follow the step-by-step techniques and make *Chicken Dijonnaise* and *Orange Duck with Cranberries* your family's home-cooked favorites.

Chicken with Porcini Mushrooms

◆

(4 SERVINGS)

1 oz	dried porcini mushrooms	30 g
1 cup	vegetable stock, heated	250 mL
4 lb	chicken, cleaned, cut in 8 pieces and skinned	1.8 kg
½ cup	all-purpose flour	125 mL
2 tbsp	olive oil	30 mL
2	garlic cloves, peeled	2
½ cup	dry white wine	125 mL
10	fresh basil leaves	10
3	tomatoes, peeled and puréed	3
	salt and freshly ground pepper	

■ Place dried mushrooms in vegetable stock and set aside to soak.

■ Season chicken pieces well and dredge in flour. Heat oil in large sauté pan over medium heat. Add chicken and cook 15 minutes, turning pieces over 3 times during cooking.

■ Add garlic and cook 1 minute. Pour in wine and cook 2 minutes.

■ Drain mushrooms and strain stock through sieve lined with cheesecloth. Add mushrooms and stock to chicken; cook 10 minutes over low heat.

■ Season well; add basil and tomatoes. Cook 20 minutes over medium-low heat. Remove chicken breasts as soon as white meat is cooked.

■ When all chicken is done, remove pieces from pan and set aside. Cook sauce 4 minutes over medium heat.

■ Pour sauce over chicken, and serve with herb rice and rapini.

1 SERVING			
Calories	219	Fat	9 g
Carbohydrate	20 g	Fiber	2.1 g
Protein	12 g	Cholesterol	28 mg

Chicken Fricassee

◆

(4 SERVINGS)

2 tbsp	olive oil	30 mL
2	onions, peeled and diced	2
2	garlic cloves, peeled and sliced	2
4	chicken legs, skinned, boned and diced	4
4	potatoes, peeled and diced	4
1	red bell pepper, diced	1
2½ cups	chicken stock, heated	625 mL
1 tbsp	chopped basil	15 mL
	salt and freshly ground pepper	
	pinch of paprika	
	chopped fresh parsley	

■ Heat oil in large frying pan over medium heat. Add onions and garlic; cook 6 minutes.

■ Add diced chicken and season well. Reduce heat to low and cook 10 minutes, partly covered. Stir occasionally during cooking.

■ Add remaining ingredients, except parsley, and mix well. Correct seasoning and add paprika. Cook 15 minutes over low heat or until potatoes are done.

■ Sprinkle with parsley and serve.

1 SERVING			
Calories	375	Fat	15 g
Carbohydrate	30 g	Fiber	3.7 g
Protein	30 g	Cholesterol	89 mg

Chicken Cutlets

◆

(4 SERVINGS)

1	large whole boneless chicken breast, skinned	1
1 cup	all-purpose flour	250 mL
2	large eggs	2
¼ cup	light cream	50 mL
2 cups	breadcrumbs	500 mL
3 tbsp	olive oil	45 mL
	salt and freshly ground pepper	
	lemon wedges	

- Preheat oven to 375°F (190°C).

- Split chicken breast in half and slice each half in two, lengthwise. Place each piece of chicken between two sheets of waxed paper and pound until pieces are ⅛-in (3-mm) thick.

- Season meat well and dredge in flour. Beat eggs with cream, dip chicken in mixture and coat with breadcrumbs.

- Heat oil in large ovenproof frying pan over medium heat. Use 2 pans if necessary. Add chicken and brown each side 2 minutes.

- Transfer pan to oven and cook 8 minutes. Serve with lemon wedges.

1 SERVING

Calories	542	Fat	18 g
Carbohydrate	68 g	Fiber	1.8 g
Protein	27 g	Cholesterol	149 mg

Sweet and Tangy Chicken Wings

◆

(4 SERVINGS)

32	chicken wings	32
½ cup	maple syrup	125 mL
6 tbsp	balsamic vinegar	90 mL
6 tbsp	olive oil	90 mL
4	garlic cloves, peeled, crushed and chopped	4
½ tsp	crushed chilies	2 mL
	juice of 2 lemons	
	freshly ground pepper	

■ Cut off wing tips at joint and discard. Place wings in large bowl and season well.

■ In separate bowl, mix remaining ingredients together; pour over wings. Mix well, cover and refrigerate 1 hour.

■ Preheat oven to 450°F (230°C).

■ Place wings in large roasting pan. Tent with foil and cook 8 minutes in oven.

■ Remove foil and cook 8 to 10 minutes, or according to size. Serve.

1 SERVING			
Calories	639	Fat	35 g
Carbohydrate	30 g	Fiber	0.1 g
Protein	51 g	Cholesterol	144 mg

Chicken Livers with Bell Peppers

◆

(4 SERVINGS)

3 tbsp	olive oil	45 mL
1½ lbs	chicken livers, cleaned, trimmed of fat and halved	675 g
1	onion, peeled and chopped	1
2	garlic cloves, peeled, crushed and chopped	2
1	green bell pepper, diced	1
1	red bell pepper, diced	1
1	yellow bell pepper, diced	1
2 tbsp	chopped fresh basil	30 mL
	salt and freshly ground pepper	

■ Heat 2 tbsp (30 mL) of oil in large frying pan over high heat. Add chicken livers and season well. Cook 2 minutes.

■ Turn livers over and cook 2 minutes. Remove livers from pan and set aside.

■ Add remaining oil to pan. When hot, add onion, garlic and bell peppers. Season well and cook 5 minutes over medium heat.

■ Return chicken livers to pan and mix well. Sprinkle in basil and simmer 3 minutes over low heat.

■ Serve over rice.

1 SERVING			
Calories	309	Fat	17 g
Carbohydrate	8 g	Fiber	1.4 g
Protein	31 g	Cholesterol	788 mg

Chicken – Hunter Style

◆

(4 SERVINGS)

4 lb	chicken, cleaned and cut in 8 pieces	1.8 kg
2 tbsp	olive oil	30 mL
3	shallots, peeled and chopped	3
3	garlic cloves, peeled, crushed and chopped	3
2	small onions, peeled and quartered	2
½ cup	dry white wine	125 mL
3	tomatoes, peeled, seeded and chopped	3
2 tbsp	chopped fresh basil	30 mL
2 tbsp	butter	30 mL
½ lb	fresh mushroom caps, cleaned	225 g
	salt and freshly ground pepper	

■ Preheat oven to 350°F (180°C).

■ Skin chicken pieces and season well. Heat oil in large ovenproof sauté pan over high heat. Add chicken and cook 6 minutes, browning all sides.

■ Add shallots, garlic and onions. Mix and cook 3 minutes. Pour in wine and cook 2 minutes.

■ Stir in tomatoes and basil; season well. Cover and cook 20 minutes in oven. Remove chicken breasts and keep warm.

■ Return pan to oven and cook remaining chicken 10 to 20 minutes, or according to size.

■ Meanwhile, heat butter in frying pan over medium heat. Add mushroom caps and season well. Sauté 3 minutes and add to chicken in oven.

■ Return chicken breasts to pan, mix well and serve.

1 SERVING

Calories	263	Fat	15 g
Carbohydrate	15 g	Fiber	3.9 g
Protein	12 g	Cholesterol	45 mg

Add shallots, garlic and onions. Mix and cook 3 minutes.

Pour in wine and cook 2 minutes.

Stir in tomatoes and basil; season well. Cover and cook 20 minutes in oven.

Remove chicken breasts
and keep warm.

Add mushroom caps to butter
and season well.

Sauté 3 minutes and
add to chicken in oven.

Orange Duck with Cranberries

◆

(4 SERVINGS)

5 lb	duck, cleaned	2.3 kg
4	oranges, halved	4
2	lemons, halved	2
1	carrot, pared and diced	1
1	onion, pared and chopped	1
½	celery rib, diced	½
1	bay leaf	1
1	fresh thyme sprig	1
2	fresh parsley sprigs	2
2 tbsp	chopped fresh basil	30 mL
3 tbsp	all-purpose flour	45 mL
1 cup	dry red wine	250 mL
1½ cups	beef stock, heated	375 mL
2 cups	frozen cranberries, defrosted	500 mL
	salt and freshly ground pepper	
	fresh squeezed orange juice	

- Preheat oven to 450°F (230°C).

- Remove extra fat from duck. Season cavity with salt and pepper. Rub skin with cut side of 1 orange and 1 lemon. Fill cavity with fruit and truss bird. Sprinkle skin with salt and pepper. Prick in several places with needle to allow fat to drain during cooking.

- Place in roasting pan. Roast 1 hour. Remove some of fat during cooking and baste bird with fresh squeezed fruit juice.

- Reduce heat to 375°F (190°C) and continue roasting duck 30 minutes. When duck is cooked, transfer bird to serving platter and tent with foil.

- Reserve ¼ cup (50 mL) of fat in roasting pan, discarding the rest. Place pan on stove over high heat. Add vegetables and seasonings; cook 3 minutes. Sprinkle in flour and reduce heat to low. Mix well and cook 4 minutes.

- Meanwhile, place wine in small saucepan and reduce by one third.

- Add wine and beef stock to roasting pan. Mix well and cook 10 minutes over medium heat.

- Strain sauce into clean saucepan. Add cranberries and simmer 2 minutes over low heat.

- Carve duck and serve with sauce.

1 SERVING			
Calories	674	Fat	18 g
Carbohydrate	37 g	Fiber	6.8 g
Protein	88 g	Cholesterol	327 mg

Chicken in White Wine with Ginger Root

◆

(4 SERVINGS)

3½ lb	chicken, cleaned and cut in 8 pieces	1.6 kg
1 cup	all-purpose flour	250 mL
3 tbsp	olive oil	45 mL
1	cucumber, peeled, seeded and sliced ½-in (1-cm) thick	1
½ lb	fresh mushrooms, cleaned and sliced	225 g
2	shallots, peeled and chopped	2
2	apples, cored, peeled and sliced	2
2 tbsp	chopped fresh ginger	30 mL
½ cup	dry white wine	125 mL
1½ cups	chicken stock, heated	375 mL
1 tbsp	cornstarch	15 mL
2 tbsp	cold water	30 mL
	salt and freshly ground pepper	
	chopped fresh chives	

■ Skin chicken pieces and season well; dredge in flour.

■ Heat 2 tbsp (30 mL) of oil in large frying pan over medium heat. Add chicken pieces and brown on all sides. Cover and cook chicken 30 to 35 minutes, or according to size. When done, transfer chicken to platter and tent with foil.

■ Add remaining oil to pan. When hot, add cucumber, mushrooms and shallots. Season well and cook 5 minutes over high heat.

■ Add apples and ginger; cook 3 minutes. Pour in white wine and cook 2 minutes. Stir in chicken stock.

■ Dilute cornstarch in cold water; incorporate to sauce. Season generously and return chicken to pan. Simmer 3 minutes, sprinkle with chives and serve.

1 SERVING

Calories	369	Fat	13 g
Carbohydrate	44 g	Fiber	4.6 g
Protein	14 g	Cholesterol	26 mg

Turkey Vol-au-Vent Suprême

◆

(4 SERVINGS)

2 tbsp	butter	30 mL
4	green onions, chopped	4
½ lb	fresh mushrooms, cleaned and diced	225 g
1	red bell pepper, grilled and diced	1
3	garlic cloves, blanched and puréed	3
2 cups	diced cooked turkey	500 mL
2 cups	Suprême Sauce (see page 166)	500 mL
2 tbsp	grated Parmesan cheese	30 mL
8	small vol-au-vent pastry shells	8
	salt and freshly ground pepper	
	pinch of nutmeg	
	chopped fresh parsley	

■ Heat butter in saucepan over medium heat. Add onions and mushrooms; season well. Cook 4 minutes.

■ Add bell pepper and garlic; mix well. Stir in cooked turkey and Suprême Sauce. Simmer 4 minutes over low heat. Correct seasoning, add nutmeg and cheese; mix well.

■ Meanwhile, heat pastry shells in warm oven.

■ Fill vol-au-vent with mixture and sprinkle with parsley. Serve.

1 SERVING

Calories	443	Fat	27 g
Carbohydrate	23 g	Fiber	3.1 g
Protein	27 g	Cholesterol	93 mg

Chicken Legs Paprika

◆

(4 SERVINGS)

4	chicken legs	4
½ cup	all-purpose flour	125 mL
3 tbsp	olive oil	45 mL
1	Spanish onion, peeled and sliced	1
1 tbsp	paprika	15 mL
4	tomatoes, peeled, seeded and chopped	4
3	garlic cloves, peeled, crushed and chopped	3
1½ cups	chicken stock, heated	375 mL
2 tbsp	chopped fresh basil	30 mL
	salt and freshly ground pepper	

■ Preheat oven to 350°F (180°C).

■ Cut chicken legs at the joint between the thigh and drumstick. Remove skin and season pieces well; dredge in flour.

■ Heat 2 tbsp (30 mL) of oil in ovenproof casserole over medium heat. Add chicken pieces and cook 8 minutes, browning all sides. Remove chicken and set aside.

■ Add remaining oil to casserole. When hot, cook onion 10 minutes over low heat. Sprinkle in paprika, mix well and cook 2 minutes.

■ Add tomatoes and garlic; season well. Cook 4 minutes.

■ Incorporate chicken stock and return chicken to casserole. Add basil and season well. Transfer partly-covered casserole to oven and cook 35 minutes, or according to size.

■ When chicken is cooked, transfer pieces to serving platter. Tent with foil.

■ Place casserole on stove over high heat. Cook sauce 4 minutes, pour over chicken and serve.

1 SERVING			
Calories	395	Fat	19 g
Carbohydrate	26 g	Fiber	3.3 g
Protein	30 g	Cholesterol	89 mg

Chicken with Tomatoes and Olives

◆

(4 SERVINGS)

3 tbsp	olive oil	45 mL
4 lb	chicken, cleaned, cut in 8 pieces and skinned	1.8 kg
3	large tomatoes, peeled, seeded and diced coarsely	3
2	garlic cloves, peeled, crushed and chopped	2
1 tbsp	tomato paste	15 mL
1 cup	dry white wine	250 mL
½ cup	gravy, heated	125 mL
1	fresh thyme sprig	1
3	fresh basil sprigs	3
1	bay leaf	1
20	pitted green olives	20
¾ lb	fresh mushrooms, cleaned	350 g
	salt and freshly ground pepper	
	grated rind of 1 small orange	

- Preheat oven to 350°F (180°C).

- Heat 2 tbsp (30 mL) of oil in large sauté pan over medium heat. Add chicken pieces and brown 5 minutes; season well. Remove chicken from pan and set aside.

- Add tomatoes and garlic to hot pan; season well. Cook 3 minutes over medium heat. Transfer mixture to ovenproof casserole.

- Mix in tomato paste, wine, gravy and all seasonings, including orange rind. Place chicken pieces in sauce and bring to a boil. Cover and cook 25 minutes in oven.

- Meanwhile, heat remaining oil in frying pan over medium heat. Add olives and mushrooms; cook 3 minutes.

- Transfer olives and mushrooms to casserole. Cook 5 minutes and remove chicken breasts; keep warm. Cook remaining chicken 5 more minutes and return chicken breasts. Cook 5 minutes and serve.

1 SERVING			
Calories	247	Fat	15 g
Carbohydrate	11 g	Fiber	4.6 g
Protein	12 g	Cholesterol	28 mg

Chicken Wings with Curry

◆

(2 SERVINGS)

2 lbs	chicken wings, tips trimmed	900 g
1 tsp	cumin	5 mL
1 tsp	curry powder	5 mL
¼ tsp	salt	1 mL
1 tsp	white pepper	5 mL
½ cup	distilled white vinegar	125 mL
1 tbsp	apple cider (optional)	15 mL
1 tbsp	Worcestershire sauce	15 mL
	vegetable oil	

■ Preheat oven to 475°F (240°C).

■ Split chicken wings at joint. Place in large bowl with cumin, curry powder, salt and pepper.

■ Oil large baking dish generously. Spread wings over bottom of dish and bake 7 to 8 minutes on each side. Drizzle with half of vinegar and cook 5 minutes.

■ Combine remaining vinegar with apple cider and Worcestershire sauce. Drizzle mixture over wings and bake 10 minutes, turning wings over once. Serve.

1 SERVING

Calories	679	Fat	27 g
Carbohydrate	5 g	Fiber	0 g
Protein	104 g	Cholesterol	286 mg

Chicken Shish Kebabs

◆

(4 SERVINGS)

1	large whole boneless chicken breast	1
1	zucchini, diced	1
1	red bell pepper, diced	1
1	green bell pepper, diced	1
20	fresh mushroom caps, cleaned	20
2 tbsp	olive oil	30 mL
1 tbsp	soy sauce	15 mL
2	garlic cloves, peeled, crushed and chopped	2
	salt and freshly ground pepper	
	juice of 1 lemon	

■ Skin and cube chicken.

■ Place all ingredients in large bowl. Mix well, cover and refrigerate 15 minutes.

■ Alternate pieces of chicken and vegetables on metal skewers. Season well and baste with marinade.

■ Broil 12 minutes, turning skewers over once. Baste with marinade during cooking.

■ Serve with rice.

1 SERVING

Calories	156	Fat	8 g
Carbohydrate	6 g	Fiber	1.2 g
Protein	15 g	Cholesterol	37 mg

Cashew Chicken
with Grilled Peppers

◆

(4 SERVINGS)

2	red bell peppers	2
2	whole boneless chicken breasts	2
2	egg whites	2
2 tbsp	cornstarch	30 mL
2 tbsp	soy sauce	30 mL
3 tbsp	olive oil	45 mL
¾ cup	sliced canned bamboo shoots, drained	175 mL
½ cup	cashews, halved	125 mL
3	green onions, chopped	3
2 cups	chicken stock, heated	500 mL
2 tbsp	cold water	30 mL
	salt and freshly ground pepper	

■ Cut bell peppers in half and remove seeds. Oil skin and place cut-side-down on cookie sheet; broil 6 minutes. Remove from oven and cool. Peel off skin, slice peppers and set aside.

■ Skin chicken and cut in strips about ⅓ in (8 mm) wide. Place chicken in bowl and season well.

■ Beat egg whites with 1 tbsp (15 mL) of cornstarch and soy sauce. Pour over chicken, mix and chill 10 minutes.

■ Heat 2 tbsp (30 mL) of oil in large frying pan over medium heat. Add chicken and stir-fry 4 to 5 minutes. Remove chicken and set aside.

■ Add remaining oil to pan. When hot, add bell peppers, bamboo shoots, cashews and green onions; cook 2 minutes.

■ Pour in chicken stock and season well. Dilute remaining cornstarch in cold water; incorporate to sauce.

■ Return chicken to pan, mix and simmer 3 minutes over low heat. Serve.

1 SERVING

Calories	398	Fat	22 g
Carbohydrate	16 g	Fiber	1.5 g
Protein	34 g	Cholesterol	73 mg

Chicken Chow-Mein

◆

(4 SERVINGS)

2	whole boneless chicken breasts	2
3 tbsp	olive oil	45 mL
4	shallots, peeled and sliced	4
1	celery rib, sliced	1
1	garlic clove, peeled and sliced	1
1 cup	sliced Chinese cabbage	250 mL
1½ cups	bean sprouts	375 mL
1½ cups	chicken stock, heated	375 mL
1 tbsp	cornstarch	15 mL
2 tbsp	cold water	30 mL
2 tbsp	soy sauce	30 mL
	salt and freshly ground pepper	

■ Skin chicken and cut in strips about ⅓-in (8-mm) wide. Heat 2 tbsp (30 mL) of oil in frying pan over medium heat. Add chicken, season well and stir-fry 4 minutes. Remove chicken from pan and set aside.

■ Add remaining oil to pan. When hot, add shallots, celery, garlic and Chinese cabbage. Cook 4 to 5 minutes over medium heat.

■ Add bean sprouts, season with pepper and cook 2 minutes.

■ Pour in chicken stock. Dilute cornstarch in cold water; incorporate to mixture. Reduce heat to low.

■ Return chicken to pan and add soy sauce. Mix and simmer 2 minutes. Serve over noodles.

1 SERVING			
Calories	253	Fat	13 g
Carbohydrate	5 g	Fiber	0.7 g
Protein	29 g	Cholesterol	73 mg

Braised Rock Cornish Game Hens

◆

(4 SERVINGS)

4	2 lb (900 g) Rock Cornish game hens, cleaned	4
1 tsp	olive oil	5 mL
3.5 oz	bacon, diced finely	100 g
12	shallots, peeled	12
12	baby carrots	12
2 tbsp	chopped fresh basil	30 mL
1½ tbsp	all-purpose flour	25 mL
1½ cups	light chicken stock, heated	375 mL
	salt and freshly ground pepper	

- Preheat oven to 375°F (190°C). Season cavities and truss cornish hens.

- Heat oil in large ovenproof casserole over medium heat. Add bacon and cook 3 minutes.

- Place hens in casserole and brown all sides; season generously.

- Add whole shallots, carrots and basil. Cover and cook 30 to 35 minutes in oven.

- When cooked, transfer hens and vegetables to serving platter. Tent with foil.

- Reserve 1½ tbsp (25 mL) of fat in casserole; discard the rest. Place on stove over medium heat and sprinkle in flour. Mix well.

- Whisk in chicken stock; mix until well-incorporated. Cook sauce 4 minutes over low heat.

- Serve hens with sauce and vegetables.

1 SERVING			
Calories	872	Fat	40 g
Carbohydrate	9 g	Fiber	1.5 g
Protein	119 g	Cholesterol	255 mg

Chicken with Prunes

◆

(4 SERVINGS)

12	prunes	12
¼ cup	rum	50 mL
2½ tbsp	olive oil	40 mL
4 lb	chicken, cleaned, cut in 8 pieces and skinned	1.8 kg
12	spring carrots, quartered	12
12	shallots, peeled	12
2	garlic cloves, peeled, crushed and chopped	2
3 cups	dry white wine	750 mL
2	fresh parsley sprigs	2
2	fresh basil sprigs	2
1	fresh thyme sprig	1
2	bay leaves	2
2 tbsp	cornstarch	30 mL
3 tbsp	cold water	45 mL
	salt and freshly ground pepper	

■ Place prunes in bowl; add water until prunes are ¾-covered. Pour in rum and marinate for 2 hours.

■ Preheat oven to 350°F (180°C).

■ Heat oil in large sauté pan over medium heat. Add chicken pieces and brown 4 to 5 minutes; season well. Remove chicken and set aside.

■ Add carrots and whole shallots to hot pan. Cook 3 to 4 minutes. Add garlic, mix well and cook 1 minute. Transfer vegetables to ovenproof casserole.

■ Place chicken on top of vegetables in casserole. Drain prunes and add to casserole. Pour in wine and add all seasonings. Cover and cook 30 minutes in oven. Remove breasts and keep warm; cook remaining chicken 10 more minutes.

■ When remaining chicken is cooked, remove from casserole. Discard herb sprigs and place casserole on stove over medium heat. Bring sauce to a boil and cook 3 minutes.

■ Dilute cornstarch in cold water; incorporate to sauce. Return all chicken pieces to casserole and simmer 2 minutes. Serve.

1 SERVING			
Calories	416	Fat	12 g
Carbohydrate	46 g	Fiber	7.9 g
Protein	12 g	Cholesterol	28 mg

Pour rum into soaking prunes and marinate for 2 hours.

Add chicken pieces to sauté pan and brown 4 to 5 minutes; season well.

Add carrots and whole shallots to hot pan; cook 3 to 4 minutes. Add garlic, mix well and cook 1 minute.

Place chicken on top of vegetables in casserole.

Drain prunes and add to casserole.

Pour in wine and add all seasonings. Cover and cook 30 minutes in oven.

Brandy Braised Whole Chicken

◆

(4 SERVINGS)

4 lb	chicken, cleaned	1.8 kg
3 tbsp	butter	45 mL
¼ cup	brandy	50 mL
2	shallots, peeled and chopped	2
½ lb	fresh mushrooms, cleaned and diced	225 g
1 tsp	tarragon	5 mL
2 tbsp	all-purpose flour	30 mL
1½ cups	chicken stock, heated	375 mL
½ cup	Port wine	125 mL
1 tbsp	chopped fresh parsley	15 mL
	salt and freshly ground pepper	

■ Preheat oven to 350°F (180°C). Season cavity of chicken generously and truss bird.

■ Heat butter in large ovenproof casserole over medium heat. Add bird and sear all sides; season well.

■ Pour in brandy and flambé. Cover casserole and braise 1¼ to 1½ hours in oven. Turn bird over on each side during cooking.

■ When chicken is cooked, remove from casserole. Set aside and tent with foil.

■ Place casserole on stove over medium heat. Add shallots, mushrooms and tarragon; cook 4 minutes.

■ Sprinkle in flour and mix well. Whisk in chicken stock, add Port wine and cook 4 minutes.

■ Carve chicken, sprinkle with parsley and serve with sauce.

1 SERVING			
Calories	208	Fat	12 g
Carbohydrate	8 g	Fiber	2.2 g
Protein	12 g	Cholesterol	52 mg

Pan-Fried Chicken with Peanut Sauce

◆

(2 SERVINGS)

¼ cup	peanut butter	50 mL
1 tbsp	dry sherry	15 mL
1 tbsp	teriyaki sauce	15 mL
1½ tbsp	lime juice	25 mL
1 tbsp	brown sugar	15 mL
1	garlic clove, peeled, crushed and chopped	1
⅓ cup	water	75 mL
1	large whole boneless chicken breast, split in half and skinned	1
1½ tbsp	peanut oil	25 mL
	salt and freshly ground pepper	
	a few drops of Tabasco sauce	

■ Mix peanut butter, sherry, teriyaki sauce, lime juice, brown sugar and garlic together in small saucepan. Season well and add a few drops of Tabasco sauce.

■ Pour in water and bring to a boil over medium heat, stirring frequently. Remove immediately from heat and cover to keep warm.

■ Season chicken well on both sides with salt and pepper. Heat oil in large cast iron frying pan over medium heat. When oil starts to smoke, add chicken. Cover and cook 5 minutes. Turn chicken over, cover and cook 7 to 8 minutes, or according to size.

■ Slice chicken into thin pieces and arrange on heated plates. Drizzle with peanut sauce and serve immediately. Accompany with mixed vegetables, if desired.

1 SERVING			
Calories	394	Fat	22 g
Carbohydrate	13 g	Fiber	1.7 g
Protein	34 g	Cholesterol	73 mg

Hot Curry Chicken with Coconut

◆

(4 SERVINGS)

1 cup	chicken stock, heated	250 mL
¼ cup	fresh shredded coconut	50 mL
3½ lb	chicken, cleaned, cut in 8 pieces and skinned	1.6 kg
3 tbsp	olive oil	45 mL
2	onions, peeled and diced	2
1 tbsp	coriander	15 mL
1 tsp	cumin	5 mL
1 tbsp	chili powder	15 mL
1 tsp	turmeric	5 mL
3	tomatoes, peeled, seeded and chopped	3
3 tbsp	toasted almonds	45 mL
	salt and freshly ground pepper	

■ Pour hot chicken stock over coconut; let stand 10 minutes. Drain coconut, reserving chicken stock in bowl. Squeeze out excess liquid from coconut into bowl. Set liquid aside and discard coconut.

■ Season chicken pieces well. Heat half of oil in large frying pan over medium heat. Add chicken and cook 12 minutes, or until browned on all sides. Remove chicken from pan and set aside.

■ Add remaining oil to hot pan. Cook onions 3 minutes over low heat. Add all seasonings, mix well and cook 2 minutes.

■ Incorporate reserved chicken stock to pan. Stir in tomatoes and reserved chicken; season well. Cover and cook 35 minutes over low heat.

■ Add almonds and serve.

1 SERVING

Calories	257	Fat	17 g
Carbohydrate	14 g	Fiber	2.9 g
Protein	12 g	Cholesterol	26 mg

Chicken with Caramelized Apples

◆

(4 SERVINGS)

4 lb	chicken, cleaned and cut in 8 pieces	1.8 kg
3 tbsp	olive oil	45 mL
3 tbsp	finely chopped shallots	45 mL
1 cup	apple cider	250 mL
½ cup	light chicken stock, heated	125 mL
¼ cup	butter	50 mL
4	large apples, cored, peeled and sliced	4
¼ tsp	cinnamon	1 mL
1½ cups	heavy cream (35% MF)	375 mL
	salt and white pepper	

■ Season chicken pieces generously. Heat oil in large frying pan over medium heat. Add chicken and sauté 10 minutes, turning pieces over frequently. When chicken is golden brown, transfer pieces to platter and set aside.

■ Add shallots to hot pan and cook 2 to 3 minutes over medium-low heat. Pour in apple cider and chicken stock; cook 2 minutes.

■ Return chicken to pan, cover and cook 20 minutes over low heat, or according to size. Remove breasts after about 10 minutes of cooking; keep warm.

■ While remaining chicken is cooking, melt butter in separate frying pan over medium heat. Add apples and cinnamon. Cook 15 to 18 minutes over medium heat, stirring occasionally. As soon as apples have caramelized, remove from pan and set aside.

■ When remaining chicken is cooked, transfer pieces to heated platter.

■ Place pan containing chicken juices on stove. Skim off fat and cook juice 3 to 4 minutes over high heat. Stir in cream, reduce heat to low and cook 2 to 3 minutes to thicken.

■ Return chicken to sauce and simmer 5 minutes, basting pieces frequently.

■ Arrange chicken on serving platter. Garnish with caramelized apples and top with cream sauce. Serve.

1 SERVING			
Calories	666	Fat	54 g
Carbohydrate	33 g	Fiber	2.7 g
Protein	12 g	Cholesterol	175 mg

Turkey Pot Pie Suprême

◆

(4 SERVINGS)

2	carrots, pared and sliced ½-in (1-cm) thick	2
½	celery rib, sliced ½-in (1-cm) thick	½
2	potatoes, peeled and diced large	2
2 tbsp	butter	30 mL
2	shallots, peeled and chopped	2
1	onion, peeled and chopped	1
1½ cups	diced cooked turkey	375 mL
2½ cups	Suprême Sauce, heated (see page 166)	625 mL
	salt and freshly ground pepper	
	paprika and nutmeg to taste	
	flaky dough (see page 342)	
	milk	

- Preheat oven to 350°F (180°C).

- Precook carrots, celery and potatoes in salted, boiling water. Drain well and set aside.

- Heat butter in saucepan over medium heat. Add shallots and onion; cook 2 minutes. Stir in turkey and vegetables. Season well and simmer 1 minute.

- Incorporate Suprême Sauce. Season with paprika and nutmeg. Transfer contents of saucepan to ovenproof baking dish.

- Cover top with pastry and cut small opening in dough. Brush with milk. Bake 16 to 18 minutes and serve.

1 SERVING

Calories	525	Fat	29 g
Carbohydrate	43 g	Fiber	3.3 g
Protein	23 g	Cholesterol	90 mg

Chicken Livers with Mushrooms

◆

(4 SERVINGS)

4 tbsp	olive oil	60 mL
1½ lbs	chicken livers, cleaned, trimmed of fat and halved	675 g
1	onion, peeled and chopped	1
2	garlic cloves, peeled, crushed and chopped	2
1 lb	fresh mushrooms, cleaned and diced	450 g
1 tbsp	chopped fresh basil	15 mL
	salt and freshly ground pepper	
	lemon juice to taste	

■ Heat half of oil in large frying pan over high heat. Add chicken livers and season well; cook 2 minutes.

■ Turn livers over and cook 2 minutes. Remove livers from pan and set aside.

■ Add remaining oil to pan. When hot, cook onion and garlic 1 minute over medium heat.

■ Add mushrooms and basil, and season well; cook 4 minutes, stirring once.

■ Return chicken livers to pan and mix well; simmer 2 minutes over low heat. Add lemon juice and serve with sliced zucchini.

1 SERVING

Calories	357	Fat	21 g	
Carbohydrate	9 g	Fiber	3.7 g	
Protein	33 g	Cholesterol	788 mg	

Sauté of Chicken with Eggplant

◆

(4 SERVINGS)

1	small eggplant	1
4 lb	chicken, cleaned and cut in 8 pieces	1.8 kg
3 tbsp	olive oil	45 mL
½ cup	dry white wine	125 mL
2	garlic cloves, peeled, crushed and chopped	2
3	tomatoes, peeled, seeded and chopped	3
1 tbsp	chopped fresh tarragon	15 mL
	salt and freshly ground pepper	

- Preheat oven to 400°F (200°C).

- Cut eggplant in half lengthwise. Score flesh in criss-cross pattern and brush with oil. Place, skin-side-up, on cookie sheet and bake 40 minutes. Scoop out flesh, chop and set aside.

- Skin chicken pieces and season well. Heat oil in large ovenproof casserole over medium heat. Add chicken pieces and brown all sides. Pour in wine and cook 3 minutes.

- Add all remaining ingredients and season well; cook 4 minutes. Cover casserole and cook 30 minutes in oven.

- Remove cooked chicken breasts, set aside and tent with foil. Cook remaining chicken 10 more minutes or according to size.

- Return chicken breasts to casserole along with reserved eggplant; serve with rice and fresh asparagus, if desired.

1 SERVING			
Calories	186	Fat	13 g
Carbohydrate	6 g	Fiber	1.7 g
Protein	10 g	Cholesterol	28 mg

Chicken Dijonnaise

◆

2 tbsp	butter	30 mL
1 tsp	olive oil	5 mL
1	large whole boneless chicken breast, split in half and skinned	1
4	green onions, chopped	4
½ cup	dry white wine	125 mL
1 cup	Suprême Sauce, heated (see page 166)	250 mL
1 tsp	chopped fresh tarragon	5 mL
1 tsp	Dijon mustard	5 mL
	salt and freshly ground pepper	

■ Heat butter and oil in frying pan over medium heat. Add chicken and onions; cook 12 minutes over medium heat. Season twice during cooking. Do not let onions burn.

■ When chicken is cooked, remove from pan and keep warm.

■ Add wine to pan and cook 2 minutes over high heat. Stir in Suprême Sauce and tarragon; season well and simmer 4 minutes.

■ Stir in mustard, return chicken to pan and simmer 3 minutes over low heat. Serve.

1 SERVING			
Calories	183	Fat	12 g
Carbohydrate	3 g	Fiber	0.4 g
Protein	14 g	Cholesterol	62 mg

Key-Side Chicken

◆

(4 SERVINGS)

2	bay leaves	2
1	fresh thyme sprig	1
2	fresh parsley sprigs	2
¼ cup	olive oil	50 mL
4 lb	chicken, cleaned, cut in 8 pieces and skinned	1.8 kg
2	onions, peeled and chopped	2
1	celery rib, chopped	1
3	garlic cloves, peeled, crushed and chopped	3
1	green bell pepper, diced	1
1	red bell pepper, diced	1
4	large tomatoes, peeled, seeded and chopped	4
2 cups	long grain white rice, rinsed	500 mL
2 cups	chicken stock, heated	500 mL
½ tsp	saffron	2 mL
1 cup	frozen green peas	250 mL
¼ cup	sliced pimiento pepper	50 mL
	salt and freshly ground pepper	

■ Preheat oven to 350°F (180°C).

■ Bundle bay leaves, thyme and parsley in piece of cheesecloth and tie with string; set bouquet garni aside.

■ Heat half of oil in large ovenproof sauté pan over medium heat. Add chicken pieces and cook 10 minutes until browned on all sides. Season well during cooking. Remove chicken from pan and set aside.

■ Add remaining oil to hot pan. Cook onions, celery and garlic 3 minutes over medium heat. Add bell peppers and cook 3 minutes.

■ Stir in tomatoes, season well and cook 4 minutes. Add rice, chicken stock and bouquet garni. Return chicken pieces to pan and add saffron. Mix well, season and bring to a boil.

■ Cover and cook 10 minutes in oven. Remove chicken breasts and cook remaining chicken 5 minutes.

■ Add peas, pimiento pepper and chicken breasts to pan. Cook 5 minutes, remove bouquet garni and serve.

1 SERVING			
Calories	482	Fat	14 g
Carbohydrate	70 g	Fiber	7.5 g
Protein	19 g	Cholesterol	28 mg

1

Place celery, fresh herbs, chicken
and vegetables in large saucepan.
Cover with 6 cups (1.5 L) of water
and season well.

2

Check vegetables regularly and
remove from pan when cooked;
tent with foil.

3

When chicken is done,
cool and cube.

Chicken and Vegetable Pot Pie

◆

(4 SERVINGS)

1	celery rib	1
1	fresh thyme sprig	1
2	fresh parsley sprigs	2
2	large whole chicken breasts, skinned	2
2	large carrots, pared and cut in ¾-in (2-cm) strips	2
2	potatoes, peeled and diced large	2
24	pearl onions, peeled	24
½ lb	fresh mushroom caps, cleaned	225 g
4 tbsp	butter	60 mL
4 tbsp	all-purpose flour	60 mL
	salt and freshly ground pepper	
	pie dough	

- Preheat oven to 375°F (190°C).

- Tie celery rib and fresh herb sprigs together. Place in large saucepan and add chicken and vegetables. Cover with 6 cups (1.5 L) of water; season well and bring to a boil.

- Reduce heat to low and cook chicken 25 minutes, or according to size. Check vegetables regularly and remove from pan when cooked; tent with foil.

- When chicken is done, cool and cube. Strain and reserve 3½ cups (875 mL) of cooking liquid.

- Heat butter in clean saucepan over medium heat. Sprinkle in flour and mix well; cook 30 seconds over low heat.

- Whisk in reserved cooking liquid; season and simmer 6 minutes.

- Combine chicken and vegetables with sauce. Pour into baking dish. Cover top with pastry and cut small opening in dough. Bake 20 minutes and serve.

1 SERVING			
Calories	551	Fat	27 g
Carbohydrate	45 g	Fiber	4.7 g
Protein	32 g	Cholesterol	117 mg

Sprinkle in flour and mix well; cook 30 seconds over low heat.

Whisk in reserved cooking liquid; season and simmer 6 minutes.

Combine chicken and vegetables with sauce. Pour into baking dish.

Chicken Livers on Skewers

◆

(4 SERVINGS)

1 tbsp	olive oil	15 mL
1½ lbs	chicken livers, cleaned, trimmed of fat and halved	675 g
6	bacon slices, halved	6
1	red onion, peeled and cut in wedges	1
1	green bell pepper, diced large	1
1	red bell pepper, diced large	1
½ cup	melted garlic butter	125 mL
	salt and freshly ground pepper	
	lemon juice to taste	

▬ Heat oil in frying pan over high heat. Add chicken livers and cook 3 minutes, stirring once. Remove livers from pan and drain well on paper towels.

▬ Alternate pieces of liver, bacon, onion and bell peppers on metal skewers. Season well and baste with garlic butter.

▬ Broil 8 minutes, turning skewers over once. Baste with garlic butter during cooking.

▬ Sprinkle with lemon juice and serve.

1 SERVING			
Calories	502	Fat	38 g
Carbohydrate	6 g	Fiber	1.1 g
Protein	34 g	Cholesterol	860 mg

Rolled Chicken Schnitzel with Prosciutto

◆

(4 SERVINGS)

2	whole boneless chicken breasts	2
8	slices prosciutto	8
8	slices Gruyère cheese	8
1 cup	all-purpose flour	250 mL
2	eggs, beaten with a few drops of oil	2
1 cup	breadcrumbs	250 mL
2 tbsp	peanut oil	30 mL
	salt and freshly ground pepper	

- Skin chicken, split into halves and remove fat. Using wooden mallet, flatten breasts between two sheets of waxed paper. Breasts should be about ⅛-in (3-mm) thick. Season meat well.

- Cover each flattened breast with two slices each of prosciutto and cheese. Season with freshly ground pepper. Roll up chicken and flatten with metal spatula.

- Dredge in flour, dip in beaten eggs and coat with breadcrumbs. Place on flat container and cover with plastic wrap; refrigerate 1 hour.

- Preheat oven to 400°F (200°C).

- Heat peanut oil in large ovenproof frying pan over high heat. Add chicken schnitzel and brown all sides. Transfer pan to oven and cook 6 minutes. Serve with chutney, if desired.

1 SERVING

Calories	784	Fat	40 g
Carbohydrate	47 g	Fiber	1.4 g
Protein	59 g	Cholesterol	263 mg

Duck in Red Wine

◆

(4 SERVINGS)

MARINADE:

2	shallots, peeled and sliced	2
1	carrot, pared and sliced	1
3	garlic cloves, peeled	3
1	fresh thyme sprig	1
2	fresh parsley sprigs	2
1	bay leaf	1
2 cups	dry red wine	500 mL
2 tbsp	olive oil	30 mL
	freshly ground pepper	

DUCK:

5 lb	duck, cleaned, cut in 8 pieces and skinned	2.3 kg
4 tbsp	olive oil	60 mL
4 tbsp	all-purpose flour	60 mL
½ cup	beef stock, heated	125 mL
24	pearl onions, peeled	24
¾ lb	fresh mushrooms, cleaned	350 g
2	garlic cloves, peeled, crushed and chopped	2
1 tbsp	chopped fresh parsley	15 mL
	freshly ground pepper	

■ Combine all marinade ingredients in a roasting pan.

■ Add duck pieces to marinade, cover with plastic wrap and refrigerate 8 hours.

■ Remove duck pieces and pat dry with paper towels. Strain marinade and set aside.

■ Preheat oven to 350°F (180°C).

■ Heat half of oil in ovenproof casserole over medium heat. Add duck and cook 8 minutes, searing all sides. Sprinkle in flour and cook 6 minutes.

■ Pour in strained marinade and beef stock; season with pepper. Cover and cook 40 to 50 minutes in oven.

■ About 20 minutes before end of cooking, heat remaining oil in frying pan over medium heat. Add onions, mushrooms, garlic and parsley. Cook 6 minutes.

■ Add vegetables to duck in casserole and resume cooking. Serve.

1 SERVING			
Calories	743	Fat	32 g
Carbohydrate	18 g	Fiber	3.7 g
Protein	88 g	Cholesterol	327 mg

163

Zesty Marinated Chicken

◆

(4 SERVINGS)

MARINADE :

¼ cup	olive oil	50 mL
¼ cup	soy sauce	50 mL
1 tbsp	Worcestershire sauce	15 mL
1 tsp	English mustard	5 mL
2	garlic cloves, peeled, crushed and chopped	2
3 tbsp	balsamic vinegar	45 mL
1 cup	cold water	250 mL
3	green onions, chopped	3
1 tbsp	sugar	15 mL
	freshly ground pepper	
	juice of 1 lemon	

CHICKEN:

4 lb	chicken, cleaned and cut in 8 pieces	1.8 kg
2 tbsp	olive oil	30 mL
1½ cups	chicken stock, heated	375 mL
1 tbsp	cornstarch	15 mL
2 tbsp	cold water	30 mL
½ cup	toasted cashew nuts, halved	125 mL

■ Combine all marinade ingredients in large bowl and mix well.

■ Skin chicken pieces and add to marinade. Cover and refrigerate 1 hour.

■ Remove chicken from liquid and pat dry with paper towels. Reserve 1 cup (250 mL) of marinade.

■ Preheat oven to 350°F (180°C).

■ Heat oil in large sauté pan over medium heat. Add chicken pieces and brown all sides.

■ Pour in chicken stock and reserved marinade. Cook 30 to 35 minutes in oven or according to size. Do not cover.

■ When chicken is cooked, remove pieces from pan and set aside. Tent with foil.

■ Place pan on stove over medium heat. Dilute cornstarch in cold water; incorporate to sauce. Stir in cashew nuts and return chicken to pan. Simmer 2 minutes and serve.

1 SERVING			
Calories	317	Fat	21 g
Carbohydrate	17 g	Fiber	0.8 g
Protein	15 g	Cholesterol	28 mg

Marinade for Poultry

◆

1 cup	dry white wine	250 mL
4 tbsp	olive oil	60 mL
3	garlic cloves, peeled, crushed and chopped	3
3 tbsp	chopped fresh basil	45 mL
1 tsp	oregano	5 mL
1	fresh thyme sprig	1
1	bay leaf	1
	salt and freshly ground pepper	
	juice of 1 lemon	
	cayenne pepper to taste	

■ Mix all ingredients together. Pour over chicken pieces and cover with plastic wrap, ensuring that wrap touches surface.

■ Refrigerate and marinate 2 hours.

1 SERVING			
Calories	602	Fat	54 g
Carbohydrate	8 g	Fiber	0.3 g
Protein	1 g	Cholesterol	0 mg

Suprême Sauce

◆

(2½ CUPS – 625 ML)

3 tbsp	butter	45 mL
3 tbsp	all-purpose flour	45 mL
2½ cups	chicken stock, heated	625 mL
1 tbsp	chopped fresh parsley	15 mL
	freshly ground pepper	

■ Heat butter in saucepan over medium heat. Sprinkle in flour and mix well; cook 1 minute.

■ Whisk in chicken stock. Stir in parsley, season and cook 12 minutes over low heat. Stir occasionally during cooking.

■ Use in a variety of meat pies and vol-au-vent recipes.

1 SERVING			
Calories	488	Fat	36 g
Carbohydrate	31 g	Fiber	3.8 g
Protein	10 g	Cholesterol	96 mg

Quick Soy Chicken and Cabbage

◆

(4 SERVINGS)

3½ lb	chicken, cleaned and cut in 8 pieces	1.6 kg
3 tbsp	olive oil	45 mL
½	red onion, sliced in rings	½
1½ cups	sliced Chinese cabbage	375 mL
1	yellow bell pepper, sliced	1
1	green bell pepper, sliced	1
2	garlic cloves, peeled, crushed and chopped	2
2 tbsp	soy sauce	30 mL
	salt and freshly ground pepper	

■ Skin and bone chicken pieces. Cut meat into 1-in (2.5-cm) cubes. Season with freshly ground pepper.

■ Heat 2 tbsp (30 mL) of oil in large frying pan over medium heat. Add chicken and stir-fry 4 to 5 minutes. Remove chicken from pan and set aside.

■ Add remaining oil to pan. When hot, cook vegetables and garlic 6 minutes over high heat. Season well.

■ Return chicken to pan and sprinkle in soy sauce. Mix well and cook 2 minutes over medium heat. Correct seasoning and serve.

1 SERVING			
Calories	164	Fat	12 g
Carbohydrate	4 g	Fiber	3.4 g
Protein	10 g	Cholesterol	26 mg

EAT

So many wonderful cuts and varieties of meat are available at the butcher's counter these days, that it is often difficult to choose. No wonder so many people fall back on standards like steak and ground beef.

A nice thick steak or a juicy burger are perennial favorites, but there are other meat dishes included in this chapter, such as *Pot-au-Feu* and *Osso Buco*, that are based on cuts that many cooks overlook.

Not only are these cuts very economically priced, but they are packed with flavor, and are as tender as the finest steak as long as they are treated to the correct cooking technique.

Also included is a selection of quick and easy lamb, veal and pork recipes. These delicious meats deserve more attention in home kitchens, as they provide wonderful alternatives to the strictly beef and potato meal.

Braised Beef with Root Vegetables

◆

(4 SERVINGS)

2 tbsp	olive oil	30 mL
3.5 oz	bacon, diced	100 g
3 lb	boneless rump roast, tied	1.4 kg
1	Spanish onion, peeled and sliced	1
2	garlic cloves, peeled and sliced	2
4 tbsp	all-purpose flour	60 mL
4 cups	beef stock, heated	1 L
½ cup	dry white wine	125 mL
1	fresh thyme sprig	1
2	fresh parsley sprigs	2
1 tbsp	chopped fresh basil	15 mL
2	bay leaves	2
4	potatoes, peeled, quartered, rinsed in cold water and drained	4
4	carrots, pared and halved	4
1	small cabbage, quartered and cored	1
	salt and freshly ground pepper	

■ Preheat oven to 350°F (180°C).

■ Heat oil and diced bacon in large ovenproof casserole over medium heat. Add meat and sear on all sides. Season well, remove from casserole and set aside.

■ Add sliced onion and garlic to casserole; cook 6 minutes over medium heat.

■ Sprinkle in flour and mix well. Reduce heat to low and cook 3 to 4 minutes, or until browned.

■ Incorporate beef stock, wine and all seasonings. Return meat to casserole and season generously; cover and cook 2 hours in oven.

■ Add all vegetables to casserole and cook 1 hour. Check vegetables regularly and remove when cooked. Keep warm in bowl with a small amount of cooking liquid.

■ When meat is done, return vegetables to casserole. Heat if necessary and serve.

1 SERVING			
Calories	926	Fat	40 g
Carbohydrate	48 g	Fiber	6.4 g
Protein	91 g	Cholesterol	206 mg

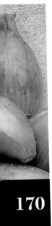

Leg of Lamb with Potatoes

◆

(4 TO 6 SERVINGS)

4-5 lb	leg of lamb, boned and prepared for roasting	1.8-2.3 kg
3	garlic cloves, peeled and sliced into thirds	3
2 tbsp	olive oil	30 mL
1	large Spanish onion, peeled and sliced	1
5	potatoes, peeled and sliced	5
	salt and freshly ground pepper	

- Preheat oven to 450°F (230°C).

- Make several small incisions in meat and insert garlic slices.

- Heat oil in roasting pan over medium heat. Add onion and cook 6 minutes over low heat. Add potatoes and season well.

- Place lamb on top of vegetables and sear 15 minutes in oven. Season meat generously and reduce heat to 350°F (180°C). Continue cooking lamb 12 minutes per lb (450 g), including searing time.

- When meat is done, let stand 10 minutes before carving. Accompany with potatoes and serve.

1 SERVING			
Calories	612	Fat	24 g
Carbohydrate	19 g	Fiber	1.8 g
Protein	80 g	Cholesterol	283 mg

Lamb Chops with Fresh Tomatoes

◆

(4 SERVINGS)

8	lamb chops, trimmed of fat	8
2 tbsp	olive oil	30 mL
4	large tomatoes, peeled, seeded and chopped	4
2	garlic cloves, peeled, crushed and chopped	2
1 tbsp	chopped fresh basil	15 mL
1 tbsp	chopped fresh parsley	15 mL
	salt and freshly ground pepper	

- Season lamb chops generously.

- Heat half of oil in large frying pan over medium heat. Add tomatoes, garlic, basil and parsley. Season and cook 15 minutes over low heat.

- Heat remaining oil in separate frying pan over medium heat. Add lamb chops and cook 3 to 4 minutes on each side, or according to size.

- Serve lamb with fresh tomato sauce.

1 SERVING			
Calories	321	Fat	17 g
Carbohydrate	6 g	Fiber	3.5 g
Protein	36 g	Cholesterol	136 mg

Beef Stroganoff

◆

(4 SERVINGS)

4 tbsp	olive oil	60 mL
1½ lbs	beef sirloin, trimmed of fat and sliced ⅓-in (8-mm) thick	675 g
1	large onion, peeled and chopped	1
1	garlic clove, peeled, crushed and chopped	1
½ lb	fresh mushrooms, cleaned and sliced	225 g
1½ tbsp	all-purpose flour	25 mL
2 cups	beef stock, heated	500 mL
1 tsp	tomato paste	5 mL
1 tbsp	chopped fresh parsley	15 mL
3 tbsp	sour cream	45 mL
	salt and freshly ground pepper	

■ Heat 1 tbsp (15 mL) of oil in large sauté pan over high heat. Add half of meat and cook 1 minute on each side; season well. Remove first batch from pan and set aside.

■ Add a little more oil and repeat cooking process for second batch of meat. Remove from pan and set aside.

■ Add remaining oil to pan. Cook onion and garlic 2 minutes. Add mushrooms, season well and cook 4 minutes over high heat.

■ Sprinkle in flour and mix well; cook 3 minutes over low heat.

■ Stir in beef stock and tomato paste; mix well. Simmer 6 minutes over low heat.

■ Return beef to pan and add parsley. Simmer 2 minutes and remove pan from heat.

■ Mix in sour cream and serve over noodles.

1 SERVING			
Calories	410	Fat	22 g
Carbohydrate	12 g	Fiber	2.9 g
Protein	41 g	Cholesterol	94 mg

174

Pork Shoulder Stew

◆

(4 SERVINGS)

3 tbsp	olive oil	45 mL
3 lbs	pork shoulder, trimmed of fat and cubed	1.4 kg
3-4 tbsp	all-purpose flour	45-60 mL
4 cups	chicken stock, heated	1 L
2 tbsp	tomato paste	30 mL
2	carrots, pared and sliced ½-in (1-cm) thick	2
2	onions, peeled and quartered	2
1	celery rib, sliced ½-in (1-cm) thick	1
2	potatoes, peeled and quartered	2
1	fresh thyme sprig	1
2	fresh parsley sprigs	2
1	bay leaf	1
2	garlic cloves, peeled, crushed and chopped	2
	salt and freshly ground pepper	
	pinch of crushed chilies	

■ Preheat oven to 325°F (160°C).

■ Heat oil in large ovenproof casserole over medium heat. Sear meat, in several batches if necessary.

■ Sprinkle in flour and mix well. Cook 4 minutes over low heat.

■ Stir in chicken stock, tomato paste and vegetables. Add seasonings and garlic. Cover and cook 1½ hours in oven. Remove bay leaf and serve.

1 SERVING

Calories	534	Fat	22 g
Carbohydrate	26 g	Fiber	4.6 g
Protein	58 g	Cholesterol	142 mg

New York Strip Steaks with Mushroom Sauce

◆

(4 SERVINGS)

3 tbsp	olive oil	45 mL
3	shallots, peeled and chopped	3
2	garlic cloves, peeled and sliced	2
½ lb	fresh mushrooms, cleaned and sliced	225 g
2 tbsp	balsamic vinegar	30 mL
1½ cups	brown sauce, heated	375 mL
1 tsp	tomato paste	5 mL
4	8-oz (225-g) strip loin steaks, trimmed of fat	4
1 tbsp	chopped fresh parsley	15 mL
	salt and freshly ground pepper	

■ Heat 2 tbsp (30 mL) of oil in large frying pan over medium heat. Add shallots and garlic; cook 1 minute.

■ Add mushrooms, season and cook 4 minutes. Sprinkle in vinegar and cook 1 minute.

■ Incorporate brown sauce and tomato paste. Simmer 8 minutes over low heat.

■ Heat remaining oil in separate large frying pan over high heat. When very hot, add meat and cook 2 minutes. Turn steaks over, season well and reduce heat to medium. Continue cooking 2 to 3 minutes or according to taste.

■ Sprinkle in parsley and serve steaks with mushroom sauce.

1 SERVING			
Calories	483	Fat	27 g
Carbohydrate	8 g	Fiber	1.9 g
Protein	52 g	Cholesterol	117 mg

Veal Scaloppine with Fresh Lemon

◆

(4 SERVINGS)

4	large veal scaloppine	4
2 tbsp	olive oil	30 mL
2 tbsp	butter	30 mL
½ lb	fresh mushrooms, cleaned and sliced	225 g
1 tbsp	all-purpose flour	15 mL
½ cup	chicken stock, heated	125 mL
1 tbsp	chopped fresh parsley	15 mL
	salt and freshly ground pepper	
	juice of 1 lemon	

- Slice each scaloppine into 4 pieces; season well.

- Heat oil in large frying pan over high heat. Add veal and cook 1 minute. Turn pieces over and cook another 30 seconds; remove and set aside.

- Melt butter in hot pan. Add mushrooms and season well. Cook 4 minutes over high heat.

- Sprinkle in flour and mix well. Add lemon juice and chicken stock. Mix to incorporate and cook sauce 2 minutes.

- Return veal to pan and sprinkle in parsley. Remove pan from heat, let stand briefly to reheat veal and serve.

1 SERVING

Calories	336	Fat	20 g
Carbohydrate	6 g	Fiber	1.9 g
Protein	33 g	Cholesterol	141 mg

Rump Roast with Red Onion and Carrot

◆

(4 TO 6 SERVINGS)

4 lb	rump roast	1.8 kg
4	garlic cloves, peeled and cut into slivers	4
3 tbsp	olive oil	45 mL
3	large carrots, pared and sliced ½-in (1-cm) thick	3
2	red onions, peeled and cut in 6 wedges	2
4 tbsp	all-purpose flour	60 mL
2 cups	dry white wine	500 mL
2 cups	beef stock, heated	500 mL
3 tbsp	tomato paste	45 mL
1	fresh thyme sprig	1
3 tbsp	chopped fresh basil	45 mL
	salt and freshly ground pepper	

- Preheat oven to 350°F (180°C).

- Make several incisions in meat and insert garlic slivers. Season meat generously with freshly ground pepper.

- Heat oil in large ovenproof casserole over medium heat. Add meat and sear on all sides; remove and set aside. Add carrots and onions. Cook 5 minutes over medium heat.

- Sprinkle in flour, mix well and cook 4 minutes over low heat to brown flour. Do not let flour burn.

- Add remaining ingredients to casserole and bring to a boil. Return meat to casserole, cover and cook 2½ hours in oven.

- When meat is cooked, remove from casserole and set aside. Place casserole on stove over medium-high heat and cook sauce 4 minutes.

- Slice meat and serve with vegetable sauce.

1 SERVING			
Calories	566	Fat	24 g
Carbohydrate	15 g	Fiber	2.7 g
Protein	68 g	Cholesterol	160 mg

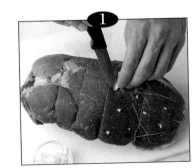

Make several incisions in meat and insert garlic slivers.

Add meat and sear on all sides; remove and set aside.

Add carrots and onions. Cook 5 minutes over medium heat.

Sprinkle in flour, mix well and cook 4 minutes over low heat to brown flour.

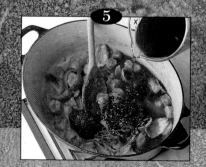

Add remaining ingredients to casserole and bring to a boil.

Return meat to casserole, cover and cook 2½ hours in oven.

Lamb Stew

◆

(4 SERVINGS)

4 tbsp	olive oil	60 mL
3 lbs	lamb shoulder, cut into ¾-in (2-cm) cubes	1.4 kg
2	garlic cloves, peeled, crushed and chopped	2
1	onion, peeled and chopped	1
5 tbsp	all-purpose flour	75 mL
4 cups	chicken stock, heated	1 L
3	tomatoes, peeled, seeded and chopped	3
2 tbsp	chopped fresh basil	30 mL
½ tsp	thyme	2 mL
1	bay leaf	1
1	small red onion, peeled and diced	1
1	celery rib, sliced ½-in (1-cm) thick	1
2	carrots, pared and sliced ½-in (1-cm) thick	2
3	potatoes, peeled and diced	3
	salt and freshly ground pepper	

- Preheat oven to 350°F (180°C).

- Heat oil in large ovenproof casserole over medium heat. Add lamb and sear on all sides.

- Add garlic and onion; cook 3 minutes.

- Sprinkle in flour and mix well. Cook over low heat until lightly browned.

- Incorporate chicken stock and tomatoes. Add all seasonings and mix well. Bring to a boil, cover and cook 40 minutes in oven.

- Add red onion, celery and carrots. Cover and cook 30 minutes.

- Add potatoes and resume cooking for 15 minutes, or until potatoes are cooked. Serve.

1 SERVING			
Calories	982	Fat	54 g
Carbohydrate	32 g	Fiber	7.0 g
Protein	92 g	Cholesterol	317 mg

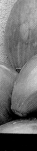

181

Medallions of Veal Loin in Wine Sauce

◆

(4 SERVINGS)

4	1-in (2.5-cm) thick veal loin medallions	4
3 tbsp	butter	45 mL
1 tbsp	olive oil	15 mL
2	shallots, peeled and chopped	2
½ lb	fresh mushrooms, cleaned and sliced	225 g
½ cup	dry white wine	125 mL
1 tbsp	chopped fresh parsley	15 mL
3 tbsp	sour cream	45 mL
	salt and freshly ground pepper	

■ Place medallions between two sheets of waxed paper. Pound lightly and season meat generously.

■ Heat 2 tbsp (30 mL) of butter and 1 tbsp (15 mL) of oil in large frying pan over medium heat. Add veal and cook 3 to 4 minutes or according to size. Turn veal over once and season well during cooking.

■ When veal is cooked, remove from pan. Set aside and keep warm.

■ Add remaining butter to hot pan. Add shallots and mushrooms. Season well and cook 4 minutes over high heat.

■ Stir in wine and parsley; cook 2 minutes. Remove pan from heat and incorporate sour cream. Pour over veal and serve.

1 SERVING			
Calories	374	Fat	22 g
Carbohydrate	4 g	Fiber	1.7 g
Protein	35 g	Cholesterol	151 mg

Pineapple Pork Tenderloin

◆

(4 SERVINGS)

2	pork tenderloins	2
3 tbsp	olive oil	45 mL
1	green bell pepper, sliced thick	1
1	red bell pepper, sliced thick	1
3	shallots, peeled and sliced	3
2	garlic cloves, peeled and sliced	2
4	pineapple rings, diced	4
¼ cup	pineapple juice	50 mL
2 cups	chicken stock, heated	500 mL
1 tbsp	soy sauce	15 mL
1½ tbsp	cornstarch	25 mL
2 tbsp	cold water	30 mL
	salt and freshly ground pepper	

■ Trim off excess fat and thin silver skin that covers tenderloin. Slice meat into strips about ½-in (1-cm) wide.

■ Divide meat into two batches. Heat 1 tbsp (15 mL) of oil in large frying pan over medium heat. Sear first batch of meat 2 minutes per side; season during cooking. Repeat technique for remaining meat. Set all meat aside.

■ Add remaining oil to hot pan. Add bell peppers, shallots and garlic; season well. Cook 4 minutes over medium heat.

■ Add diced pineapple and cook 3 minutes.

■ Pour in pineapple juice, chicken stock and soy sauce. Mix well and cook 3 minutes.

■ Dilute cornstarch in cold water; incorporate to sauce. Return meat to pan and simmer 2 minutes. Serve.

1 SERVING

Calories	376	Fat	20 g
Carbohydrate	14 g	Fiber	1.5 g
Protein	35 g	Cholesterol	82 mg

Pork with Roasted Bell Peppers

◆

(4 SERVINGS)

1	green bell pepper	1
1	red bell pepper	1
1	yellow bell pepper	1
2 tbsp	olive oil	30 mL
4	pork chops, ¾-in (2-cm) thick, trimmed of fat	4
4	garlic cloves, peeled, crushed and chopped	4
1 tbsp	chopped fresh basil	15 mL
	salt and freshly ground pepper	

■ Cut bell peppers in half and remove seeds. Oil skin and place cut-side-down on cookie sheet; broil 6 minutes. Remove from oven and let cool. Peel off skin, slice peppers and set aside.

■ Heat half of oil in large frying pan over medium heat. Add chops and sear 3 to 4 minutes on each side.

■ Add all remaining ingredients to pan, including reserved peppers. Cover and cook pork 10 to 15 minutes over low heat or according to size. Serve.

1 SERVING

Calories	232	Fat	16 g
Carbohydrate	4 g	Fiber	0.9 g
Protein	18 g	Cholesterol	40 mg

Barbecued Spareribs

◆

(4 SERVINGS)

BASTING MARINADE:

½ cup	ketchup	125 mL
½ tsp	horseradish	2 mL
2 tbsp	molasses	30 mL
2 tbsp	oil	30 mL
2 tbsp	wine vinegar	30 mL
2	garlic cloves, peeled, crushed and chopped	2
1 tbsp	soy sauce	15 mL
	juice of 1 lemon	
	a few drops of hot pepper sauce	
	salt and freshly ground pepper	

■ Mix ingredients together in bowl and set aside.

SPARERIBS:

5 lbs	pork spareribs	2.3 kg
	salt and freshly ground pepper	

■ Place spareribs in large pot filled with salted, boiling water. Boil 4 to 5 minutes. Remove meat and pat dry with paper towels.

■ Cook spareribs 35 to 42 minutes on preheated barbecue over medium heat. Baste frequently with marinade and turn ribs over 3 to 4 times during cooking process. Season generously.

■ Serve with baked potatoes and fresh green salad.

1 SERVING			
Calories	1070	Fat	62 g
Carbohydrate	8 g	Fiber	0.5 g
Protein	120 g	Cholesterol	246 mg

Mushroom and Herb Stuffed Beef Flank

◆

(4 SERVINGS)

STUFFING:

2 tbsp	olive oil	30 mL
2	onions, peeled and chopped	2
2	garlic cloves, peeled, crushed and chopped	2
½ lb	fresh mushrooms, cleaned and chopped	225 g
1 tbsp	chopped fresh parsley	15 mL
2 tbsp	chopped fresh basil	30 mL
2 tbsp	chopped fresh chives	30 mL
¼ cup	breadcrumbs	50 mL
3 tbsp	heavy cream (35% MF)	45 mL
	salt and freshly ground pepper	
	pinch of crushed chilies	

- Heat oil in large frying pan over high heat. Add onions and garlic. Reduce heat to low and cook 3 minutes.

- Add remaining ingredients, except breadcrumbs and cream. Mix well and cook 6 minutes over high heat.

- Remove pan from heat. Stir in breadcrumbs and cream. Correct seasoning and set aside.

BEEF FLANK:

2	small flank steaks	2
2 tbsp	olive oil	30 mL
2	onions, peeled and cubed	2
2	garlic cloves, peeled, crushed and chopped	2
1 cup	dry white wine	250 mL
5	tomatoes, peeled, seeded and chopped	5
3 tbsp	chopped fresh basil	45 mL
3 tbsp	chopped sun-dried tomatoes	45 mL
	salt and freshly ground pepper	

- Preheat oven to 350°F (180°C).

- Using a sharp knife, split flank steaks lengthwise to make a larger, thinner piece of meat. Do not cut all the way through meat. Spread stuffing over meat, roll and tie.

- Heat oil in large ovenproof sauté pan over high heat. Add meat and sear on all sides. Add onions and garlic; cook 4 minutes over low heat. Pour in wine and cook 2 minutes.

- Add tomatoes, basil and sun-dried tomatoes. Season well, cover and cook 1½ to 2 hours in oven.

- When meat is cooked, remove and set aside. Place pan on stove over high heat and cook 4 minutes to reduce sauce.

- Slice stuffed flank and serve with sauce and seasonal vegetables.

1 SERVING			
Calories	430	Fat	22 g
Carbohydrate	28 g	Fiber	5.7 g
Protein	20 g	Cholesterol	40 mg

Beef Bourguignon

◆

(4 SERVINGS)

5 tbsp	olive oil	75 mL
3½ lbs	beef chuck, cut into ¾-in (2-cm) cubes	1.6 kg
4	garlic cloves, peeled, crushed and chopped	4
5 tbsp	all-purpose flour	75 mL
2½ cups	beef stock, heated	625 mL
2 cups	dry red wine	500 mL
1	fresh thyme sprig	1
2	fresh parsley sprigs	2
2	bay leaves	2
12	shallots, peeled	12
½ lb	fresh mushrooms, cleaned and halved	225 g
	salt and freshly ground pepper	

■ Preheat oven to 350°F (180°C).

■ Heat 1½ tbsp (25 mL) of oil in large ovenproof casserole over medium heat. Sear half of meat and set aside. Add more oil and sear remaining meat.

■ Return all meat to casserole, season well and stir in garlic. Cook 1 minute.

■ Sprinkle in flour and mix well. Cook 5 minutes over low heat until lightly browned. Stir in beef stock and simmer over low heat.

■ Pour wine into small saucepan and cook 8 minutes over high heat. Incorporate to stew.

■ Tie fresh herbs and bay leaves together. Add to casserole and season well. Bring to boil, cover and cook 1 hour in oven.

■ Add whole shallots to stew. Continue cooking 1 hour.

■ Twenty-five minutes before stew is cooked, prepare mushrooms. Heat remaining oil in frying pan over high heat. Cook mushrooms 4 minutes; season well. Add mushrooms to stew and resume cooking.

■ Serve stew over noodles.

1 SERVING			
Calories	712	Fat	29 g
Carbohydrate	16 g	Fiber	2.9 g
Protein	94 g	Cholesterol	195 mg

Broiled Beef Tenderloin Shish Kebabs

◆

(4 SERVINGS)

1½ lbs	beef tenderloin, cut into ¾-in (2-cm) pieces	675 g
8	bay leaves	8
8	bacon slices, cooked lightly and halved	8
1	yellow bell pepper, cut in bite-size pieces	1
1	small red onion, peeled and cut in 6 wedges	1
30	fresh mushroom caps, cleaned	30
2 tbsp	olive oil	30 mL
1 tbsp	teriyaki sauce	15 mL
	salt and freshly ground pepper	
	juice of 1 lemon	

■ Alternate beef, bay leaves, bacon and vegetables on metal skewers.

■ Mix remaining ingredients together and brush over skewers. Place in oven 5 in (13 cm) below top element. Broil 4 minutes, rotating skewers once during cooking. Baste several times.

■ Season well and serve with green salad.

1 SERVING			
Calories	412	Fat	24 g
Carbohydrate	8 g	Fiber	1.5 g
Protein	41 g	Cholesterol	95 mg

Veal Chops with Fresh Tarragon

◆

(4 SERVINGS)

1 tsp	olive oil	5 mL
2 tbsp	butter	30 mL
4	¾-in (2-cm) thick veal chops, trimmed of fat	4
3 tbsp	chopped fresh tarragon	45 mL
½ cup	dry white wine	125 mL
1½ cups	light cream, heated	375 mL
	salt and freshly ground pepper	

■ Heat oil and butter in large frying pan over high heat. Add veal chops and cook 2 minutes. Turn chops over, season well and cook 2 minutes; reduce heat to medium. Cook 5 to 6 minutes or according to size. Remove from pan and set chops aside; keep warm.

■ Add tarragon to hot pan and cook 1 minute. Pour in wine, increase heat to high and cook 2 minutes. Mix in cream and season well. Cook 3 minutes or until thickened.

■ Pour sauce over veal. Accompany with fresh beans, turnips and rutabaga and serve.

1 SERVING

Calories	416	Fat	30 g
Carbohydrate	6 g	Fiber	0 g
Protein	28 g	Cholesterol	138 mg

Osso Buco

◆

(4 SERVINGS)

8	veal shanks, sawed into ¾-in (2-cm) wide pieces	8
1 cup	all-purpose flour	250 mL
3 tbsp	olive oil	45 mL
3	shallots, peeled and chopped	3
1	onion, peeled and chopped	1
3	garlic cloves, peeled and sliced	3
1 cup	dry white wine	250 mL
4	large tomatoes, peeled, seeded and chopped	4
1	fresh thyme sprig	1
12	fresh basil leaves	12
2	fresh parsley sprigs	2
1	bay leaf	1
1 cup	chicken stock, heated	250 mL
	salt and freshly ground pepper	
	pinch of crushed chilies	

■ Preheat oven to 350°F (180°C).

■ Season meat well and dredge in flour. Heat oil in large ovenproof casserole over medium heat. Add meat and sear on all sides. Remove meat and set aside.

■ Add shallots, onion and garlic; cook 2 minutes. Pour in wine and cook 2 minutes.

■ Stir in tomatoes and all seasonings. Return meat to casserole and pour in chicken stock. Mix, cover and cook 1½ to 2 hours in oven.

■ When meat is cooked, transfer to serving platter; keep warm.

■ Place casserole on stove over high heat; cook sauce 12 minutes.

■ Return meat to casserole, simmer 3 minutes and serve.

1 SERVING			
Calories	661	Fat	21 g
Carbohydrate	35 g	Fiber	3.2 g
Protein	78 g	Cholesterol	270 mg

Season meat well and dredge in flour.

Heat oil in large ovenproof casserole over medium heat. Add meat and sear on all sides.

Add shallots, onion and garlic; cook 2 minutes.

4 Pour in wine and cook 2 minutes.

5 Stir in tomatoes and all seasonings.

6 Return meat to casserole
and pour in chicken stock.

193

Easy Beef and Vegetable Stew

◆

(4 SERVINGS)

3 tbsp	olive oil	45 mL
3 lbs	beef chuck, cut into ¾-in (2-cm) cubes	1.4 kg
1	onion, peeled and chopped	1
2	garlic cloves, peeled and sliced	2
4	potatoes, peeled and sliced	4
3	carrots, pared and sliced	3
4 cups	beef stock, heated	1 L
2 tbsp	tomato paste	30 mL
1	fresh thyme sprig	1
2	fresh parsley sprigs	2
2	bay leaves	2
2 tbsp	chili powder	30 mL
	salt and freshly ground pepper	

■ Preheat oven to 300°F (150°C).

■ Heat half of oil in large ovenproof casserole over medium heat. Sear half of meat and set aside. Add more oil and sear remaining meat.

■ Return all meat to casserole; add onion and garlic. Cook 2 minutes and transfer contents of casserole to bowl. Set aside.

■ Place potatoes in bottom of casserole and cover with layer of carrots. Add seared meat and remaining ingredients; mix well. Cover and cook 3 hours in oven. Serve.

1 SERVING			
Calories	707	Fat	23 g
Carbohydrate	28 g	Fiber	5.0 g
Protein	97 g	Cholesterol	195 mg

Beef Tournedos with Poivre Vert Sauce

◆

(4 SERVINGS)

1 tbsp	green peppercorns	15 mL
1 cup	heavy cream (35% MF)	250 mL
¼ cup	Madeira wine	50 mL
4	6-oz (170-g) beef tournedos, about 1-in (2.5-cm) thick	4
½ cup	basic beef stock (see page 9)	125 mL
	olive oil	
	salt and freshly ground pepper	

■ Rinse peppercorns under cold, running water. Drain and place in small bowl with 1 tbsp (15 mL) of cream. Mash.

■ Place peppercorns, remaining heavy cream, wine and beef stock in small saucepan; season well. Cook over low heat, stirring frequently, until flavors are nicely blended.

■ Brush meat on both sides with olive oil. Sear meat quickly on both sides in large frying pan over high heat. Season well. Transfer meat to ovenproof tray and broil 3 minutes on each side.

■ Serve with peppercorn sauce.

1 SERVING

Calories	406	Fat	26 g
Carbohydrate	3 g	Fiber	0.1 g
Protein	38 g	Cholesterol	152 mg

195

Veal Scaloppine with Mixed Vegetables

◆

(4 SERVINGS)

2 tbsp	olive oil	30 mL
2 tbsp	butter	30 mL
½ lb	fresh mushrooms, cleaned and diced	225 g
2	shallots, peeled and chopped	2
½ cup	dry white wine	125 mL
1½ cups	chicken stock, heated	375 mL
1 tbsp	cornstarch	15 mL
2 tbsp	cold water	30 mL
12	new potatoes, cooked	12
2	carrots, pared, in thick julienne and cooked	2
12	pearl onions, peeled and cooked	12
4	large veal scaloppine	4
½ cup	all-purpose flour	125 mL
1 tbsp	chopped fresh basil	15 mL
	salt and freshly ground pepper	

■ Heat half of oil and half of butter in sauté pan over medium heat. Add mushrooms and shallots; season and cook 4 minutes.

■ Pour in wine and cook 3 minutes. Add chicken stock, mix and season well. Simmer 2 minutes.

■ Dilute cornstarch in cold water; incorporate to sauce. Add cooked vegetables and simmer until ready to serve.

■ Season veal well and dredge in flour. Heat remaining oil and butter in large frying pan over high heat. Add meat and cook 2 minutes. Turn veal over and cook 1 minute.

■ Top with vegetables, sprinkle with fresh basil and serve.

1 SERVING			
Calories	573	Fat	21 g
Carbohydrate	53 g	Fiber	6.2 g
Protein	38 g	Cholesterol	141 mg

Calf's Liver with Dijon

◆

(4 SERVINGS)

1½ tbsp	olive oil	25 mL
1	Spanish onion, peeled and sliced	1
4	slices fresh calf's liver	4
½ cup	all-purpose flour	125 mL
2 tbsp	butter	30 mL
½ cup	chicken stock, heated	125 mL
1 tsp	Dijon mustard	5 mL
1 tbsp	chopped fresh parsley	15 mL
	salt and freshly ground pepper	
	lemon juice to taste	

■ Heat oil in large frying pan over medium heat. Add onion and cook 12 minutes. Season and add lemon juice. Mix well and remove onion from pan; set aside.

■ Season pieces of liver well and dredge in flour. Add butter to hot pan and cook liver 3 minutes on each side over medium heat. Do not overcook. Transfer liver to serving platter.

■ Return cooked onion to pan and pour in chicken stock. Mix well, season and cook 1 minute.

■ Remove pan from heat and stir in mustard. Add parsley, mix, pour over liver and serve.

1 SERVING			
Calories	313	Fat	17 g
Carbohydrate	19 g	Fiber	1.6 g
Protein	21 g	Cholesterol	519 mg

Hungarian Goulash

◆

(4 SERVINGS)

2 tbsp	olive oil	30 mL
2	onions, peeled and chopped	2
2½ lbs	beef chuck, cut into ¾-in (2-cm) cubes	1.2 kg
2	garlic cloves, peeled, crushed and chopped	2
1 tsp	caraway seeds	5 mL
2 tbsp	paprika	30 mL
8 cups	tepid water	2 L
3	tomatoes, peeled, seeded and chopped	3
4	large potatoes, peeled and cubed	4
	salt and freshly ground pepper	

■ Preheat oven to 350°F (180°C).

■ Heat oil in large ovenproof casserole over medium heat. Add onions and cook 10 minutes over low heat. Do not let onions burn. Add meat and brown well on all sides.

■ Add garlic, caraway seeds and paprika. Mix well and cook 1 minute. Pour in water, season and bring to a boil. Cover and cook stew 1 hour in oven.

■ Stir in tomatoes. Cover and cook 1 hour.

■ Add potatoes and cook until potatoes are done. Serve.

1 SERVING			
Calories	569	Fat	17 g
Carbohydrate	32 g	Fiber	5.2 g
Protein	72 g	Cholesterol	146 mg

199

Barbecued Pork Cutlets and Tomatoes

◆

(4 SERVINGS)

½ cup	ketchup	125 mL
3 tbsp	balsamic vinegar	45 mL
3 tbsp	olive oil	45 mL
½ cup	water	125 mL
3	shallots, peeled and chopped	3
2	garlic cloves, peeled, crushed and chopped	2
1 tsp	paprika	5 mL
2 tbsp	honey	30 mL
8	pork cutlets, fat removed	8
4	tomatoes, cored and halved	4
	salt and freshly ground pepper	
	cayenne pepper to taste	
	a few drops of lemon juice	

■ Place all ingredients, except pork and tomatoes, in saucepan. Cook 16 minutes over medium heat. Remove from heat and let cool.

■ Season cutlets generously and baste with marinade. Cook over hot grill 5 minutes per side or according to size. Baste with marinade during cooking.

■ Baste tomatoes with marinade and grill 5 minutes. Serve chops and tomatoes with green salad.

1 SERVING

Calories	477	Fat	21 g
Carbohydrate	24 g	Fiber	2.0 g
Protein	48 g	Cholesterol	84 mg

Country Veal Chops

◆

(4 SERVINGS)

4	¾-in (2-cm) thick veal chops, trimmed of fat	4
2 tbsp	olive oil	30 mL
3.5 oz	bacon, diced	100 g
½ lb	fresh mushrooms, cleaned and diced	225 g
24	pearl onions, peeled and cooked	24
1 tbsp	fresh chopped parsley	15 mL
½ cup	dry white wine	125 mL
	salt and freshly ground pepper	

■ Season chops with freshly ground pepper.

■ Heat half of oil in large frying pan over medium heat. Add veal chops and bacon. Cook 10 to 12 minutes, turning chops over 2 to 3 times.

■ When veal is cooked, remove from pan; set aside and keep warm.

■ Add remaining oil to pan. Add mushrooms, onions and parsley; season well. Cook 4 minutes.

■ Pour in wine and cook 1 minute. Correct seasoning, pour over chops and serve.

1 SERVING

Calories	476	Fat	28 g
Carbohydrate	8 g	Fiber	2.7 g
Protein	43 g	Cholesterol	146 mg

Rib Roast – English Style

◆

(6 SERVINGS)

4-5 lb	rib roast, prepared for roasting	1.8-2.3 kg
1 tbsp	olive oil	15 mL
1	onion, peeled and diced	1
1	carrot, pared and diced finely	1
½ tsp	thyme	2 mL
1 tbsp	chopped fresh parsley	15 mL
1	garlic clove, peeled and chopped	1
1 tbsp	all-purpose flour	15 mL
1½ cups	beef stock, heated	375 mL
	salt and freshly ground pepper	

■ Preheat oven to 500°F (260°C). Baste meat with oil and place roast, bone-side-down, in roasting pan.

■ Place roast in hot oven and cook until nicely browned, about 10 minutes. Season meat generously and reduce heat to 350°F (180°C). Cook according to taste: 15 minutes per lb (450 g) for rare, 20 minutes for medium or 25 minutes for well done.

■ When roast is cooked, remove from pan and set aside on serving platter. Wait 15 minutes before carving.

■ Add vegetables, seasonings and garlic to roasting pan. Cook 5 minutes over high heat.

■ Sprinkle in flour and mix well. Cook 4 minutes until flour browns. Stir in beef stock and cook 10 minutes over medium heat.

■ Strain sauce through sieve and serve with roast. Carve meat in very thin slices and serve with new potatoes.

1 SERVING			
Calories	522	Fat	22 g
Carbohydrate	5 g	Fiber	0.9 g
Protein	76 g	Cholesterol	185 mg

Stuffed Leg of Lamb

◆

(4 SERVINGS)

STUFFING:

3 tbsp	butter	45 mL
4	shallots, peeled and chopped	4
2 tbsp	chopped fresh parsley	30 mL
1 tsp	rosemary	5 mL
2 tbsp	chopped basil	30 mL
½ lb	fresh mushrooms, cleaned and chopped	225 g
8	blanched garlic cloves, puréed	8
1½ cups	croûtons	375 mL
1	egg, beaten	1
	salt and freshly ground pepper	

■ Heat butter in frying pan over medium heat. Add shallots and cook 2 minutes.

■ Add parsley, rosemary, basil and mushrooms. Season and cook 4 minutes.

■ Transfer mixture to food processor. Add garlic and croûtons; blend 10 seconds. Add beaten egg and blend to incorporate. Season well and set aside.

LAMB:

4-5 lb	leg of lamb	1.8-2.3 kg
1 tbsp	olive oil	15 mL
1	onion, peeled and diced	1
1	carrot, pared and diced finely	1
2 tbsp	all-purpose flour	30 mL
1 cup	dry white wine	250 mL
2 cups	light beef stock	500 mL
	salt and freshly ground pepper	

■ Preheat oven to 450°F (230°C).

■ Peel back thin skin (the fell) that covers meat. Spread stuffing about ¼-in (5-mm) thick over meat. Replace fell and truss edges to keep stuffing in place.

■ Place lamb in roasting pan and baste with oil. Sear 10 minutes in oven.

■ Season meat generously and reduce heat to 350°F (180°C). Cook lamb 12 minutes per lb (450 g), including searing time. When meat is cooked, let stand 10 minutes before carving.

■ Place roasting pan on stove over high heat. Add vegetables and cook 4 minutes. Sprinkle in flour and brown 4 minutes over medium heat. Remove from pan and set aside.

■ Add wine to roasting pan and cook 2 minutes over high heat. Stir in beef stock and return vegetables to pan. Mix well, season and cook 6 minutes.

■ Strain sauce and serve with lamb.

1 SERVING			
Calories	1054	Fat	47 g
Carbohydrate	29 g	Fiber	4.0 g
Protein	126 g	Cholesterol	503 mg

Quick Beef Stir-Fry

◆

(4 SERVINGS)

4 tbsp	olive oil	60 mL
1 lb	beef tenderloin, sliced	450 g
2	garlic cloves, peeled and sliced	2
1	head broccoli, in florets	1
1	red bell pepper, sliced	1
1	green bell pepper, sliced	1
4	green onions, cut in short sticks	4
½ lb	fresh mushrooms, cleaned and sliced	225 g
1 tbsp	chopped fresh ginger	15 mL
2 tbsp	soy sauce	30 mL
	salt and freshly ground pepper	
	pinch of crushed chilies	

■ Heat 2 tbsp (30 mL) of oil in large frying pan over high heat. Add meat and cook 1 minute. Turn over and cook 1 minute; remove and set aside.

■ Add remaining oil to pan. When hot, add garlic and vegetables. Season well, cover and cook 3 minutes. Stir in ginger and crushed chilies; uncover and cook 3 minutes.

■ Return meat to pan and sprinkle in soy sauce. Mix well and cook 1 minute, or according to taste. Serve over rice, if desired.

1 SERVING			
Calories	341	Fat	21 g
Carbohydrate	10 g	Fiber	4.1 g
Protein	28 g	Cholesterol	57 mg

Deep-Fried Pork Tenderloin

◆

(4 SERVINGS)

2	pork tenderloins	2
1½ cups	all-purpose flour	375 mL
1 tsp	olive oil	5 mL
3	eggs, beaten	3
1½ cups	breadcrumbs	375 mL
	salt and freshly ground pepper	
	peanut oil for deep-frying	

■ Preheat peanut oil to 350°F (180°C).

■ Trim off excess fat and thin silver skin that covers tenderloin. Cut meat into ½-in (1-cm) slices and season well. Dredge in flour.

■ Add olive oil to beaten eggs and mix well. Dip pork slices into egg mixture and coat with breadcrumbs.

■ Deep-fry in peanut oil until cooked through and golden brown. Drain on paper towels before serving.

1 SERVING			
Calories	663	Fat	23 g
Carbohydrate	66 g	Fiber	1.9 g
Protein	48 g	Cholesterol	245 mg

207

Pot-au-Feu

◆

(4 SERVINGS)

4	leeks, white part only	4
2 lbs	cleaned beef bones, cut into 2-in (5-cm) pieces	900 g
3 lb	bottom round roast, tied	1.4 kg
12 cups	cold water	3 L
1 tbsp	salt	15 mL
12	spring carrots, pared	12
1	medium turnip, peeled and cut in 12 pieces	1
2	onions, peeled and studded with cloves	2
2	celery ribs, cut in 4 pieces	2
	freshly ground pepper	
	sea salt	
	Dijon mustard	
	red wine vinegar	

■ Slit leeks from top to bottom twice, leaving 1 in (2.5 cm) intact at base. Wash leeks under cold, running water to remove dirt and sand. Set aside.

■ Place bones in stock pot. Add roast, water and 1 tbsp (15 mL) of salt. Bring to a slow boil over medium heat. This process should take about 30 minutes. Skim as needed.

■ When water is boiling, reduce heat to low and simmer 30 minutes. Skim as needed.

■ When liquid is clear, add all vegetables, including leeks. Season well with pepper. Cook 3 hours over very low heat. Remove vegetables when done; keep warm in bowl with some of cooking liquid.

■ Serve meat with vegetables and sea salt. Accompany with Dijon mustard and red wine vinegar.

1 SERVING			
Calories	592	Fat	16 g
Carbohydrate	30 g	Fiber	6.1 g
Protein	82 g	Cholesterol	195 mg

Pork Chops with Honey and Apples

◆

(4 SERVINGS)

4	¾-in (2-cm) thick pork chops, trimmed of fat	4
2 tbsp	olive oil	30 mL
3	apples, cored, peeled and sliced thick	3
2 tbsp	honey	30 mL
1 tbsp	chopped fresh parsley	15 mL
	salt and freshly ground pepper	

■ Season chops with freshly ground pepper.

■ Heat half of oil in frying pan over medium heat. Add pork and cook 3 to 4 minutes on each side. Season meat generously and reduce heat to low. Cover and cook 12 minutes, or according to thickness.

■ When pork is cooked, remove from pan and set aside; keep warm.

■ Add remaining oil to hot pan. Add apples, honey and parsley; season well. Cook 6 to 7 minutes.

■ Serve apples over pork chops.

1 SERVING

Calories	304	Fat	16 g
Carbohydrate	23 g	Fiber	1.9 g
Protein	17 g	Cholesterol	40 mg

Lamb Shish Kebabs

◆

(4 SERVINGS)

1½ lbs	loin of lamb, cut into ¾-in (2-cm) pieces	675 g
½ cup	dry white wine	125 mL
3 tbsp	olive oil	45 mL
1 tbsp	rosemary	15 mL
½ tsp	thyme	2 mL
8	bay leaves	8
12	blanched garlic cloves	12
16	fresh mushroom caps, cleaned	16
8	bacon slices, cooked lightly and halved	8
1	red onion, peeled and cut in 6 wedges	1
1	large green bell pepper, cubed	1
1	large red bell pepper, cubed	1
	salt and freshly ground pepper	
	juice of 1 lemon	

■ Place meat in bowl. Add wine, oil, rosemary, thyme, bay leaves, salt, pepper and lemon juice. Mix, cover and marinate 1 hour in refrigerator.

■ Alternate pieces of lamb, garlic, bay leaves, mushrooms, folded pieces of bacon, onion wedges and bell peppers on metal skewers. Baste with marinade.

■ Place skewers in oven and broil 3 to 4 minutes, rotating two or three times during cooking. Serve with rice.

1 SERVING

Calories	473	Fat	27 g
Carbohydrate	12 g	Fiber	2.2 g
Protein	43 g	Cholesterol	152 mg

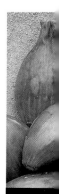

Roast Loin of Pork with Garlic and Onions

◆

(4 SERVINGS)

3½ lb	boneless pork loin, trimmed of fat and tied	1.6 kg
2	garlic cloves, peeled and halved	2
2 tbsp	rosemary	30 mL
2 tbsp	olive oil	30 mL
1	Spanish onion, peeled and chopped	1
1	celery rib, diced	1
2	apples, cored, peeled and sliced thick	2
1½ cups	chicken stock, heated	375 mL
1 tsp	cornstarch	5 mL
2 tbsp	cold water	30 mL
1 tbsp	chopped fresh basil	15 mL
	salt and freshly ground pepper	

■ Preheat oven to 400°F (200°C).

■ Make several small incisions in meat and insert garlic pieces. Sprinkle rosemary over pork and rub into meat. Baste with oil and place in roasting pan. Sear 10 minutes in oven.

■ Reduce heat to 325°F (160°C). Cook meat 25 minutes per lb (450 g), including searing time. Season well during cooking.

■ About 15 minutes before end of cooking, add onion, celery and apples to pan.

■ When roast is cooked, remove from pan and set aside on platter. Wait 15 minutes before carving.

■ Place roasting pan on stove over medium heat. Pour in chicken stock and bring to a boil.

■ Reduce heat to medium. Dilute cornstarch in cold water; incorporate to sauce. Cook 4 minutes.

■ Add basil, mix and cook 1 minute. Strain sauce and serve with roast.

1 SERVING			
Calories	808	Fat	36 g
Carbohydrate	19 g	Fiber	2.7 g
Protein	102 g	Cholesterol	248 mg

Lamb Chops with Watercress

◆

(4 SERVINGS)

2 tbsp	olive oil	30 mL
2	garlic cloves, peeled, crushed and chopped	2
1 tbsp	rosemary	15 mL
8	lamb chops, trimmed of fat	8
1 tsp	vegetable oil	5 mL
2	bunches watercress, cleaned and dried	2
	a few drops of lemon juice	
	salt and freshly ground pepper	

■ Mix olive oil with garlic, rosemary and lemon juice. Season well. Brush over lamb chops.

■ Heat vegetable oil in large frying pan over high heat. Add lamb chops and cook 2 minutes. Turn chops over and cook 2 minutes. Baste with olive oil mixture during cooking.

■ Reduce heat to medium and cook 2 minutes more, or according to size.

■ Serve lamb chops on bed of watercress.

1 SERVING			
Calories	193	Fat	13 g
Carbohydrate	1 g	Fiber	0 g
Protein	18 g	Cholesterol	68 mg

Pork Tenderloin with Bordelaise Sauce

◆

(4 SERVINGS)

2	pork tenderloins	2
2 tbsp	olive oil	30 mL
3.5 oz	bacon, diced	100 g
2	shallots, peeled and chopped	2
½ lb	fresh mushrooms, cleaned and quartered	225 g
2	garlic cloves, peeled and sliced	2
¼ tsp	thyme	1 mL
1 tbsp	basil	15 mL
2 tbsp	all-purpose flour	30 mL
1 cup	dry red wine	250 mL
1 cup	beef stock, heated	250 mL
	salt and freshly ground pepper	

- Preheat oven to 350°F (180°C).

- Trim off excess fat and thin silver skin that covers tenderloin.

- Heat oil in large ovenproof sauté pan over medium heat. Add pork and sear on all sides. Remove pork from pan and set aside.

- Add bacon to hot pan and cook 3 minutes. Cook shallots, mushrooms, garlic and seasonings 2 minutes.

- Sprinkle in flour and mix well. Incorporate wine and beef stock. Season well.

- Return pork to pan, cover and cook in oven 30 to 40 minutes, or according to size. Serve.

1 SERVING

Calories	482	Fat	29 g
Carbohydrate	8 g	Fiber	2.1 g
Protein	37 g	Cholesterol	104 mg

215

When liquid is clear, add whole onion, carrots, leeks and herb sprigs.

Strain cooking liquid, reserving 3 cups (750 mL).

Add mushrooms and shallots; season well. Cook 4 minutes over medium heat.

Veal Blanquette

◆

(4 SERVINGS)

2½ lbs	veal shoulder, cut into ¾-in (2-cm) cubes	1.2 kg
1	onion, peeled and studded with cloves	1
2	carrots, pared and cut in three	2
2	leeks, cleaned (white part only)	2
1	fresh thyme sprig	1
2	fresh parsley sprigs	2
4 tbsp	butter	60 mL
24	pearl onions, peeled	24
½ lb	fresh mushrooms, cleaned and diced	225 g
2	shallots, peeled and chopped	2
4 tbsp	all-purpose flour	60 mL
2 tbsp	chopped fresh basil	30 mL
	salt and freshly ground pepper	

■ Place veal in large saucepan. Cover with cold water and bring to a boil. Cook 15 minutes, skimming constantly.

■ When liquid is clear, add whole onion, carrots, leeks and herb sprigs. Season well and cook 40 minutes over low heat.

■ When veal is tender, remove from saucepan and set aside. Strain cooking liquid, reserving 3 cups (750 mL).

■ Heat butter in clean saucepan over medium heat. Add pearl onions and cook 10 minutes.

■ Add mushrooms and shallots; season well. Cook 4 minutes over medium heat.

■ Sprinkle in flour and mix well. Incorporate reserved cooking liquid and cook 4 minutes over medium heat.

■ Place meat in sauce, add basil and simmer 4 minutes. Serve.

1 SERVING			
Calories	586	Fat	26 g
Carbohydrate	26 g	Fiber	5.2 g
Protein	62 g	Cholesterol	285 mg

Sprinkle in flour and mix well.

Incorporate reserved cooking liquid and cook 4 minutes over medium heat.

Place meat in sauce, add basil and simmer 4 minutes.

Carbonnade of Beef

◆

(4 TO 6 SERVINGS)

3 tbsp	olive oil	45 mL
3 lbs	sliced round steak, trimmed of fat and pounded	1.4 kg
6	onions, peeled and sliced thinly	6
1 tbsp	butter	15 mL
1 tbsp	brown sugar	15 mL
2 tbsp	all-purpose flour	30 mL
1 cup	beef stock, heated	250 mL
1½ cups	beer	375 mL
1 tbsp	wine vinegar	15 mL
1	fresh thyme sprig	1
2	parsley sprigs	2
2	fresh basil sprigs	2
	salt and freshly ground pepper	

■   Preheat oven to 325°F (160°C).

■   Heat half of oil in large frying pan over high heat. Sear sliced meat in two batches. Remove from pan and set aside.

■   Heat remaining oil in hot pan. Add onions and season well. Cook 16 minutes over low heat, stirring occasionally. Do not let onions burn.

■   Alternate layers of meat and onions in large baking dish. Season well.

■   Add butter and brown sugar to hot frying pan. When melted, stir in flour and cook 2 minutes over low heat.

■   Incorporate beef stock; add beer and vinegar. Mix very well and pour over meat. Add fresh herbs, cover and cook 2 hours in oven.

■   Serve with buttered or glazed yellow turnips, if desired.

1 SERVING			
Calories	396	Fat	14 g
Carbohydrate	16 g	Fiber	2.2 g
Protein	50 g	Cholesterol	98 mg

Veal Scaloppine Island Sauté

◆

(4 SERVINGS)

4	large veal scaloppine	4
2 tbsp	green peppercorns, mashed	30 mL
1 tbsp	olive oil	15 mL
1	onion, peeled and chopped	1
1	Boston lettuce, cleaned and cut in julienne	1
½ lb	bean sprouts	225 g
1	large, ripe mango, pitted, peeled and sliced	1
1 tbsp	soy sauce	15 mL
2 tbsp	butter	30 mL
	juice of 2 limes	
	salt and freshly ground pepper	

■ Slice veal into 1-in (2.5-cm) strips and spread on large platter. Mix mashed peppercorns with lime juice; pour over veal. Season with salt and freshly ground pepper. Cover with plastic wrap and chill 30 minutes.

■ Heat oil in frying pan over high heat. Add onion and cook 2 minutes. Add lettuce, season well and cook 3 minutes.

■ Add bean sprouts and mango; season well. Cook 3 minutes over high heat. Sprinkle in soy sauce, mix and cook 1 minute.

■ Meanwhile, heat butter in separate large frying pan over high heat. Add half of veal and sauté 1 minute on each side. Remove first batch of veal and repeat for remaining meat.

■ Serve veal on bed of vegetables.

1 SERVING			
Calories	361	Fat	17 g
Carbohydrate	17 g	Fiber	3.7 g
Protein	35 g	Cholesterol	141 mg

Short Ribs Braised in Red Wine

◆

(4 SERVINGS)

3 tbsp	olive oil	45 mL
5 lbs	short ribs, trimmed of fat and cut into 2-in (5-cm) pieces	2.3 kg
1	Spanish onion, peeled and chopped finely	1
3	garlic cloves, peeled and sliced	3
¼ cup	all-purpose flour	50 mL
3 cups	beef stock, heated	750 mL
2 cups	red wine	500 mL
3	large tomatoes, peeled, seeded and chopped	3
1	fresh thyme sprig	1
2	fresh parsley sprigs	2
2	bay leaves	2
1 tsp	tarragon	5 mL
	salt and freshly ground pepper	
	pinch of crushed chilies	

■ Preheat oven to 350°F (180°C).

■ Heat 2 tbsp (30 mL) of oil in large ovenproof casserole over medium heat. Add short ribs and sear on all sides. Season well, remove ribs and set aside.

■ Add remaining oil to casserole. Cook onion and garlic 5 minutes over low heat.

■ Sprinkle in flour and mix well. Cook 3 to 4 minutes to brown flour.

■ Stir in beef stock and wine; season well. Return ribs to casserole and mix in tomatoes and seasonings. Cover and cook 2 to 2½ hours in oven. About 20 minutes before ribs are cooked, remove cover and resume cooking. Serve.

1 SERVING			
Calories	1086	Fat	58 g
Carbohydrate	20 g	Fiber	4.5 g
Protein	116 g	Cholesterol	234 mg

Veal Chops with Tomatoes and Onions

◆

(4 SERVINGS)

2 tbsp	olive oil	30 mL
4	¾-in (2-cm) thick veal chops, trimmed of fat	4
1 tbsp	butter	15 mL
1	onion, peeled and chopped	1
2	garlic cloves, peeled, crushed and chopped	2
2	shallots, peeled and chopped	2
2 tbsp	all-purpose flour	30 mL
2	large tomatoes, peeled, seeded and diced	2
1 cup	chicken stock, heated	250 mL
1 tbsp	chopped fresh basil	15 mL
	salt and freshly ground pepper	

■ Heat half of oil in large frying pan over high heat. Add veal chops and cook 2 minutes. Turn chops over, season well and cook 2 minutes. Correct seasoning and reduce heat to medium. Cook 5 to 6 minutes or according to size. Remove from pan and set chops aside; keep warm.

■ Add remaining oil and butter to hot pan. Cook onion, garlic and shallots 2 minutes. Sprinkle in flour, mix well and cook 1 minute.

■ Add tomatoes, chicken stock and basil. Season and cook 8 minutes over low heat.

■ Add veal to sauce and simmer 2 to 3 minutes. Accompany with pasta and serve.

1 SERVING			
Calories	355	Fat	19 g
Carbohydrate	10 g	Fiber	2.7 g
Protein	36 g	Cholesterol	132 mg

RICE, POTATOES AND PASTA

Carbohydrate-rich foods like rice, potatoes and pasta play an important role in our diets, and for many of us they are also inexpensive "comfort foods". But that doesn't mean they have to be boring.

It takes only a few extra minutes to turn potatoes or rice into something special, and to embellish an otherwise ordinary meal.

For example, a baked potato stuffed with mushrooms is a wonderful way to dress up a grilled steak, and a creamy risotto paired with a veal chop makes for a delicious Italian meal in minutes.

As for pasta, the focus of this chapter is on light, simple sauces. Made with the freshest ingredients, *Pasta Verdura* or *Fettuccine à la Rouille* are examples of how to bring out the full flavor of vegetables and herbs.

Risotto

◆

(4 SERVINGS)

2 tbsp	butter	30 mL
1	large onion, peeled and chopped finely	1
1 cup	Arborio rice, rinsed and drained	250 mL
2-3 cups	light chicken stock, heated	500-750 mL
4 tbsp	grated Pecorino cheese	60 mL
	salt and white pepper	

■ Heat butter in heavy-bottomed saucepan over medium heat. Add onion and cook 3 minutes over low heat.

■ Add rice, season and mix well; cook 2 minutes.

■ Add ½ cup (125 mL) of hot chicken stock to saucepan, stirring constantly. Cook over medium-low heat. As liquid is absorbed, add more chicken stock, about ⅓ cup (75 mL) at a time. The trick to making a good risotto is to gradually add liquid while stirring constantly.

■ When rice is cooked, remove pan from heat and stir in cheese. Season well and serve immediately.

1 SERVING			
Calories	197	Fat	7 g
Carbohydrate	30 g	Fiber	2.1 g
Protein	7 g	Cholesterol	18 mg

Potatoes Sautéed with Leeks

◆

(4 SERVINGS)

2	large leeks, white part only	2
2 tbsp	olive oil	30 mL
2	shallots, peeled and quartered	2
4	large cooked potatoes, peeled and sliced thickly	4
½	red bell pepper, roasted and sliced	½
1 tbsp	chopped fresh basil	15 mL
	salt and freshly ground pepper	

■ Slit leeks from top to bottom twice, leaving 1 in (2.5 cm) intact at base. Wash leeks under cold, running water to remove dirt and sand. Drain and slice.

■ Heat oil in large frying pan over medium heat. Add leeks and shallots; cook 2 minutes.

■ Add potatoes and red pepper. Season well and cook 8 to 10 minutes over medium heat. Do not allow leeks to burn; reduce heat if necessary.

■ Add basil, season and cook 2 to 3 minutes. Serve.

1 SERVING			
Calories	175	Fat	7 g
Carbohydrate	25 g	Fiber	2.7 g
Protein	3 g	Cholesterol	0 mg

Potatoes in Cream au Gratin

◆

(6 SERVINGS)

3 tbsp	butter	45 mL
5	medium potatoes, peeled and sliced very thinly	5
1½ cups	scalded milk, cooled	375 mL
2	eggs, beaten	2
¼ cup	heavy cream (35% MF)	50 mL
2	garlic cloves, peeled and chopped	2
1 cup	grated Gruyère cheese	250 mL
	salt and freshly ground pepper	
	chopped fresh parsley	

■ Preheat oven to 350°F (180°C).

■ Coat large cast iron pan with butter. Arrange potato slices to cover bottom of pan; season well. Layer remaining potatoes, seasoning each layer well.

■ Mix milk with eggs and cream; season well and pour over potatoes. Add garlic and top with cheese.

■ Place pan on stove over low heat; cook 15 minutes. Transfer to oven and cook 50 to 60 minutes, or until potatoes are tender.

■ Sprinkle with chopped parsley and serve.

1 SERVING			
Calories	224	Fat	13 g
Carbohydrate	13 g	Fiber	1.4 g
Protein	12 g	Cholesterol	108 mg

Pan-Fried Potato Cakes

◆

(4 SERVINGS)

4	large potatoes, unpeeled	4
1	egg yolk	1
2 tbsp	heavy cream (35% MF)	30 mL
1	onion, peeled and grated	1
3 tbsp	all-purpose flour	45 mL
1 tbsp	butter	15 mL
3 tbsp	olive oil	45 mL
	salt and freshly ground pepper	
	sour cream	

■ Cook unpeeled potatoes in salted, boiling water until tender. Drain well and cool 5 minutes before peeling.

■ Pass potatoes through food mill or potato ricer into bowl.

■ Mix egg yolk with cream; incorporate to mashed potatoes. Add remaining ingredients, except oil and sour cream; cover with plastic wrap. Chill 15 minutes.

■ Shape potato mixture into small patties. Heat oil in large frying pan over medium heat. Add patties and cook 3 to 4 minutes on each side or until heated through.

■ Serve with sour cream.

1 SERVING			
Calories	277	Fat	17 g
Carbohydrate	27 g	Fiber	2.3 g
Protein	4 g	Cholesterol	70 mg

Rice with Fresh Herbs

◆

(4 SERVINGS)

2 tbsp	butter	30 mL
2	green onions, chopped	2
1 tbsp	chopped fresh basil	15 mL
1 tbsp	chopped fresh chives	15 mL
1 tsp	chopped fresh fennel	5 mL
1 cup	long grain white rice, rinsed and drained	250 mL
1½ cups	chicken stock, heated	375 mL
	salt and freshly ground pepper	

■ Preheat oven to 350°F (180°C).

■ Heat butter in ovenproof casserole over medium heat. Add green onions and fresh herbs. Cook 1 minute over very low heat.

■ Add rice, mix and season well. Cook 2 minutes.

■ Pour in chicken stock, season and bring to a boil. Cover and cook 18 minutes in oven. Serve.

1 SERVING			
Calories	157	Fat	5 g
Carbohydrate	25 g	Fiber	1.4 g
Protein	3 g	Cholesterol	14 mg

Fettuccine à la Rouille

◆

(4 SERVINGS)

4	red bell peppers	4
14	garlic cloves, unpeeled	14
¼ cup	white breadcrumbs	50 mL
½ cup	olive oil	125 mL
1 lb	fettuccine, cooked *al dente*	450 g
¼ cup	cooking liquid from pasta	50 mL
	salt and freshly ground pepper	
	paprika to taste	

■ Cut bell peppers in half and remove seeds. Oil skin and place cut-side-down on cookie sheet; broil 6 minutes. Remove from oven and let cool. Peel off skin and set aside.

■ Place unpeeled garlic cloves in saucepan with 1 cup (250 mL) of water. Bring to a boil and cook 4 minutes. Remove garlic from water and let cool. Peel cloves and place in food processor.

■ Add roasted peppers to garlic; blend in food processor for 30 seconds. Add breadcrumbs and blend to combine; add oil and blend to incorporate.

■ Return hot pasta to cooking pot. Add roasted pepper mixture and mix well. Pour in ¼ cup (50 mL) of reserved cooking liquid and combine.

■ Season pasta with salt, pepper and paprika. Toss and serve.

1 SERVING			
Calories	458	Fat	30 g
Carbohydrate	40 g	Fiber	4.3 g
Protein	7 g	Cholesterol	0 mg

233

Potatoes Lyonnaise

◆

(4 SERVINGS)

4	large potatoes, peeled and sliced thinly	4
3 tbsp	olive oil	45 mL
1	Spanish onion, peeled and sliced	1
2	garlic cloves, peeled and sliced	2
1 tbsp	chopped fresh chives	15 mL
1 tbsp	chopped fresh basil	15 mL
	salt and freshly ground pepper	

■ Soak potatoes in cold water for 5 minutes. Drain well and pat dry with paper towels.

■ Heat 1 tbsp (15 mL) of oil in frying pan over medium heat. Add onion and garlic; season well. Cook 10 minutes over low heat. Transfer contents to bowl and set aside.

■ Add remaining oil to hot pan and heat. Add potatoes, season and cook 10 minutes. Stir frequently to avoid burning.

■ Add onion mixture and fresh herbs. Season well and cook 5 to 6 minutes, or until potatoes are tender. Serve.

1 SERVING

Calories	206	Fat	10 g
Carbohydrate	26 g	Fiber	2.9 g
Protein	3 g	Cholesterol	0 mg

Potato Galette

◆

(4 SERVINGS)

4	large potatoes, peeled and in fine julienne	4
1	onion, peeled and grated	1
1	apple, peeled and grated	1
1	egg, beaten	1
3 tbsp	all-purpose flour	45 mL
1 tsp	baking powder	5 mL
2½ tbsp	peanut oil	40 mL
	salt and freshly ground pepper	
	pinch of nutmeg	

■ Preheat oven to 375°F (190°C)

■ Mix all ingredients, except peanut oil, in large bowl. Season generously.

■ Heat oil in large frying pan over medium heat. Add potatoes and spread evenly with backside of spoon. Cook 5 minutes to brown underside of potatoes.

■ Lightly grease a separate ovenproof frying pan with oil. When hot, transfer potato galette, browned side up, to frying pan. Cook 30 minutes in oven.

■ Slice and serve.

1 SERVING

Calories	234	Fat	10 g
Carbohydrate	32 g	Fiber	2.9 g
Protein	4 g	Cholesterol	54 mg

Potatoes Anna

◆

(4 TO 6 SERVINGS)

½ cup	butter	125 mL
5	medium potatoes	5
	salt and freshly ground pepper	

- Preheat oven to 400°F (200°C).

- Coat large ovenproof frying pan with butter. Set aside.

- Peel potatoes and slice paper thin – use a mandoline if available.

- Arrange potato slices in overlapping circles to fill pan. Dot layers with butter and season frequently. Top with butter and cover with foil.

- Place pan on stove over medium heat and cook 10 minutes.

- Transfer pan to oven and bake 30 minutes.

- Invert onto serving platter, slice and serve.

1 SERVING			
Calories	198	Fat	14 g
Carbohydrate	16 g	Fiber	1.4 g
Protein	2 g	Cholesterol	39 mg

Saffron Rice

◆

(4 SERVINGS)

1 tbsp	butter	15 mL
2	shallots, peeled and chopped	2
1 cup	long grain white rice, rinsed and drained	250 mL
1½ cups	light chicken stock, heated	375 mL
¼ tsp	saffron	1 mL
1	small bay leaf	1
3 tbsp	grated Parmesan cheese	45 mL
	salt and freshly ground pepper	

- Preheat oven to 350°F (180°C).

- Heat butter in ovenproof casserole over medium heat. Add shallots and cook 1 minute.

- Add rice, season generously and mix. Cook over low heat until rice browns and starts to stick to bottom of casserole.

- Pour in chicken stock and increase heat to high. Stir in saffron and bay leaf; bring to a boil.

- Season, cover and cook rice 18 minutes in oven.

- Stir in cheese with fork and serve.

1 SERVING

Calories	160	Fat	4 g
Carbohydrate	26 g	Fiber	1.2 g
Protein	5 g	Cholesterol	10 mg

Macaroni with Black Olives

◆

(4 SERVINGS)

2 tbsp	olive oil	30 mL
3	shallots, peeled and chopped	3
2	garlic cloves, peeled, crushed and chopped	2
1	small marinated pimiento pepper, chopped	1
28 oz	can tomatoes, drained and chopped	796 mL
2 tbsp	chopped fresh basil	30 mL
1 tbsp	chopped fresh parsley	15 mL
2 tbsp	capers	30 mL
24	pitted black olives	24
4	portions of macaroni, cooked *al dente* and kept warm	4
½ cup	grated Pecorino cheese	125 mL
	salt and freshly ground pepper	

■ Heat oil in large sauté pan over medium heat. Add shallots, garlic and pimiento pepper; cook 2 minutes over low heat.

■ Add tomatoes, fresh herbs and capers. Season well and cook 8 minutes over high heat.

■ Stir in olives and hot pasta. Simmer 2 minutes. Sprinkle with cheese and serve.

1 SERVING			
Calories	394	Fat	14 g
Carbohydrate	54 g	Fiber	5.6 g
Protein	13 g	Cholesterol	8 mg

Pasta Verdura

◆

(4 SERVINGS)

2 tbsp	olive oil	30 mL
1½ cups	broccoli florets	375 mL
1	carrot, pared and sliced very thinly	1
1	zucchini, diced small	1
1	red bell pepper, sliced	1
1 tbsp	chopped fresh basil	15 mL
1 cup	light cream	250 mL
1 lb	pasta, cooked *al dente*	450 g
½ cup	grated Parmesan cheese	125 mL
	salt and freshly ground pepper	
	paprika to taste	

■ Heat oil in frying pan over medium heat. Add broccoli and carrot; season well. Cover and cook 3 minutes over low heat.

■ Add zucchini, red pepper and basil. Season and cook 3 minutes over high heat, uncovered.

■ Heat cream in saucepan over medium heat. Add paprika and season with pepper. Cook 3 minutes.

■ Mix hot pasta with cream in bowl. Mix in cheese and add vegetables. Mix and serve.

1 SERVING

Calories	370	Fat	18 g
Carbohydrate	38 g	Fiber	5.4 g
Protein	14 g	Cholesterol	28 mg

Spaghetti with Garlic-Basil Purée

◆

(4 SERVINGS)

12	garlic cloves	12
2 cups	fresh basil leaves, washed and dried	500 mL
½ cup	pine nuts, roasted	125 mL
½ cup	grated Parmesan cheese	125 mL
½ cup	olive oil	125 mL
1 lb	spaghetti, cooked *al dente*	450 g
	salt and freshly ground pepper	

■ Place unpeeled garlic cloves in saucepan with 1 cup (250 mL) of water. Bring to a boil and cook 4 minutes. Remove garlic from water and let cool. Peel cloves and purée flesh in mortar.

■ Place all ingredients, except pasta, in food processor. Blend 30 seconds or until fully incorporated.

■ Place hot spaghetti in heated mixing bowl. Add garlic mixture and toss to coat evenly. Season with freshly ground pepper and serve with grated Asiago cheese, if desired.

1 SERVING

Calories	623	Fat	47 g
Carbohydrate	33 g	Fiber	2.7 g
Protein	17 g	Cholesterol	8 mg

Garlic Potatoes with Rosemary

◆

(4 SERVINGS)

6	small red potatoes, scrubbed	6
2 tbsp	olive oil	30 mL
4	garlic cloves, peeled and sliced	4
1 tsp	rosemary	5 mL
	salt and freshly ground pepper	

■ Cook potatoes in steamer until tender. Remove and cut into quarters.

■ Heat oil in frying pan over high heat. Add potatoes, garlic and rosemary. Mix and cook until lightly browned on all sides.

■ Season with salt and pepper to taste; serve.

1 SERVING			
Calories	199	Fat	7 g
Carbohydrate	31 g	Fiber	2.8 g
Protein	3 g	Cholesterol	0 mg

Linguine with Quick Fresh Tomato Sauce

◆

(4 SERVINGS)

4	large tomatoes, cored	4
1 tbsp	olive oil	15 mL
1	small onion, peeled and chopped	1
3	garlic cloves, peeled, crushed and chopped	3
2 tbsp	chopped fresh parsley	30 mL
2 tbsp	chopped fresh basil	30 mL
¼ tsp	crushed chilies	1 mL
1 lb	linguine, cooked *al dente*	450 g
	pinch sugar	
	salt and pepper	
	grated Pecorino cheese	

■ Plunge tomatoes in boiling water. Remove tomatoes after 1 minute. When cool enough to handle, remove skins. Cut tomatoes in half horizontally, and squeeze out seeds. Chop pulp and set aside.

■ Heat oil in frying pan over medium heat. Add onion and garlic and cook 3 minutes. Add chopped tomatoes, parsley, basil and all other seasonings. Cook 8 minutes over medium-low heat. Do not cover.

■ Toss tomato sauce with hot pasta. Serve with grated cheese.

1 SERVING			
Calories	221	Fat	5 g
Carbohydrate	37 g	Fiber	5.0 g
Protein	7 g	Cholesterol	0 mg

Baked Potatoes Stuffed with Mushrooms

◆

(4 SERVINGS)

4	large baking potatoes, scrubbed	4
3 tbsp	olive oil	45 mL
2	shallots, peeled and chopped	2
⅓ lb	fresh mushrooms, cleaned and chopped finely	150 g
1 tbsp	chopped fresh parsley	15 mL
1 tbsp	chopped fresh basil	15 mL
½ cup	heavy cream (35% MF)	125 mL
2 tbsp	butter	30 mL
½ cup	grated Gruyère cheese	125 mL
	salt and freshly ground pepper	

▪ Preheat oven to 450°F (200°C).

▪ Wrap potatoes in foil and prick several times with fork. Place in oven and bake 1 hour.

▪ When done, remove potatoes and cut off slice from long side of potato. Carefully scoop out flesh and place in bowl. Set shells aside.

▪ Heat oil in frying pan over high heat. Add shallots, mushrooms, parsley and basil; season well. Cook 6 minutes.

▪ Incorporate half of cream and cook 2 minutes. Combine with potato flesh in bowl. Add butter and remaining cream. Season and mix well.

▪ Fill potato skins with mixture and top with cheese. Broil 8 minutes in oven and serve.

1 SERVING			
Calories	402	Fat	30 g
Carbohydrate	25 g	Fiber	2.5 g
Protein	8 g	Cholesterol	62 mg

Cut off slice from long side of potato.

Carefully scoop out flesh and place in bowl. Set shells aside.

Add shallots, mushrooms, parsley and basil; season well. Cook 6 minutes.

Incorporate half of cream
and cook 2 minutes.

Combine with potato flesh in bowl.
Add butter and remaining cream.

Fill potato skins with mixture
and top with cheese.

245

Basic Wild Rice

◆

(4 TO 6 SERVINGS)

2 tbsp	butter	30 mL
1	onion, peeled and chopped finely	1
1 cup	wild rice, rinsed and drained	250 mL
5 cups	water	1.2 L
	salt and freshly ground pepper	

■ Heat butter in large saucepan over medium heat. Add onion and cook 3 minutes over low heat.

■ Add rice, mix and season well. Cook 3 minutes.

■ Pour in water, season and bring to a boil over medium heat. Cover tightly and cook rice 35 to 45 minutes over low heat.

■ Drain off excess liquid and serve.

1 SERVING			
Calories	103	Fat	3 g
Carbohydrate	17 g	Fiber	0.9 g
Protein	2 g	Cholesterol	9 mg

Spaghettini with Zesty Anchovy Sauce

◆

(4 SERVINGS)

1 tbsp	olive oil	15 mL
1	medium onion, peeled and chopped finely	1
2	garlic cloves, peeled, crushed and chopped	2
6	anchovy fillets, drained and chopped	6
4	tomatoes, peeled, seeded and chopped	4
½ tsp	finely chopped jalapeño pepper	2 mL
1 tbsp	basil	15 mL
1 lb	spaghettini, cooked *al dente*	450 g
	salt and pepper	
	grated cheese of your choice	

■ Heat oil in frying pan over medium heat. Add onion and garlic; cook 3 minutes. Add chopped anchovies, mixing well to combine.

■ Add remaining ingredients, except pasta and cheese, and cook sauce 10 minutes over medium-low heat.

■ Pour sauce over hot pasta and serve with grated cheese of your choice.

1 SERVING

Calories	230	Fat	6 g
Carbohydrate	36 g	Fiber	4.6 g
Protein	8 g	Cholesterol	4 mg

247

Mushroom Rice Pilaf

◆

(4 SERVINGS)

2 tbsp	butter	30 mL
4	shallots, peeled and chopped	4
1 tbsp	chopped fresh basil	15 mL
1 cup	long grain white rice, rinsed and drained	250 mL
1½ cups	light chicken stock, heated	375 mL
1 tbsp	olive oil	15 mL
½ lb	fresh mushrooms*, cleaned and sliced	225 g
1	garlic clove, peeled, crushed and chopped	1
1 tbsp	chopped fresh parsley	15 mL
	salt and freshly ground pepper	
	lemon juice to taste	

■ Preheat oven to 350°F (180°C).

■ Heat half of butter in oven-proof casserole over medium heat. Add half of shallots and all of basil; cook 1 minute.

■ Add rice, season generously and mix. Cook over low heat until rice starts to stick to bottom of casserole.

■ Pour in chicken stock and increase heat to high. Bring to a boil.

■ Season, cover and cook rice 18 minutes in oven.

■ Heat remaining butter with oil in frying pan over high heat. Add remaining shallots, mushrooms, garlic and parsley. Season well and cook 5 minutes.

■ Add lemon juice and mix well. Serve over cooked rice.

* You can use any kind of fresh mushrooms in this dish.

1 SERVING			
Calories	201	Fat	9 g
Carbohydrate	28 g	Fiber	3.2 g
Protein	2 g	Cholesterol	14 mg

EGETABLES

There is an old saying that a good restaurant can be judged by the attention it pays to vegetables. It is certainly true that great chefs are almost fanatical about the quality of the vegetables allowed in their kitchens, and pay a great deal of attention to their preparation and presentation.

But it doesn't take a professional chef to realize that vegetables, when not overcooked, can add to the flavor, color, taste and texture of a meal, and to the overall pleasure of dining.

This chapter provides a wealth of different techniques and combinations to bring out the best in vegetables, ranging from *Artichokes in Hollandaise Sauce* to *Grilled Tomato Halves* to *Creamed Onions and Peppers*. The possibilities are truly endless.

Mixed Vegetables with Ginger

◆

(4 SERVINGS)

1	head broccoli	1
3 tbsp	olive oil	45 mL
1	green bell pepper, sliced thinly	1
1	red bell pepper, sliced thinly	1
1	zucchini, sliced	1
½	celery rib, sliced	½
2 tbsp	chopped fresh ginger	30 mL
1 tbsp	soy sauce	15 mL
1½ cups	chicken stock, heated	375 mL
1 tsp	cornstarch	5 mL
3 tbsp	cold water	45 mL
	salt and freshly ground pepper	

■ Divide broccoli into small florets. Reserve remaining stems for later use.

■ Heat oil in large frying pan over high heat. Add all vegetables and season well. Stir-fry 3 minutes over high heat.

■ Add ginger and soy sauce. Mix well and cook 2 minutes. Pour in chicken stock, mix and cook 2 minutes.

■ Reduce heat to low. Dilute cornstarch in cold water; incorporate to sauce. Cook 1 minute and serve.

1 SERVING			
Calories	146	Fat	10 g
Carbohydrate	10 g	Fiber	3.0 g
Protein	4 g	Cholesterol	0 mg

Cauliflower with Jack Cheese

◆

(4 SERVINGS)

1	head cauliflower	1
2 tbsp	butter	30 mL
1	small onion, peeled and chopped	1
2 tbsp	all-purpose flour	30 mL
3	tomatoes, peeled, seeded and chopped	3
¼ cup	diced green chilies	50 mL
1 cup	grated Monterey Jack cheese	250 mL
	salt and freshly ground pepper	
	a few drops of hot pepper sauce	

■ Preheat oven to 400°F (200°C).

■ Wash cauliflower, remove dark leaves and core. Place cauliflower, core-side-down, in pot of salted, boiling water. Cook until tender. Drain and cool under cold water. Drain again and divide head into large florets; set aside in buttered baking dish.

■ Heat butter in large saucepan over medium heat. Add onion and cook 3 minutes. Sprinkle in flour and cook 10 seconds.

■ Stir in tomatoes and season well. Cook 7 minutes over medium heat.

■ Add chilies, all seasonings and cheese. Mix well and cook 3 minutes.

■ Pour sauce over cauliflower and cook 5 minutes in oven. Serve.

1 SERVING

Calories	172	Fat	8 g
Carbohydrate	18 g	Fiber	3.1 g
Protein	7 g	Cholesterol	22 mg

Deep-Fried Eggplant

◆

(4 SERVINGS)

1	eggplant, peeled and cut in thick sticks	1
½ cup	all-purpose flour	125 mL
4	egg whites, beaten stiff	4
	salt and freshly ground pepper	
	peanut oil for deep-frying	

■ Arrange eggplant sticks in single layer on cookie sheet. Sprinkle with salt and let stand 1 hour at room temperature. Rinse off excess salt and drain well. Pat dry with paper towels.

■ Preheat peanut oil to 350°F (180°C).

■ Season eggplant with pepper and dredge in flour. Dip sticks into beaten egg whites.

■ Deep-fry in peanut oil until golden brown. Drain on paper towels, season well and serve.

1 SERVING

Calories	112	Fat	4 g
Carbohydrate	14 g	Fiber	1.1 g
Protein	5 g	Cholesterol	0 mg

Marinated Rapini with Garlic

◆

(4 SERVINGS)

2	large bunches rapini	2
3	garlic cloves, peeled, crushed and chopped	3
	wine vinegar to taste	
	olive oil to taste	
	lemon juice to taste	
	salt and freshly ground pepper	

■ Trim stalk ends and wash rapini in plenty of cold water. Drain and blanch 3 minutes in salted, boiling water. Place briefly under cold, running water to stop cooking process. Drain well and squeeze out all excess liquid.

■ Spread rapini in baking dish. Sprinkle remaining ingredients over greens and mix well. The proportion of oil to vinegar to use is 2 to 1. Marinate 1 hour.

■ Serve cold with toasted French bread.

1 SERVING

Calories	292	Fat	28 g
Carbohydrate	6 g	Fiber	3.7 g
Protein	4 g	Cholesterol	0 mg

French Peas with Lettuce

◆

(4 SERVINGS)

1	head Boston lettuce, washed	1
4 lbs	fresh peas, shelled	1.8 kg
¼ cup	butter	50 mL
6	shallots, peeled and sliced	6
2	fresh parsley sprigs	2
1	fresh thyme sprig	1
1 tsp	sugar	5 mL
½ cup	chicken stock	125 mL
	salt and white pepper	

■ Stack lettuce leaves on work surface and cut lengthwise into 3. Place lettuce, peas, butter, shallots, herbs, sugar and chicken stock in sauté pan. Season well, cover and cook 30 minutes over very low heat. If mixture is too dry, add a little cold water.

■ Season and serve.

1 SERVING			
Calories	242	Fat	10 g
Carbohydrate	27 g	Fiber	2.4 g
Protein	11 g	Cholesterol	26 mg

Baby Corn with Assorted Vegetables

◆

(4 SERVINGS)

3 tbsp	olive oil	45 mL
1½ cups	canned baby corn, drained	375 mL
2	carrots, pared and in julienne	2
½	celery rib, in julienne	½
1	red bell pepper, in thick julienne	1
½	zucchini, in thick julienne	½
12	cherry tomatoes, halved	12
½	jalapeño pepper, seeded and chopped	½
2	garlic cloves, peeled and sliced	2
1 tbsp	soy sauce	15 mL
	salt and freshly ground pepper	

- Heat oil in large frying pan over high heat. Add all vegetables and garlic; season well. Mix and cook 3 minutes over high heat.

- Continue cooking vegetables until tender-firm. Stir occasionally and season during cooking.

- Sprinkle in soy sauce, mix and serve.

1 SERVING			
Calories	178	Fat	10 g
Carbohydrate	20 g	Fiber	3.1 g
Protein	2 g	Cholesterol	0 mg

Brussels Sprouts with Bacon

◆

(4 SERVINGS)

1½ lbs	**Brussels sprouts**	675 g
3.5 oz	**bacon, diced finely**	100 g
1½ cups	**cooked pearl onions**	375 mL
1 tbsp	**chopped Italian parsley**	15 mL
	lemon juice to taste	
	salt and freshly ground pepper	

■ Remove outer leaves from Brussels sprouts and discard. Wash Brussels sprouts well. Using a paring knife, score an "X" on stems. This technique promotes even cooking.

■ Cook Brussels sprouts in salted, boiling water 10 minutes or until tender. When cooked, place pan under cold, running water and let cool slightly. Drain well and set aside.

■ Heat heavy-bottomed frying pan over medium heat. Add bacon and cook 3 minutes.

■ Add onions and Brussels sprouts. Season well, mix and cook 8 to 10 minutes.

■ Add remaining ingredients, mix well and serve.

1 SERVING

Calories	244	Fat	12 g
Carbohydrate	22 g	Fiber	8.7 g
Protein	12 g	Cholesterol	21 mg

258

Garlic Fried Tomatoes

◆

(4 SERVINGS)

5	tomatoes, cored	5
1 cup	seasoned flour	250 mL
2	eggs, beaten with a few drops of oil	2
1½ cups	breadcrumbs	375 mL
4	garlic cloves, peeled, crushed and chopped	4
¼ cup	olive oil	50 mL
	salt and freshly ground pepper	
	chopped fresh basil	

■ Cut tomatoes into thick slices and season generously. Dredge in flour and dip in beaten eggs.

■ Mix breadcrumbs and garlic together. Coat tomato slices thoroughly and arrange on plate. Cover with plastic wrap and refrigerate 1 hour.

■ Heat oil in deep frying pan over high heat. Add tomato slices and brown 3 minutes on each side. Correct seasoning.

■ Drain slices on paper towels, sprinkle with fresh basil and serve.

1 SERVING

Calories	444	Fat	16 g
Carbohydrate	62 g	Fiber	5.6 g
Protein	13 g	Cholesterol	108 mg

259

Broiled Vegetables on Skewers

◆

(4 SERVINGS)

12	large garlic cloves	12
1	Italian eggplant, sliced 1-in (2.5-cm) thick	1
24	large fresh mushroom caps, cleaned	24
1	zucchini, sliced ½-in (1-cm) thick	1
1 tbsp	lemon juice	15 mL
½ cup	dry white wine	125 mL
½ cup	water	125 mL
4 tbsp	olive oil	60 mL
1	red bell pepper, diced large	1
1	green bell pepper, diced large	1
1	red onion, peeled and cut in 6 wedges	1
8	cherry tomatoes	8
	salt and freshly ground pepper	
	extra lemon juice	

■ Set oven to broil.

■ Blanch garlic cloves 3 minutes in boiling water. Remove, peel and set aside.

■ Place eggplant, mushrooms and zucchini in large saucepan. Add lemon juice, wine, water and 1 tbsp (15 mL) of oil. Season well with freshly ground pepper. Cover and cook 3 minutes. Drain well.

■ Alternate garlic with vegetables on metal skewers. Set aside on ovenproof tray.

■ Place remaining oil in bowl; add lemon juice and freshly ground pepper. Mix well and brush over vegetables. Broil skewers 4 to 5 minutes in oven or according to size. Serve with rice.

1 SERVING			
Calories	218	Fat	14 g
Carbohydrate	15 g	Fiber	3.6 g
Protein	3 g	Cholesterol	0 mg

Carrots and Onions in Foil

◆

(4 SERVINGS)

3	shallots, peeled and chopped	3
2	garlic cloves, peeled, crushed and chopped	2
1	jalapeño pepper, seeded and chopped	1
1	tomato, peeled, seeded and chopped	1
2 tbsp	lime juice	30 mL
3 tbsp	olive oil	45 mL
6	carrots, pared	6
6	medium onions, peeled	6
	salt and freshly ground pepper	

■ Preheat oven to 400°F (200°C).

■ Place shallots, garlic, jalapeño pepper and tomato in bowl. Mix well and season generously. Incorporate lime juice and oil.

■ Arrange carrots and onions on large doubled sheet of foil. Fold up long sides to hold vegetables. Pour sauce over vegetables and season well. Close package securely. Tie with string if necessary.

■ Place package in roasting pan and cook 35 to 40 minutes in oven.

■ Slit foil open and serve.

1 SERVING			
Calories	243	Fat	11 g
Carbohydrate	32 g	Fiber	6.5 g
Protein	4 g	Cholesterol	0 mg

Mexican-Style Vegetables

◆

(4 SERVINGS)

3 tbsp	safflower oil	45 mL
2	onions, peeled and chopped	2
2	garlic cloves, peeled and sliced	2
1-2	serrano chili peppers, seeded and chopped finely	1-2
1	zucchini, diced small	1
½	cucumber, peeled, seeded and diced	½
1	large tomato, peeled, seeded and chopped	1
1 cup	cooked baby corn	250 mL
½ cup	cooked green peas	125 mL
2 tbsp	chopped fresh cilantro	30 mL
	salt and freshly ground pepper	

■ Heat oil in large sauté pan over medium heat. Add onions and cook 6 minutes over low heat. Do not let onions burn.

■ Add garlic, serrano peppers, zucchini and cucumber. Season well and cook 6 minutes over medium heat.

■ Stir in tomato and cook 3 minutes.

■ Add remaining ingredients, season and mix well. Simmer 4 minutes and serve.

1 SERVING			
Calories	210	Fat	10 g
Carbohydrate	26 g	Fiber	4.8 g
Protein	4 g	Cholesterol	0 mg

Trim stem ends of asparagus.

Pare asparagus if necessary.

Place in salted, boiling water with juice of ½ lemon and cook until tender. Drain well and pat dry with paper towels.

Asparagus with Cheese Sauce

◆

(4 SERVINGS)

2	large bunches fresh asparagus	2
4 tbsp	butter	60 mL
1	onion, peeled and chopped	1
3 tbsp	all-purpose flour	45 mL
2½ cups	milk, heated	625 mL
1 cup	grated Gruyère cheese	250 mL
	juice of ½ lemon	
	pinch of nutmeg	
	pinch of ground clove	
	salt and white pepper	
	pinch of paprika	

■ Trim stem ends of asparagus and pare if necessary. Place in salted, boiling water with juice of ½ lemon and cook until tender. Drain well and pat dry with paper towels.

■ Meanwhile, heat butter in saucepan over medium heat. Add onion and cook 2 minutes over low heat. Sprinkle in flour and mix well; cook 15 seconds.

■ Incorporate milk, nutmeg and clove. Mix well, season and cook sauce 12 minutes over low heat, whisking frequently.

■ When sauce is cooked, strain through sieve into clean saucepan. Add cheese and paprika; mix well. Simmer several minutes to melt cheese. Pour over asparagus and serve.

1 SERVING

Calories	343	Fat	19 g
Carbohydrate	27 g	Fiber	2.1 g
Protein	16 g	Cholesterol	56 mg

Heat butter in saucepan over medium heat. Add onion and cook 2 minutes over low heat. Sprinkle in flour and mix well.

Incorporate milk, nutmeg and clove. Mix well, season and cook sauce 12 minutes over low heat, whisking frequently.

When sauce is cooked, strain through sieve into clean saucepan. Add cheese and paprika; mix well.

Broccoli with Paprika Sauce

◆

(4 SERVINGS)

2	large heads broccoli	2
2 tbsp	butter	30 mL
1	onion, peeled and chopped	1
2	garlic cloves, peeled and sliced	2
1 tbsp	paprika	15 mL
1 tbsp	all-purpose flour	15 mL
1½ cups	chicken stock, heated	375 mL
1 tbsp	chopped fresh parsley	15 mL
	juice of ½ lemon	
	salt and freshly ground pepper	

■ Trim stalk ends of broccoli. Slice heads lengthwise into several pieces.

■ Heat butter in saucepan over medium heat. Add onion and garlic; cook 4 minutes. Sprinkle in paprika and mix well; cook 1 minute.

■ Sprinkle in flour and mix well. Incorporate chicken stock and cook sauce 10 minutes over low heat. Season well during cooking.

■ Meanwhile, cook broccoli in salted, boiling water with lemon juice until tender.

■ Drain well and arrange on serving platter. Top with paprika sauce, sprinkle with parsley and serve.

1 SERVING			
Calories	134	Fat	6 g
Carbohydrate	14 g	Fiber	4.5 g
Protein	6 g	Cholesterol	14 mg

Marinated Fresh Vegetables

◆

(6 TO 8 SERVINGS)

VEGETABLES:

2	large potatoes	2
1	yellow bell pepper, diced large	1
1	red bell pepper, diced large	1
1	green bell pepper, diced large	1
1	celery rib, sliced ¾-in (2-cm) thick	1
24	fresh mushroom caps, cleaned	24

■ Peel potatoes and dice large. Place in bowl of cold water. Set remaining vegetables aside.

MARINADE:

2 ½ cups	water	625 mL
⅓ cup	olive oil	75 mL
4	garlic cloves, peeled	4
1 tsp	coriander	5 mL
1 tsp	whole black peppercorns	5 mL
1	fresh thyme sprig	1
2	fresh parsley sprigs	2
3	fresh fennel sprigs	3
2	bay leaves	2
	salt	

■ Place all ingredients in large saucepan and bring to a boil.

■ Drain potatoes and place in marinade with all remaining vegetables. Cook over medium heat until tender. Check vegetables regularly and remove from marinade as soon as they are cooked.

■ Once all vegetables are cooked, return to marinade. Using a slotted spoon, serve warm or cold and accompany with garlic bread, if desired.

1 SERVING

Calories	108	Fat	8 g
Carbohydrate	8 g	Fiber	1.3 g
Protein	1 g	Cholesterol	0 g

Carrots with Parsnips in Honey

◆

(4 SERVINGS)

3	carrots, pared and sliced ¼-in (5-mm) thick	3
3	parsnips, pared and sliced	3
2 tbsp	butter	30 mL
1 tbsp	honey	15 mL
1 tbsp	chopped fresh chives	15 mL
	salt and freshly ground pepper	

■ Place carrots and parsnips in salted, boiling water. Cook over medium heat until done.

■ When vegetables are cooked, place saucepan under cold, running water for 2 minutes. Drain well.

■ Heat butter in frying pan over medium heat. Add vegetables, honey and chives; season well. Cook 2 to 3 minutes, stirring occasionally. Season well and serve.

1 SERVING			
Calories	137	Fat	5 g
Carbohydrate	22 g	Fiber	3.9 g
Protein	1 g	Cholesterol	14 mg

Sautéed Zucchini

◆

(4 SERVINGS)

2 tbsp	olive oil	30 mL
4	small zucchini, sliced thinly	4
½ cup	toasted pine nuts	125 mL
1 tbsp	chopped fresh basil	15 mL
1 tsp	chopped lemon rind	5 mL
	salt and freshly ground pepper	

■ Heat oil in frying pan over high heat. Add zucchini and cook until soft, turning slices over during cooking. Season well.

■ When cooked, add remaining ingredients to pan. Mix well, simmer 1 minute and serve.

1 SERVING

Calories	236	Fat	20 g
Carbohydrate	6 g	Fiber	2.4 g
Protein	8 g	Cholesterol	0 mg

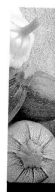

Vegetables with Sun-Dried Tomatoes

◆

(4 SERVINGS)

2 tbsp	olive oil	30 mL
4	green onions, cut in short sticks	4
1	yellow bell pepper, in fine julienne	1
1	red bell pepper, in fine julienne	1
1	yellow summer squash, in julienne	1
¼	celery rib, in short julienne	¼
2	garlic cloves, peeled and sliced	2
2 tbsp	chopped fresh basil	30 mL
2 tbsp	thinly sliced sun-dried tomatoes	30 mL
	salt and freshly ground pepper	
	extra virgin olive oil	
	grated Asiago cheese	

■ Heat olive oil in sauté pan over high heat. Add all vegetables, except sun-dried tomatoes, and cook *al dente*. Season well.

■ Add basil and sun-dried tomatoes; mix well.

■ Serve vegetables and sprinkle with extra-virgin olive oil and grated cheese.

1 SERVING			
Calories	107	Fat	7 g
Carbohydrate	9 g	Fiber	2.2 g
Protein	2 g	Cholesterol	1 mg

Braised Cabbage in Wine

◆

(4 SERVINGS)

2 tbsp	olive oil	30 mL
1	medium cabbage, cored and cut in 8 pieces	1
4	shallots, peeled and sliced	4
½	celery rib, sliced	½
2	garlic cloves, peeled and sliced	2
2 tbsp	chopped fresh basil	30 mL
½ cup	dry white wine	125 mL
½ cup	chicken stock, heated	125 mL
2 tbsp	balsamic vinegar	30 mL
1 tbsp	chopped fresh parsley	15 mL
	salt and freshly ground pepper	

- Preheat oven to 350°F (180°C).

- Heat oil in large ovenproof casserole over medium heat. Add cabbage, shallots, celery and garlic. Season well and cook 8 minutes over high heat, stirring occasionally.

- Add basil, wine, chicken stock, vinegar, salt and pepper. Mix well, cover and cook 30 minutes in oven.

- Sprinkle with parsley and serve.

1 SERVING			
Calories	101	Fat	7 g
Carbohydrate	7 g	Fiber	2.2 g
Protein	1 g	Cholesterol	0 mg

Grilled Tomato Halves

◆

(4 TO 6 SERVINGS)

6	large tomatoes, halved	6
3 tbsp	olive oil	45 mL
2	onions, peeled and chopped	2
2	garlic cloves, peeled, crushed and chopped	2
2 tbsp	chopped fresh parsley	30 mL
½ cup	white breadcrumbs	125 mL
	salt and freshly ground pepper	
	crushed chilies to taste	

- Preheat oven to 375°F (190°C).

- Gently squeeze out some of tomato seeds and juice. Arrange halves, cut-side-up, in baking dish and season generously.

- Heat oil in frying pan over high heat. Add onions and garlic. Cook 8 minutes over medium heat; add parsley and cook 1 minute.

- Season well and mix in breadcrumbs. Add crushed chilies and cook 2 minutes.

- Spread mixture over tomato halves, bake 10 minutes in oven and serve.

1 SERVING			
Calories	123	Fat	7 g
Carbohydrate	13 g	Fiber	1.7 g
Protein	2 g	Cholesterol	0 mg

Braised Fennel Bulbs

◆

(4 SERVINGS)

3	fennel bulbs	3
2 tbsp	olive oil	30 mL
3	garlic cloves	3
3	shallots, peeled	3
1	carrot, pared and sliced	1
½ cup	dry white wine	125 mL
1 cup	chicken stock, heated	250 mL
1	fresh thyme sprig	1
2	fresh parsley sprigs	2
1	bay leaf	1
	salt and freshly ground pepper	

- Preheat oven to 350°F (180°C).

- Trim most of stems and cut fennel bulbs in half. Peel off outer rib and remove core.

- Heat oil in large ovenproof casserole over medium heat. Add fennel, garlic, shallots and carrot. Cook 6 minutes over medium heat.

- Pour in wine and cook 3 minutes. Add chicken stock and all seasonings. Cover and cook 20 to 25 minutes in oven. Remove bay leaf and serve.

1 SERVING			
Calories	129	Fat	7 g
Carbohydrate	13 g	Fiber	0.8 g
Protein	2 g	Cholesterol	0 mg

Place eggplants in roasting pan and sprinkle with salt.

Score flesh in criss-cross pattern.

Baste with oil and arrange, skin-side-up, on baking sheet. Bake 35 minutes.

Stuffed Eggplant

◆

(4 SERVINGS)

2	eggplants, halved lengthwise	2
3 tbsp	olive oil	45 mL
2	garlic cloves, peeled, crushed and chopped	2
2	onions, peeled and chopped	2
1	yellow bell pepper, diced small	1
3	tomatoes, peeled, seeded and chopped	3
¼ cup	chopped sun-dried tomatoes	50 mL
2 tbsp	chopped fresh basil	30 mL
1 tbsp	chopped fresh parsley	15 mL
1¼ cups	grated mozzarella cheese	300 mL
	salt and freshly ground pepper	

■ Preheat oven to 400°F (200°C).

■ Place eggplants in roasting pan and sprinkle with salt. Let stand 1 hour at room temperature. Rinse off excess salt and drain well; pat dry and score flesh in criss-cross pattern. Baste with oil and arrange, skin-side-up, on baking sheet. Bake 35 minutes.

■ Remove eggplants from oven and scoop out flesh, reserving sturdy shells. Chop flesh and set aside.

■ Heat oil in large frying pan over medium heat. Add garlic and onions; cook 4 minutes over low heat.

■ Add yellow pepper, tomatoes, sun-dried tomatoes and eggplant flesh. Stir in all seasonings and cook 16 minutes over medium heat.

■ Fill eggplant shells with stuffing. Top with cheese and broil 8 minutes in oven or until golden brown. Serve.

1 SERVING			
Calories	245	Fat	17 g
Carbohydrate	16 g	Fiber	3.7 g
Protein	7 g	Cholesterol	22 mg

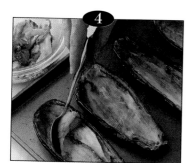

Remove eggplants from oven and scoop out flesh, reserving sturdy shells.

Fill eggplant shells with stuffing.

Top with cheese and broil 8 minutes in oven or until golden brown.

Sauerkraut with Apples

◆

(4 SERVINGS)

2 lbs	sauerkraut	900 g
1 tbsp	olive oil	15 mL
4	back bacon slices, diced	4
1	onion, peeled and chopped	1
1 cup	dry white wine	250 mL
1 cup	chicken stock, heated	250 mL
1	bay leaf	1
1	fresh thyme sprig	1
2 tbsp	butter	30 mL
2	tart apples, cored, peeled and sliced	2
	salt and freshly ground pepper	
	a few juniper berries	

■ Preheat oven to 350°F (180°C).

■ Rinse sauerkraut under cold water and drain well. Set aside.

■ Heat oil in ovenproof casserole over medium heat. Add bacon and cook 2 minutes; add onion and cook 2 minutes.

■ Add sauerkraut and mix well. Increase heat to high and cook 5 minutes.

■ Mix in wine, chicken stock and all seasonings. Cover and cook 1½ hours in oven.

■ Heat butter in frying pan over medium heat. Add apples and cook 3 minutes over high heat. Incorporate to sauerkraut mixture. Cover and cook 30 minutes in oven. Add more liquid if necessary. Remove bay leaf and serve.

1 SERVING			
Calories	232	Fat	11 g
Carbohydrate	22 g	Fiber	1.8 g
Protein	8 g	Cholesterol	27 mg

Creamed Onions and Peppers

◆

(4 TO 6 SERVINGS)

¼ cup	butter	50 mL
3	medium onions, peeled and sliced thinly	3
2	green bell peppers, sliced thinly	2
1 tbsp	all-purpose flour	15 mL
1½ cups	light cream, heated	375 mL
½ tsp	celery seeds	2 mL
1 tbsp	chopped fresh parsley	15 mL
	pinch of nutmeg	
	salt and freshly ground pepper	

■ Heat half of butter in saucepan over medium heat. Add onions and cook 16 minutes over low heat, stirring frequently. Season half-way through cooking. Remove onions from pan and set aside.

■ Add remaining butter to hot pan. Cook bell peppers 12 minutes over low heat, stirring frequently. Season half-way through cooking.

■ Return onions to pan with peppers and sprinkle in flour; mix well. Incorporate cream and all remaining ingredients. Simmer 6 minutes over low heat and serve.

1 SERVING			
Calories	156	Fat	12 g
Carbohydrate	10 g	Fiber	1.5 g
Protein	2 g	Cholesterol	35 mg

Fresh Green Beans Niçoise

◆

(4 SERVINGS)

1½ lbs	fresh green beans, pared	675 g
3 tbsp	olive oil	45 mL
3	shallots, peeled and chopped	3
3	garlic cloves, peeled, crushed and chopped	3
3	tomatoes, peeled, seeded and chopped	3
¼ cup	chopped sun-dried tomatoes	50 mL
2 tbsp	chopped fresh basil	30 mL
	salt and freshly ground pepper	
	chopped black olives to taste	

■ Cook beans in salted, boiling water about 8 to 10 minutes. Place saucepan under cold, running water briefly, then drain well and set beans aside.

■ Heat 2 tbsp (30 mL) of oil in large frying pan over medium heat. Add shallots and garlic; cook 2 minutes over low heat.

■ Add tomatoes, sun-dried tomatoes and basil. Season well and cook 7 minutes over medium heat.

■ Heat remaining oil in separate frying pan over high heat. Add green beans and cook 3 minutes; season well.

■ Add tomato mixture to beans. Mix well, top with chopped black olives and serve.

1 SERVING

Calories	178	Fat	10 g
Carbohydrate	18 g	Fiber	4.2 g
Protein	4 g	Cholesterol	0 mg

Flageolets in White Wine and Tomatoes

◆

2 cups	flageolets*	500 mL
2 tbsp	olive oil	30 mL
1	large onion, peeled and chopped	1
½ cup	dry white wine	125 mL
3	large tomatoes, peeled, seeded and chopped	3
3 tbsp	chopped fresh parsley	45 mL
	salt and freshly ground pepper	

■ Soak beans 8 hours in plenty of cold water. Drain well.

■ Place beans in large saucepan and cover with fresh water. Water should cover beans by 1 in (2.5 cm). Bring to a boil and simmer 1½ to 2 hours over medium heat. Add water to keep beans covered. When cooked, drain well and set aside.

■ Heat oil in large frying pan over medium heat. Add onion and cook 5 minutes over low heat.

■ Increase heat to high and pour in wine; cook 3 minutes. Add tomatoes and half of parsley. Season well and cook 8 minutes over medium heat.

■ Transfer tomato mixture to large saucepan. Incorporate beans and remaining parsley; season generously. Cover, simmer 15 minutes and serve.

Flageolets are young, white kidney beans, cultivated mainly in France and Italy. If not available in your area, substitute with another white bean.

1 SERVING

Calories	233	Fat	7 g
Carbohydrate	31 g	Fiber	5.0 g
Protein	10 g	Cholesterol	0 mg

Zucchini with Garlic and Parmesan

◆

2	large zucchini, sliced ¼-in (5-mm) thick	2
2 tbsp	olive oil	30 mL
1	garlic clove, peeled and chopped	1
3 tbsp	grated Parmesan cheese	45 mL
1 tbsp	breadcrumbs	15 mL
	salt and freshly ground pepper	

■ Season zucchini generously with salt and pepper.

■ Heat oil in frying pan over high heat. Add garlic and zucchini; cook 2 minutes. Turn slices over and cook 2 to 3 minutes.

■ Mix cheese with breadcrumbs. Add to zucchini, mix and cook 1 minute. Season and serve.

1 SERVING

Calories	92	Fat	8 g
Carbohydrate	3 g	Fiber	1.2 g
Protein	2 g	Cholesterol	3 mg

Baked Eggplant with Ricotta Cheese

♦

(4 TO 6 SERVINGS)

1	large eggplant, sliced ½-in (1-cm) thick	1
4 tbsp	olive oil	60 mL
2	onions, peeled and chopped	2
3	garlic cloves, peeled, crushed and chopped	3
4	tomatoes, peeled, seeded and chopped	4
¼ tsp	thyme	1 mL
½ tsp	oregano	2 mL
½ cup	ricotta cheese	125 mL
½ cup	grated Parmesan cheese	125 mL
½ cup	heavy cream (35% MF)	125 mL
1	egg, beaten	1
	salt and freshly ground pepper	
	cayenne pepper to taste	

■ Preheat oven to 400°F (200°C).

■ Arrange eggplant slices in single layer on cookie sheet. Brush with oil and cook 6 minutes in oven. Turn slices over and cook 6 minutes.

■ Cover bottom of oiled baking dish with eggplant slices. Season well and set aside. Change oven setting to 375°F (190°C).

■ Heat remaining oil in large frying pan over high heat. Add onions and garlic; cook 3 minutes over medium heat.

■ Add tomatoes and all seasonings. Increase heat to high and cook 8 minutes. Pour mixture over eggplant.

■ Mix both cheeses with cream and egg. Season well and pour over tomatoes. Bake 20 minutes and serve.

1 SERVING			
Calories	278	Fat	22 g
Carbohydrate	12 g	Fiber	2.1 g
Protein	8 g	Cholesterol	79 mg

Mashed Yellow Turnips

◆

(4 SERVINGS)

3	medium yellow turnips, peeled and diced large	3
3 tbsp	butter	45 mL
¼ cup	light cream or milk, heated	50 mL
	salt and freshly ground pepper	
	pinch of nutmeg	

■ Cook turnips in salted, boiling water until tender.

■ When cooked, drain well and pass through food mill into bowl. Add butter and hot cream. Mix very well. Season to taste with salt, pepper and nutmeg. Serve hot.

1 SERVING

Calories	95	Fat	7 g
Carbohydrate	7 g	Fiber	2.0 g
Protein	I g	Cholesterol	21 mg

284

Ratatouille

◆

(4 TO 6 SERVINGS)

⅓ cup	olive oil	75 mL
4	onions, peeled and chopped	4
3	large tomatoes, peeled, seeded and chopped	3
4	large zucchini, sliced	4
1	medium eggplant, peeled and diced	1
1	red bell pepper, sliced	1
3	garlic cloves, peeled, crushed and chopped	3
1 tbsp	chopped fresh basil	15 mL
½ tsp	thyme	2 mL
1 tbsp	chopped fresh parsley	15 mL
	salt and freshly ground pepper	

■ Heat oil in large sauté pan over medium heat. Add onions and cook 10 minutes over low heat. Do not let onions burn.

■ Add tomatoes and season well. Mix and cook 4 minutes over high heat.

■ Add remaining ingredients and mix well. Season generously, cover and cook 1 hour over low heat. Stir occasionally during cooking.

■ Remove cover and cook 15 minutes or until most of liquid evaporates. Serve.

1 SERVING			
Calories	176	Fat	12 g
Carbohydrate	15 g	Fiber	4.3 g
Protein	2 g	Cholesterol	0 mg

Artichokes with Hollandaise Sauce

◆

(4 SERVINGS)

4	large artichokes	4
4	lemon slices	4
2	egg yolks	2
1 tbsp	cold water	15 mL
¾ cup	melted clarified butter	175 mL
	strained lemon juice to taste	
	salt and white pepper	
	cayenne pepper to taste	

■ Cut off tip and stem ends from artichokes. Using kitchen scissors, snip off triangular tips of outer leaves. Rub lemon over cut edges and secure lemon slices to bottom of artichokes with kitchen string.

■ Place artichokes in salted, boiling water. Cook 30 to 40 minutes or according to size. Centre leaves should detach easily when cooked.

■ When artichokes are done, place pot under cold, running water to stop cooking process. Drain very well and arrange artichokes on serving dishes.

■ Fill saucepan with 2 in (5 cm) of water. Simmer over low heat.

■ Place egg yolks and 1 tbsp (15 mL) of cold water in stainless steel bowl. Set bowl over simmering water in saucepan. Beat egg yolks until smooth. Incorporate some of clarified butter and beat until thickened. Repeat procedure several times until all of butter is incorporated and sauce is very thick. Maintain water at simmer or sauce may curdle.

■ Season with salt, pepper, cayenne pepper and lemon juice. Serve Hollandaise sauce with artichokes.

1 SERVING			
Calories	351	Fat	31 g
Carbohydrate	13 g	Fiber	0 g
Protein	5 g	Cholesterol	186 mg

Beat egg yolks until smooth.

Gradually incorporate clarified
butter and beat until sauce
is very thick.

Season with salt, pepper,
cayenne pepper and lemon juice.

287

Fresh Snow Peas with Apple

◆

(4 SERVINGS)

1 lb	snow peas, pared	450 g
2 tbsp	butter	30 mL
1	shallot, peeled and chopped	1
1	small red onion, peeled and sliced in rings	1
2	apples, cored, peeled and sliced ¼-in (5-mm) thick	2
¼ cup	sliced almonds	50 mL
	salt and freshly ground pepper	

■ Steam snow peas 3 minutes. Place under cold, running water to stop cooking process and let cool. Drain well and set aside.

■ Heat butter in large frying pan over medium heat. Add shallot and red onion. Cook 3 minutes.

■ Add snow peas and apples; season well and mix. Cook 4 minutes over high heat.

■ Add almonds, season and cook 1 minute. Mix and serve.

1 SERVING			
Calories	176	Fat	8 g
Carbohydrate	22 g	Fiber	5.5 g
Protein	4 g	Cholesterol	12 mg

Warm Navy Bean Salad

◆

(4 TO 6 SERVINGS)

1¼ cups	dried navy beans	300 mL
1	large onion, peeled and quartered	1
1	celery rib, cut in 3	1
1	fresh thyme sprig	1
2	fresh parsley sprigs	2
1	bay leaf	1
2 tbsp	olive oil	30 mL
2	garlic cloves, peeled and sliced	2
12	pearl onions, cooked	12
1	green bell pepper, sliced	1
1	red bell pepper, sliced	1
1 tsp	chili powder	5 mL
	salt and freshly ground pepper	

■ Soak navy beans 8 hours in cold water. Drain well.

■ Place beans, quartered onion, celery, fresh herbs, bay leaf and freshly ground pepper in large saucepan. Cover beans with cold water; water should cover beans by 2 in (5 cm). Bring to a boil over medium heat. Reduce heat to low and cook 2 hours, adding water as needed. When cooked, drain well and set beans aside.

■ Heat oil in frying pan over medium heat. Add garlic, pearl onions, bell peppers and chili powder. Season well and cook 7 minutes.

■ Place beans in clean saucepan and incorporate vegetable mixture. Season generously and cook 10 minutes over low heat. If necessary, add a little liquid. Serve warm.

1 SERVING			
Calories	193	Fat	5 g
Carbohydrate	29 g	Fiber	4.6 g
Protein	8 g	Cholesterol	0 mg

Mushrooms with Fresh Herbs

◆

(4 SERVINGS)

3 tbsp	olive oil	45 mL
1 lb	fresh mushrooms, cleaned and cut in 3	450 g
3	shallots, peeled and chopped	3
2 tbsp	chopped fresh parsley	30 mL
1 tbsp	chopped fresh chives	15 mL
¼ cup	toasted pine nuts	50 mL
	lemon juice to taste	
	salt and freshly ground pepper	

- Heat oil in frying pan over high heat. Add mushrooms, season and cook 4 minutes.

- Add remaining ingredients, mix well and cook 2 to 3 minutes.

- Add more lemon juice, mix and serve.

1 SERVING

Calories	188	Fat	16 g
Carbohydrate	6 g	Fiber	3.1 g
Protein	5 g	Cholesterol	0 mg

Fresh Spinach with Julienne of Sweet Peppers

◆

(4 SERVINGS)

½	red bell pepper	½
½	yellow bell pepper	½
½	green bell pepper	½
1	carrot, pared	1
2 lbs	fresh spinach	900 g
2 tbsp	olive oil	30 mL
1	garlic clove, peeled and sliced thinly	1
	salt and freshly ground pepper	
	pinch of nutmeg	

■ Slice bell peppers and carrot into very fine julienne. Set aside.

■ Remove stems from spinach. Wash leaves and place in ½ cup (125 mL) of boiling water; cook 2 to 3 minutes or until wilted. Transfer spinach to sieve and press with back of spoon to squeeze out excess water. Set aside.

■ Heat oil in saucepan over medium heat. Add julienned vegetables and garlic; season well. Cover and cook 3 minutes over low heat.

■ Add spinach and nutmeg. Mix well, simmer 1 minute and serve.

1 SERVING			
Calories	135	Fat	7 g
Carbohydrate	11 g	Fiber	6.6 g
Protein	7 g	Cholesterol	0 mg

Vegetables with Curry

◆

(4 TO 6 SERVINGS)

CURRY SAUCE:

3 tbsp	butter	45 mL
1	large onion, peeled and chopped	1
1	garlic clove, peeled, crushed and chopped	1
3 tbsp	curry powder	45 mL
3 tbsp	all-purpose flour	45 mL
2 cups	chicken stock, heated	500 mL
	salt and freshly ground pepper	

■ Heat butter in saucepan over medium heat. Add onion and cook 10 minutes over low heat. Add garlic and cook 2 minutes.

■ Sprinkle in curry powder and mix well; cook 3 minutes. Sprinkle in flour, mix well and season to taste.

■ Incorporate chicken stock and season well. Cook sauce 12 minutes over low heat, stirring occasionally.

VEGETABLES:

1 tbsp	olive oil	15 mL
1	zucchini, sliced	1
1	green bell pepper, sliced thickly	1
1	yellow bell pepper, sliced thickly	1
2	carrots, pared and sliced	2
1	bunch asparagus, cooked and cut in short sticks	1
½	head cauliflower, in florets and cooked	½
	salt and freshly ground pepper	
	crushed chilies to taste	

■ Heat oil in frying pan over medium heat. Add zucchini, bell peppers and carrots. Season well and cook 5 minutes.

■ Add remaining vegetables and mix well. Add crushed chilies and cook 3 minutes.

■ Incorporate curry sauce and simmer 3 minutes. Serve with rice.

1 SERVING			
Calories	152	Fat	8 g
Carbohydrate	16 g	Fiber	3.3 g
Protein	4 g	Cholesterol	14 mg

DESSERTS

A special meal does not seem complete without a special dessert finale. But desserts need not be reserved for special occasions. Many people enjoy a little something sweet at the end of the simplest everyday meal, or during an afternoon break. Whatever the occasion, this chapter explores the many options at your disposal for quick and easy delights.

From an exquisite *Fresh Strawberry Tart with Kirsch* to a simple *Banana-Nut Cake*, to a rich and delicious *Chocolate Quatre Quart*, you can turn out these recipes successfully every time, as long as you follow the simple directions.

Also included in this chapter for those truly last-minute gatherings, are several desserts like the *Quick Blueberry Pie* that are sure to please everyone. Why not treat yourself, as well as your guests?

Balthazar Cake

◆

(6 TO 8 SERVINGS)

1 cup	all-purpose flour	250 mL
1¼ cups	powdered almonds	300 mL
¾ cup	granulated sugar	175 mL
3	egg yolks	3
¾ cup	rum	175 mL
1 cup	chopped candied fruit	250 mL
4	egg whites, beaten stiff	4
1 tbsp	butter	15 mL
2 tbsp	slivered almonds	30 mL

■ Preheat oven to 350°F (180°C).

■ Sift flour into bowl; set aside.

■ Mix powdered almonds and sugar together in separate bowl. Add egg yolks and beat with electric hand mixer. As mixture thickens, blend into batter using spatula.

■ Add rum and mix well; incorporate candied fruit.

■ Sift in flour. Fold in half of egg whites using a spatula*, mix to incorporate. Repeat the same process with the remaining egg whites.

■ Grease cake mold with butter and sprinkle with slivered almonds. Pour in batter and cook 35 to 45 minutes. Cool before serving.

It is important to mix the flour in with half of the egg whites; otherwise the batter will become too thick.

1 SERVING

Calories	401	Fat	15 g
Carbohydrate	45 g	Fiber	1.9 g
Protein	9 g	Cholesterol	84 mg

Bananas with Rum over Ice Cream

◆

(4 SERVINGS)

1 tbsp	butter	15 mL
1½ tbsp	granulated sugar	25 mL
4	bananas	4
¼ cup	rum	50 mL
	juice of 2 oranges	
	juice of 1 lemon	
	vanilla ice cream	

■ Heat butter in frying pan over medium heat. Add sugar and mix with small spoon until it caramelizes. Add fruit juices and cook over high heat to dissolve sugar. Mix constantly.

■ Add bananas to pan and cook 2 minutes over high heat.

■ Pour in rum and flambé; cook 1 minute. Serve over ice cream, and berries if desired.

1 SERVING			
Calories	257	Fat	7 g
Carbohydrate	44 g	Fiber	2.0 g
Protein	2 g	Cholesterol	26 mg

298

Oatmeal Drop Cookies

◆

(APPROXIMATELY 2 DOZEN)

⅓ cup	vegetable shortening	75 mL
1 cup	brown sugar	250 mL
1	large egg	1
1¼ cups	all-purpose flour	300 mL
1 tsp	baking powder	5 mL
¼ tsp	salt	1 mL
¼ cup	milk	50 mL
1 cup	rolled oats	250 mL
½ cup	raisins	125 mL
½ cup	chopped walnuts	125 mL

- Preheat oven to 375°F (190°C).

- Cream shortening and brown sugar together in large bowl. Beat in egg until smooth.

- Sift flour, baking powder and salt over batter. Incorporate with wooden spoon or hand mixer.

- Pour in milk and continue mixing. Add rolled oats, raisins and walnuts; mix to distribute evenly.

- Drop small spoonfuls of batter onto ungreased baking sheets. Bake 10 to 12 minutes. When done, cool cookies on wire racks.

1 SERVING

Calories	108	Fat	4 g
Carbohydrate	16 g	Fiber	0.4 g
Protein	2 g	Cholesterol	9 mg

Basic Crêpes

◆

(YIELD: 16 CRÊPES)

1 cup	all-purpose flour	250 mL
½ tsp	salt	2 mL
2 tbsp	granulated sugar	30 mL
3	large eggs	3
1 cup	milk	250 mL
1 cup	water	250 mL
3 tbsp	melted clarified butter, cooled until tepid	45 mL

- Combine flour, salt and sugar in mixing bowl.

- In separate bowl, beat eggs lightly with whisk. Incorporate milk and water, whisking to blend.

- Incorporate dry ingredients to wet, mixing with whisk. Batter should have consistency of heavy cream.

- Pour in clarified butter, whisking constantly.

- Strain batter through sieve into clean bowl. Cover with piece of plastic wrap, ensuring that wrap touches surface of batter. Refrigerate 1 hour, then bring to room temperature.

- Place crêpe pan over medium heat. When hot, use piece of paper towel to wipe pan with butter. Add ladle of crêpe batter and rotate smoothly to spread batter evenly. Let excess batter drip back into bowl.

- Cook crêpe over medium-high heat until underside is golden brown. Turn crêpe over carefully and cook other side. Remove pan from heat and let crêpe slide out onto plate.

- Add more butter to pan, heat and repeat process, stacking crêpes on plate.

1 SERVING			
Calories	71	Fat	3 g
Carbohydrate	8 g	Fiber	0.2 g
Protein	3 g	Cholesterol	47 mg

Crêpes with Chestnut Filling

◆

(4 SERVINGS)

1 cup	canned chestnut purée	250 mL
½ cup	heavy cream (35% MF)	125 mL
1 tsp	vanilla	5 mL
2 tbsp	confectioners' sugar	30 mL
8	crêpes	8
3 tbsp	brown sugar	45 mL
3 tbsp	maple syrup	45 mL

- Place chestnut purée in bowl and mix well; set aside.

- Using electric hand mixer, whip heavy cream and vanilla together in large bowl; mix until firm. Fold in confectioners' sugar.

- Incorporate whipped cream to chestnut purée.

- Fill crêpes with mixture, roll and arrange in baking dish. Sprinkle with brown sugar and maple syrup. Broil 5 to 6 minutes in oven and serve.

1 SERVING			
Calories	418	Fat	18 g
Carbohydrate	56 g	Fiber	5.4 g
Protein	8 g	Cholesterol	135 mg

Fresh Fruit Salad with Hot Sabayon

◆

(4 SERVINGS)

1	grapefruit	1
1	large orange	1
¼ lb	fresh blackberries	110 g
¼ lb	fresh raspberries	110 g
2	figs, cut into 6 pieces	2
2	pears, sliced	2

HOT SABAYON:

¾ cup	granulated sugar	175 mL
4	large egg yolks	4
2	large whole eggs	2
½ cup	dry white wine	125 mL
3 tbsp	liqueur of your choice	45 mL

■ Cut thin slice from top and bottom of grapefruit and orange. Use sharp knife to remove rind and white pith. Hold fruit in one hand and cut between membranes to release sections of fruit. Place in bowl.

■ Add blackberries, raspberries, figs and pears to citrus fruit. Mix well and divide between 4 ovenproof plates.

■ To prepare Sabayon, combine sugar, egg yolks and whole eggs until light and frothy, in a stainless steel bowl.

■ Place bowl over saucepan three quarters filled with simmering water. Cook 3 to 4 minutes, whisking constantly. Pour in wine and whisk vigorously until very thick. Gradually incorporate liqueur.

■ Cover fruit with hot Sabayon and broil 3 to 4 minutes or until lightly browned. Serve immediately.

1 SERVING			
Calories	439	Fat	8 g
Carbohydrate	74 g	Fiber	6.6 g
Protein	7 g	Cholesterol	317 mg

Oatmeal Date Squares

◆

(8 SERVINGS)

½ lb	soft butter	225 g
1½ cups	brown sugar	375 mL
1 cup	rolled oats	250 mL
1½ cups	all-purpose flour	375 mL
1 tsp	baking soda	5 mL
1 lb	pitted dates	450 g
1¾ cups	water	425 mL
	pinch of salt	

■ Preheat oven to 350°F (180°C). Butter 8-in (20-cm) square cake pan.

■ Cream butter and 1 cup (250 mL) of brown sugar together using electric mixer.

■ Combine rolled oats, flour, baking soda and salt together. Incorporate to creamed mixture.

■ Place dates, water and remaining brown sugar in saucepan. Mix and bring to a boil. Reduce heat to low and simmer until thickened, stirring occasionally. Remove from heat and let cool.

■ Press some of rolled oat mixture into bottom of cake pan; bottom layer should be ½-in (1-cm) thick. Cover with layer of date mixture and top with remaining oat mixture. Bake 25 minutes.

■ When cooked, remove date squares from oven. Cool completely in cake pan before cutting into squares.

1 SERVING			
Calories	595	Fat	23 g
Carbohydrate	92 g	Fiber	5.6 g
Protein	5 g	Cholesterol	61 mg

Upside-Down Peach Cake

◆

(6 TO 8 SERVINGS)

CAKE BATTER:

2 tbsp	canned peach juice	30 mL
2 tbsp	granulated sugar	30 mL
2 cups	canned sliced peaches, drained	500 mL
1 tbsp	brown sugar	15 mL
½ cup	soft butter	125 mL
½ cup	granulated sugar	125 mL
3	large eggs	3
1¼ cups	pastry flour	300 mL
	grated rind of 1 orange	
	juice of 1 orange	
	pinch of salt	

■ Preheat oven to 350°F (180°C). Generously butter 9-in (23-cm) springform cake pan.

■ Heat peach juice and 2 tbsp (30 mL) of granulated sugar in small saucepan over medium-high heat. Add sliced peaches and stir to coat thoroughly in syrup.

■ Sprinkle brown sugar over bottom of buttered cake pan. Starting from the center, arrange sliced peaches in circles, covering bottom of pan completely.

■ Cream butter with orange rind using electric mixer. Add ½ cup (125 mL) of granulated sugar. Using electric hand mixer, beat until pale and fluffy.

■ Incorporate eggs one at a time, beating well between additions.

■ Add flour, salt and fresh orange juice. Blend thoroughly.

■ Pour batter over peaches in cake pan. Bake 40 to 50 minutes or until tester inserted into center comes out clean. Let cake cool before removing mold.

■ To remove mold, run small knife around inside edge of cake pan. Invert cake onto serving platter.

GLAZE:

1 tbsp	apricot brandy	15 mL
2 tbsp	granulated sugar	30 mL
2 tbsp	water	30 mL

■ Place all ingredients in small saucepan and bring to a boil over high heat. Cook until mixture thickens, stirring constantly.

■ Brush glaze over peaches.

1 SERVING			
Calories	281	Fat	13 g
Carbohydrate	36 g	Fiber	1.3 g
Protein	4 g	Cholesterol	110 mg

Pears with Chocolate Sauce and Almonds

◆

(4 SERVINGS)

HOT CHOCOLATE SAUCE:

2 oz	semi-sweet chocolate, cut into pieces	60 g
2 tbsp	butter	30 mL
¾ cup	confectioners' sugar	175 mL
4 tbsp	evaporated milk	60 mL
¼ tsp	vanilla	1 mL

- Melt chocolate in double boiler over low heat.

- Add remaining ingredients and mix well. Cook sauce 20 minutes, stirring occasionally.

PEARS:

4	pears	4
1 cup	granulated sugar	250 mL
3 cups	cold water	750 mL
2	whole cloves	2
1 cup	hot chocolate sauce	250 mL
1 tbsp	sliced almonds	15 mL
	juice of 1 lemon	

- While chocolate sauce is cooking, peel pears without removing stems. Place in bowl and sprinkle with lemon juice.

- Place sugar, water and cloves in saucepan. Bring to a boil over high heat. Add pears, cover and poach 20 minutes over medium-low heat. When done, let pears cool in cooking liquid.

- Remove pears from liquid. Trim bases so that pears stand securely in serving platter. Ladle chocolate sauce over pears and decorate with almonds. Serve.

1 SERVING			
Calories	555	Fat	15 g
Carbohydrate	102 g	Fiber	7.7 g
Protein	3 g	Cholesterol	19 mg

Orange Cookies

◆

1 cup	soft butter	250 mL
1½ cups	granulated sugar	375 mL
1	large egg	1
1 tbsp	water	15 mL
1 tbsp	orange extract	15 mL
2½ cups	all-purpose flour	625 mL
½ tsp	salt	2 mL
1 tbsp	baking powder	15 mL
½ cup	shredded coconut	125 mL
	whole almonds	

■ Preheat oven to 350°F (180°C). Butter and flour cookie sheets.

■ Cream butter and sugar using electric mixer. Add egg, water and orange extract; mix well.

■ Sift flour, salt and baking powder together. Add to batter and blend well until dough forms. Mix in coconut.

■ Roll dough into very small balls and place on cookie sheet. Make indentation with thumb and stud with whole almond. Leave enough room for cookies to spread.

■ Bake 12 to 15 minutes in middle of oven.

■ Remove cookies from oven and transfer to wire rack. Cool completely and store in airtight container.

1 SERVING			
Calories	80	Fat	4 g
Carbohydrate	10 g	Fiber	0.3 g
Protein	1 g	Cholesterol	14 mg

Peach Salad with Candied Ginger

◆

(4 SERVINGS)

5	ripe peaches	5
2 tbsp	granulated sugar	30 mL
2 tbsp	chopped candied ginger	30 mL
¼ tsp	nutmeg	1 mL
1 tsp	cornstarch	5 mL
3 tbsp	cold water	45 mL
	juice of 1 orange	
	juice of ½ lemon	
	cottage cheese	
	candied ginger for garnishing	

■ Plunge peaches in saucepan filled with boiling water. Let stand about 30 seconds, just long enough to loosen skins. Remove peaches and peel. Cut in half and remove pit. Slice peaches and set aside.

■ Place sugar, ginger and fruit juices in saucepan. Bring to a boil and cook 2 minutes. Add peaches and nutmeg. Cover and cook 3 minutes over low heat.

■ Dilute cornstarch in cold water. Incorporate to peaches and cook until syrup thickens. Remove pan from heat and let peaches cool.

■ Divide between plates and accompany with cottage cheese and extra candied ginger.

1 SERVING			
Calories	140	Fat	0 g
Carbohydrate	29 g	Fiber	2.1 g
Protein	6 g	Cholesterol	0 mg

Open-Faced Rhubarb Pie

◆

(6 SERVINGS)

1 cup	granulated sugar	250 mL
⅓ cup	all-purpose flour	75 mL
¾ cup	heavy cream (35% MF)	175 mL
4 cups	fresh rhubarb, cut in ½-in (1-cm) pieces	1 L
	pinch of salt	
	pinch of nutmeg	
	9-in (23-cm) pie shell	

- Preheat oven to 450°F (230°C).

- Beat sugar, flour, cream, salt and nutmeg together in large bowl. When mixture is thick and smooth, stir in rhubarb.

- Pour filling into unbaked pie shell. Bake 20 minutes in oven.

- Reduce heat to 350°F (180°C). Continue baking pie until filling has thickened.

- Let cool and serve.

1 SERVING

Calories	360	Fat	20 g
Carbohydrate	42 g	Fiber	1.4 g
Protein	3 g	Cholesterol	37 mg

Lemon Bread Cake

◆

(6 SERVINGS)

1	lemon	1
1½ cups	all-purpose flour, sifted	375 mL
1 tsp	baking powder	5 mL
½ tsp	salt	2 mL
½ cup	soft butter	125 mL
1 cup	granulated sugar	250 mL
2	large eggs	2
½ cup	milk	125 mL

■ Preheat oven to 350°F (180°C). Butter and flour 9 x 5-in (23 x 13-cm) loaf pan.

■ Finely grate lemon rind and set aside. Cut lemon in half and squeeze out juice. Set aside.

■ Mix flour, baking powder and salt together in bowl. Add lemon juice and mix with fork.

■ Cream butter and sugar together using electric mixer. Add flour mixture and blend until incorporated.

■ Add eggs, milk and lemon rind to batter. Beat until well blended.

■ Pour batter into loaf pan and bake 55 to 60 minutes. Cool slightly before removing from mold. Cool completely on wire rack and serve.

1 SERVING

Calories	368	Fat	16 g
Carbohydrate	50 g	Fiber	1.2 g
Protein	6 g	Cholesterol	113 mg

Chocolate Quatre Quart

◆

(6 TO 8 SERVINGS)

8 oz	semi-sweet chocolate, cut into pieces	225 g
½ lb	unsalted butter, at room temperature	225 g
4	medium eggs, at room temperature	4
1¼ cups	granulated sugar	300 mL
1½ cups	all-purpose flour, sifted	375 mL

■ Preheat oven to 350°F (180°C). Butter and lightly flour 8-in (20-cm) square cake pan.

■ Melt chocolate and butter together in double boiler. When completely melted and smooth, set aside and cool slightly.

■ Using electric mixer, beat eggs and sugar together for 4 minutes or until foamy.

■ Stir in melted chocolate and combine. Incorporate flour thoroughly and pour batter into cake pan. Bake 45 minutes or until tester inserted into center comes out clean.

■ Remove cake from oven and let stand 3 to 4 minutes before removing from mold. Cool at least 2 hours on wire rack. Serve plain or dusted with confectioners' sugar.

1 SERVING			
Calories	584	Fat	40 g
Carbohydrate	48 g	Fiber	5.7 g
Protein	8 g	Cholesterol	169 mg

Quick Blueberry Pie

◆

(6 SERVINGS)

2 cups	fresh blueberries	500 mL
2 tbsp	lemon juice	30 mL
1 tbsp	grated lemon rind	15 mL
¼ cup	granulated sugar	50 mL
1 tsp	cornstarch	5 mL
3 tbsp	cold water	45 mL
	graham cracker pie crust, cooked	
	whipped cream	

■ Place blueberries in saucepan. Add lemon juice, rind and sugar. Cover and cook 3 to 4 minutes over medium-low heat.

■ Dilute cornstarch in cold water; stir into blueberries. Cook 2 minutes.

■ Remove pan from heat and let mixture cool. Fill pie crust and serve with whipped cream.

1 SERVING

Calories	178	Fat	6 g
Carbohydrate	30 g	Fiber	1.4 g
Protein	1 g	Cholesterol	0 mg

Little Butter Wafers

◆

(APPROXIMATELY 4 DOZEN)

1 cup	soft butter	250 mL
1½ cups	granulated sugar	375 mL
1	large egg	1
½ tsp	vanilla	2 mL
½ tsp	rum	2 mL
2½ cups	all-purpose flour	625 mL
1 tsp	baking soda	5 mL
1 tsp	cream of tartar	5 mL
¼ tsp	salt	1 mL

■ Preheat oven to 375°F (190°C).

■ Cream butter 2 minutes using electric mixer. Add sugar gradually and beat until fluffy. Incorporate egg, vanilla and rum.

■ Sift dry ingredients together. Add to batter and blend until dough forms.

■ Roll dough onto floured work surface. Cut with cookie cutter and place cookies on ungreased cookie sheet. Leave enough room for cookies to spread.

■ Bake 15 minutes in middle of oven.

■ Remove cookies from oven and transfer to wire rack. Cool completely and store in airtight container.

1 SERVING

Calories	63	Fat	3 g
Carbohydrate	9 g	Fiber	0.1 g
Protein	0 g	Cholesterol	14 mg

Oranges in Caramel

◆

(6 SERVINGS)

1 cup	granulated sugar	250 mL
½ cup	cold water	125 mL
½ cup	tepid water	125 mL
8	seedless navel oranges	8

■ Place sugar and cold water in saucepan. Cook over medium heat until golden brown. Remove from heat and soak bottom of pan in bowl of cold water to stop cooking process. Remove from bowl and immediately pour in ½ cup (125 mL) of tepid water. Return to stove and cook over medium heat 1 minute, or until sugar is dissolved.

■ Using knife, carefully remove rind from oranges and slice into fine julienne. Blanch rind 3 minutes in boiling water and drain well.

■ Cut thin slice from top and bottom of fruit. Use sharp knife to remove any remaining rind and white pith. Cut fruit into slices and reshape into oranges.

■ Arrange on serving platter and drizzle with caramel. Decorate with orange rind and chill. Serve cold.

1 SERVING			
Calories	220	Fat	0 g
Carbohydrate	54 g	Fiber	3.2 g
Protein	1 g	Cholesterol	0 mg

315

Fresh Strawberry Tart with Kirsch

◆

(6 TO 8 SERVINGS)

STRAWBERRY GLAZE:

6 tbsp	granulated sugar	90 mL
¼ lb	fresh strawberries, hulled	110 g
1 tbsp	kirsch	15 mL

■ Place all ingredients in small saucepan. Cook 7 minutes over medium heat.

■ Force mixture through sieve into clean saucepan. Return to stove and cook syrup 2 to 3 minutes over medium heat, or until very thick.

■ Transfer glaze to small bowl and set aside to cool.

STRAWBERRY TART:

1 lb	fresh strawberries, hulled	450 g
2 tbsp	kirsch	30 mL
2 tbsp	granulated sugar	30 mL
1 lb	Flaky Dough (see page 342)	450 g
1¼ cups	Pastry Cream (see page 345)	300 mL
	beaten egg	

■ Preheat oven to 400°F (200°C).

■ Place strawberries, kirsch and sugar in bowl. Mix and marinate 45 minutes at room temperature.

■ Meanwhile, prepare tart dough. Roll out flaky dough ¼-in (5-mm) thick on lightly floured work surface. Use ruler to measure a rectangle of 5 x 15 in (13 x 38 cm). Cut out shape with pastry wheel and transfer rectangle to cookie sheet. Cut out four strips of dough, ½-in (1-cm) wide, for sides and ends of rectangle.

■ Prick dough on cookie sheet with fork and brush with beaten egg. Attach strips flush with edges, using a little beaten egg to secure overlapping corners. Brush strips of dough with beaten egg.

■ Bake tart shell 18 minutes in oven. Let cool completely at room temperature before filling.

■ Spread layer of pastry cream in bottom of tart shell. Drain strawberries and arrange over cream. Brush fruit with glaze and serve.

1 SERVING

Calories	338	Fat	18 g
Carbohydrate	39 g	Fiber	2.4 g
Protein	5 g	Cholesterol	111 mg

Spice Cake

◆

(6 TO 8 SERVINGS)

¾ cup	seedless raisins	175 mL
½ cup	rum	125 mL
1½ cups	sifted all-purpose flour	375 mL
½ tsp	baking soda	2 mL
1 tsp	baking powder	5 mL
½ tsp	ground clove	2 mL
1 tsp	cinnamon	5 mL
½ cup	soft butter	125 mL
1 cup	granulated sugar	250 mL
2	large whole eggs	2
2	large egg yolks	2
½ cup	heavy cream (35% MF)	125 mL
½ cup	chopped candied fruit	125 mL
2 tbsp	honey	30 mL
2	large egg whites, beaten stiff	2

■ Preheat oven to 350°F (180°C). Butter and flour 9-in (23-cm) springform cake pan.

■ Place raisins in bowl and pour in rum. Marinate 30 minutes at room temperature.

■ Sift flour, baking soda, baking powder and spices together; set aside.

■ Cream butter and sugar together using electric mixer. When very creamy, beat in whole eggs and egg yolks. Incorporate heavy cream and mix until smooth.

■ Sift in flour and incorporate thoroughly. Stir in raisins and rum, candied fruit and honey.

■ Fold stiff egg whites into batter.

■ Pour into cake pan and bake 60 to 75 minutes, or until tester inserted into center comes out clean.

■ Let cake cool before removing from mold. Finish cooling on wire rack. When cool, cover cake with cream cheese icing (see page 336) if desired, and serve.

1 SERVING			
Calories	507	Fat	19 g
Carbohydrate	70 g	Fiber	1.5 g
Protein	6 g	Cholesterol	157 mg

Pear and Kiwi Pie

◆

(6 SERVINGS)

3	pears, cored, peeled and sliced thinly	3
3	kiwis, peeled and sliced	3
½ cup	brown sugar	125 mL
1 tbsp	cinnamon	15 mL
½ tsp	nutmeg	2 mL
1	large egg, beaten	1
	Flaky Dough (see page 342)	
	granulated sugar	
	heavy cream (35% MF – optional)	

■ Preheat oven to 400°F (200°C). Butter and flour 9 x 1½-in (23 x 4-cm) deep pie plate. Line with flaky dough and set aside.

■ Place pears and kiwis in bowl. Add brown sugar, cinnamon and nutmeg; mix well.

■ Fill pie crust with fruit mixture and top with crust of flaky dough. Crimp edges shut with cold water. Slash top crust once and brush dough with beaten egg.

■ Bake 20 minutes. Reduce heat to 375°F (190°C) and bake 20 minutes.

■ Remove pie from oven and let cool. Sprinkle with granulated sugar and broil 3 to 4 minutes in oven.

■ Serve with heavy cream if desired.

1 SERVING			
Calories	429	Fat	21 g
Carbohydrate	55 g	Fiber	4.9 g
Protein	5 g	Cholesterol	90 mg

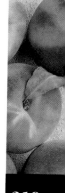

Frozen Almond Soufflé

◆

(6 TO 8 SERVINGS)

5	large egg yolks	5
¾ cup	granulated sugar	175 mL
¾ cup	ground nuts*	175 mL
2 tbsp	rum	30 mL
2 cups	heavy cream (35% MF), whipped	500 mL
5	large egg whites	5
	grated semi-sweet chocolate	
	sliced toasted almonds (optional)	

- Butter 6 individual soufflé dishes or a 9-in (23-cm) springform cake pan. Attach 2-in (5-cm) high foil collar around outside of soufflé dishes or cake pan. Secure tightly with tape and string.

- Beat egg yolks with sugar until light and foamy. Incorporate ground nuts and rum; mix well. Beat in whipped cream.

- Beat egg whites until soft peaks form. Fold whites into batter using spatula.

- Transfer batter to soufflé dishes or cake pan. Freeze until set.

- To serve, sprinkle soufflé with grated chocolate and decorate with almonds, if desired.

* Use almonds, filberts or walnuts.

1 SERVING			
Calories	433	Fat	34 g
Carbohydrate	23 g	Fiber	1.1 g
Protein	7 g	Cholesterol	215 mg

Beat egg yolks with sugar
until light and foamy.

Incorporate ground nuts
and rum; mix well.

Attach 2-in (5-cm) high foil collar
around outside of soufflé dishes
or cake pan. Secure tightly
with tape and string.

Beat in whipped cream.

Beat egg whites until soft peaks
form. Fold whites into batter
using spatula.

Transfer batter to soufflé dishes
or cake pan. Freeze until set.

Banana-Nut Cake

◆

(6 SERVINGS)

½ cup	soft butter	125 mL
1 cup	granulated sugar	250 mL
2	large eggs	2
3	bananas, mashed	3
¼ cup	chopped nuts of your choice	50 mL
½ tsp	baking soda	2 mL
1 tbsp	baking powder	15 mL
2 cups	all-purpose flour	500 mL
3 tbsp	rum	45 mL
¼ cup	buttermilk	50 mL
	pinch of salt	

■ Preheat oven to 350°F (180°C). Butter and flour 9-in (23-cm) springform cake pan.

■ Cream butter and sugar together using electric mixer. Add eggs, one at a time, beating well between additions. Incorporate mashed bananas, then mix in nuts.

■ Sift dry ingredients together. Add half of mixture to batter and incorporate well.

■ Add rum and buttermilk; mix thoroughly. Incorporate remaining dry ingredients, blending well.

■ Transfer batter to cake pan. Bake 1 hour or until tester inserted into center comes out clean. Let cool 5 minutes before removing from mold. Finish cooling on wire rack.

■ Serve with thick custard cream or top with your favorite icing.

1 SERVING			
Calories	546	Fat	19 g
Carbohydrate	82 g	Fiber	2.5 g
Protein	8 g	Cholesterol	112 mg

Thick Custard Cream

◆

(1 ¼ CUPS – 300 ML)

4	large egg yolks	4
½ cup	granulated sugar	125 mL
1 cup	scalded milk, cooled	250 mL
1 tbsp	vanilla	15 mL

▪ Beat egg yolks and sugar together in saucepan until foamy. Whisk in milk and vanilla.

▪ Place saucepan on stove over medium heat. Stir constantly with wooden spoon and cook until cream is thick enough to coat back of spoon. Do not boil.

▪ Transfer cream to stainless steel bowl and cover with piece of plastic wrap, ensuring that wrap touches surface of cream. Refrigerate 24 hours before using.

* Serve with cake, ice cream, iced soufflé, fruits and rice pudding.

1 SERVING

Calories	661	Fat	25 g
Carbohydrate	90 g	Fiber	0 g
Protein	19 g	Cholesterol	879 mg

Bread Pudding

◆

(4 TO 6 SERVINGS)

1 cup	seedless raisins	250 mL
3 tbsp	rum	45 mL
3	large eggs	3
1 tbsp	vanilla	15 mL
1 cup	brown sugar	250 mL
2 cups	milk, heated	500 mL
2½ cups	diced white bread	625 mL
2 tbsp	butter	30 mL
	pinch of salt	

■ Place raisins in bowl and pour in rum. Marinate 2 hours at room temperature.

■ Preheat oven to 350°F (180°C).

■ Place eggs in large bowl. Add vanilla, brown sugar and salt. Beat with electric hand mixer until well incorporated.

■ Stir in hot milk and bread. Add raisins with rum and butter; mix well. Pour batter into buttered 9-in (23-cm) round mold and bake 45 minutes. Serve warm with lightly whipped cream and strawberry coulis if desired.

1 SERVING

Calories	319	Fat	8 g
Carbohydrate	51 g	Fiber	1.9 g
Protein	7 g	Cholesterol	124 mg

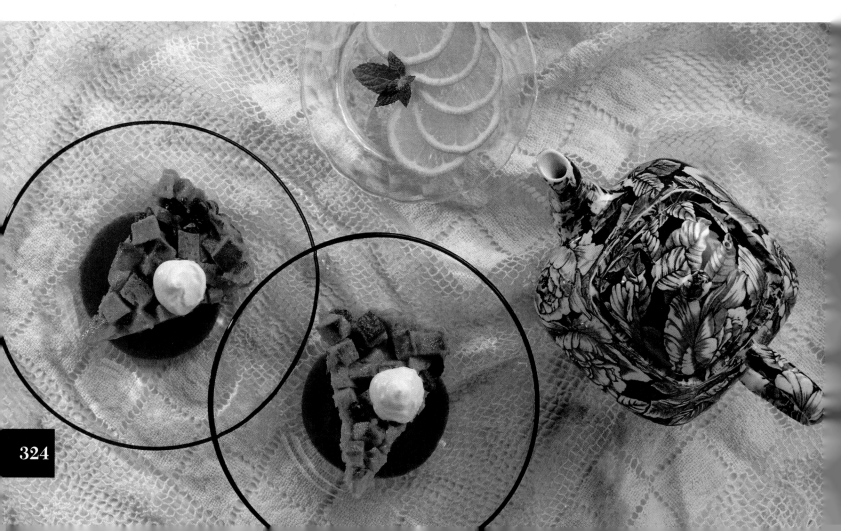

Golden Raisin Boulders

◆

(APPROXIMATELY 3 DOZEN)

1 cup	soft butter	250 mL
1¾ cups	brown sugar	425 mL
3	large eggs	3
2 cups	golden raisins	500 mL
3 cups	all-purpose flour	750 mL
1 cup	chopped pecans	250 mL
2 tsp	baking soda	10 mL
2 tsp	cinnamon	10 mL
	pinch of salt	

■ Preheat oven to 350°F (180°C). Grease and lightly flour baking sheets.

■ Cream butter in large bowl. Add brown sugar and blend well. Add eggs, one at a time, beating well between additions.

■ Dust raisins with small amount of flour. Add raisins and pecans to batter; mix well.

■ Sift remaining flour, baking soda, cinnamon and salt together. Incorporate to egg mixture; batter will become stiff.

■ Drop medium spoonfuls of batter onto baking sheets. Bake 15 minutes or until golden brown.

■ When done, cool cookies on wire rack.

1 SERVING

Calories	155	Fat	7 g
Carbohydrate	21 g	Fiber	1.1 g
Protein	2 g	Cholesterol	31 mg

Almond Cake with Cognac

◆

(6 SERVINGS)

½ cup	soft butter	125 mL
1 cup	granulated sugar	250 mL
3	large eggs	3
1¼ cups	all-purpose flour	300 mL
¼ tsp	salt	1 mL
½ tsp	baking powder	2 mL
¼ cup	ground almonds	50 mL
1 tsp	almond extract	5 mL
2 tbsp	cognac	30 mL

- Preheat oven to 350°F (180°C). Butter and flour 8 x 2¾-in (20 x 7-cm) deep square cake pan.

- Cream butter, sugar and 1 egg using electric mixer. Increase speed and beat 2 minutes.

- Sift flour, salt and baking powder together. Add half to creamed mixture and mix well.

- Add remaining eggs; beat 1 minute. Add remaining sifted ingredients; beat 1 minute.

- Incorporate ground almonds, almond extract and cognac and beat 1 minute. Pour batter into cake pan and bake 40 minutes or until tester inserted into center comes out clean.

- Let cool 5 minutes before removing from pan. Finish cooling on wire rack.

- Sprinkle with confectioners' sugar and decorate with sliced toasted almonds, or top with your favorite icing.

1 SERVING			
Calories	425	Fat	19 g
Carbohydrate	55 g	Fiber	1.1 g
Protein	6 g	Cholesterol	147 mg

Cream butter, sugar and 1 egg using electric mixer. Increase speed and beat 2 minutes.

Sift flour, salt and baking powder together. Add half to creamed mixture and mix well.

Add remaining eggs; beat 1 minute.

Add remaining sifted ingredients; beat 1 minute.

Incorporate ground almonds, almond extract and cognac and beat 1 minute.

Pour batter into cake pan and bake 40 minutes or until tester inserted into center comes out clean.

Creamy Cheesecake

(8 SERVINGS)

CRUST:

1½ cups	crushed Graham crackers	375 mL
3 tbsp	granulated sugar	45 mL
3 tbsp	butter	45 mL

■ Preheat oven to 350°F (180°C). Mix crushed Graham crackers, sugar and batter together. Coat bottom and sides of 9-in (23-cm) cake mold with mixture. Cook 10 minutes in oven and set aside.

FILLING:

1 lb	cream cheese, softened	450 g
2 tsp	vanilla	10 mL
½ cup	granulated sugar	125 mL
3 tbsp	all-purpose flour	45 mL
4	egg yolks	4
1 cup	heavy cream (35% MF)	250 mL
4	egg whites	4
	pinch of salt	

■ Preheat oven to 325°F (160°C). Combine cheese and vanilla. Add sugar, flour and salt; mix well.

■ Incorporate egg yolks; mix until creamy. Whip cream and incorporate to mixture. Beat egg whites until stiff and incorporate to cheese mixture using spatula.

■ Pour batter into coated cake mold. Cook 1 hour in oven. Remove from oven and let stand 2 hours at room temperature. Serve with raspberry coulis, if desired.

1 SERVING			
Calories	548	Fat	40 g
Carbohydrate	37 g	Fiber	1.3 g
Protein	10 g	Cholesterol	224 mg

Brownie Date Loaf

◆

(6 SERVINGS)

¾ cup	all-purpose flour	175 mL
½ tsp	baking soda	2 mL
¼ tsp	salt	1 mL
1 cup	pitted dates, chopped	250 mL
½ cup	brown sugar	125 mL
¼ cup	soft butter	50 mL
¼ cup	water	50 mL
½ cup	semi-sweet chocolate chips	125 mL
2	large eggs, beaten	2
3 tbsp	brandy	45 mL
¼ cup	buttermilk	50 mL
½ cup	chopped nuts	125 mL

■ Preheat oven to 350°F (180°C). Butter and flour 9 x 5-in (23 x 13-cm) loaf pan.

■ Sift flour, baking soda and salt into small bowl; set aside.

■ Place dates, brown sugar, butter and water in saucepan. Cook over medium-low heat until dates are softened, stirring frequently.

■ Transfer date mixture to electric mixer. Stir in chocolate chips and beaten eggs, and mix 1 minute.

■ Add half of sifted ingredients; mix well. Add brandy and buttermilk; mix until blended thoroughly. Incorporate remaining sifted ingredients and fold in nuts.

■ Pour batter into loaf pan and bake 45 minutes or until tester inserted into center comes out clean.

■ When done, remove from oven and let cool slightly before removing from mold. Finish cooling on wire rack.

■ Serve plain or dusted with confectioners' sugar.

1 SERVING			
Calories	413	Fat	18 g
Carbohydrate	53 g	Fiber	3.1 g
Protein	6 g	Cholesterol	88 mg

Caramel Custard

◆

(4 to 6 servings)

⅔ cup	granulated sugar	150 mL
3 tbsp	water	45 mL
2 cups	milk	500 mL
1 tsp	vanilla	5 mL
1 tbsp	water	15 mL
2	large whole eggs, at room temperature	2
3	large egg yolks	3
½ cup	granulated sugar	125 mL

- Preheat oven to 350°F (180°C).

- Place ⅔ cup (150 mL) of sugar and 3 tbsp (45 mL) of water in small saucepan.

- Cook over low heat to dissolve sugar. Increase heat to medium-high and continue cooking until syrup turns golden brown. Do not stir during process. Monitor closely as changes in color occur quickly. Divide syrup between ramekins and set aside.

- Bring milk, vanilla and 1 tbsp (15 mL) of water to a boil in separate saucepan.

- Place eggs and egg yolks in large bowl and beat lightly with whisk. Add remaining sugar and beat until well blended.

- Gradually incorporate heated milk mixture to beaten eggs, whisking constantly. Strain batter through sieve and pour into ramekins.

- Place ramekins in water bath and bake 40 to 45 minutes.

- When cooked, remove from water bath and let cool on counter. Refrigerate until firm.

- To remove from molds, run blade of small knife around inside edge of ramekins. Invert custard onto dessert plate and serve.

1 SERVING

Calories	193	Fat	5 g
Carbohydrate	31 g	Fiber	0 g
Protein	6 g	Cholesterol	183 mg

Viennese Crêpes

◆

(YIELD: 16 CRÊPES)

1 cup	all-purpose flour	250 mL
2 tbsp	granulated sugar	30 mL
4	large eggs	4
2 cups	milk	500 mL
3 tbsp	melted clarified butter, cooled until tepid	45 mL
	pinch of salt	
	unsalted butter	

- Combine flour, sugar and salt in mixing bowl.

- In separate bowl, beat eggs lightly with whisk. Incorporate milk; blend well.

- Incorporate dry ingredients to wet, mixing with whisk. Batter should have consistency of heavy cream.

- Pour in clarified butter, whisking constantly.

- Strain batter through sieve into clean bowl. Cover with piece of plastic wrap, ensuring that wrap touches surface. Refrigerate 1 hour. Bring to room temperature before using.

- Place crêpe pan over medium heat. When hot, use piece of paper towel to wipe pan with butter. Pour out any excess.

- Add ladle of crêpe batter and, holding pan above stove, rotate smoothly to spread batter evenly. Turn pan on a 90 degree angle and let excess batter drip back into bowl.

- Return pan to stove and cook crêpe over medium-high heat until underside is golden brown. Using long, metal spatula, turn crêpe over carefully and cook other side.

- Remove pan from heat and let crêpe slide out onto large dinner plate.

- Add more butter to pan, heat and repeat process. Stack crêpes on plate as they are cooked.

1 SERVING

Calories	84	Fat	4 g
Carbohydrate	9 g	Fiber	0.2 g
Protein	3 g	Cholesterol	62 mg

Viennese Crêpe Cake

◆

(4 SERVINGS)

1 cup	heavy cream (35% MF)	250 mL
½ lb	semi-sweet chocolate, in pieces	225 g
2 tbsp	boiling water	30 mL
2 tbsp	Tia Maria liqueur, heated	30 mL
12	Viennese crêpes	12

- Whip cream until firm and spoon ⅓ into pastry bag fitted with star tip. Leave remaining whipped cream in bowl and chill until ready to use.

- Melt chocolate in double boiler over low heat.

- Mix water with liqueur; incorporate to melted chocolate.

- Place one crêpe flat on serving platter. Pour small amount of chocolate sauce over crêpe and top with reserved whipped cream. Repeat layers until all ingredients are used.

- Decorate with whipped cream from pastry bag and any remaining chocolate sauce. Cut into wedges and serve.

1 SERVING

Calories	598	Fat	52 g
Carbohydrate	22 g	Fiber	10 g
Protein	7 g	Cholesterol	92 mg

Pears in Sabayon

◆

(4 SERVINGS)

2 cups	water	500 mL
¾ cup	granulated sugar	175 mL
4	pears, peeled	4
3	large egg yolks	3
1	large egg white	1
3 tbsp	granulated sugar	45 mL
½ cup	dry white wine	125 mL
	juice of ¼ lemon	

■ Place water and ¾ cup (175 mL) of sugar in large saucepan. Bring to a boil. Add lemon juice and cook 3 minutes.

■ Reduce heat to medium-low and add whole pears. Cover and cook 15 to 16 minutes. Rotate pears several times during cooking.

■ As soon as pears are cooked, remove pan from heat and let cool on counter.

■ Meanwhile, prepare sabayon. Place egg yolks and egg white in large stainless steel bowl. Add remaining granulated sugar and wine.

■ Set bowl over saucepan containing 3 cups (750 mL) of simmering water. Cook over very low heat, whisking until mixture thickens. If water is too hot, eggs will cook.

■ Top pears with generous ladle of warm sabayon and serve.

1 SERVING			
Calories	329	Fat	4 g
Carbohydrate	68 g	Fiber	5.1 g
Protein	3 g	Cholesterol	157 mg

Chocolate Tart

♦

(6 SERVINGS)

5	large eggs, separated	5
1 cup	granulated sugar	250 mL
4 oz	semi-sweet chocolate, grated finely	115 g
½ cup	unsalted butter, softened	125 mL
1 cup	pastry flour	250 mL

■ Preheat oven to 325°F (160°C). Butter and flour 8 in (20 cm) springform cake pan.

■ Place egg yolks and sugar in stainless steel bowl. Beat 2 to 3 minutes or until ingredients become light and creamy.

■ Mix in grated chocolate. Stir in soft butter and beat 1 to 2 minutes until thoroughly incorporated.

■ Gradually incorporate flour to batter, mixing thoroughly with spatula.

■ Beat egg whites until stiff. Fold into chocolate mixture. Transfer batter to cake pan and bake 45 to 50 minutes or until tester inserted into center comes out clean.

■ Let tart cool before removing from pan. Serve plain, dusted with icing sugar or with whipped cream.

1 SERVING

Calories	512	Fat	28 g
Carbohydrate	56 g	Fiber	4.0 g
Protein	9 g	Cholesterol	212 mg

Harvest Carrot Cake

◆

(6 SERVINGS)

CAKE:

1 cup	granulated sugar	250 mL
½ cup	vegetable oil	125 mL
1 cup	all-purpose flour, sifted	250 mL
1 tsp	baking powder	5 mL
1 tsp	cinnamon	5 mL
1 tsp	baking soda	5 mL
½ tsp	salt	2 mL
2	large eggs	2
1½ cups	grated carrots	375 mL
¼ cup	chopped nuts of your choice	50 mL
¼ cup	golden seedless raisins	50 mL

- Preheat oven to 325°F (160°C). Butter and flour 8½-in (22-cm) springform cake pan.

- Place sugar and oil in electric mixer; blend well.

- Combine dry ingredients together. Add half to electric mixer; blend well.

- Incorporate eggs, one at a time, mixing well between additions.

- Blend in remaining dry ingredients. Incorporate carrots, nuts and raisins.

- Pour batter into cake pan and bake 1¼ hours or until tester inserted into center comes out clean.

- Let cool slightly before removing from mold. Finish cooling on wire rack and prepare icing.

CREAM CHEESE ICING:

½ lb	cream cheese, softened	225 g
2 tbsp	orange juice	30 mL
½ tsp	vanilla	2 mL
2 cups	icing sugar	500 mL

- Beat cream cheese with orange juice and vanilla. Gradually add icing sugar, mixing constantly until well-blended.

- Spread over carrot cake and serve.

1 SERVING			
Calories	758	Fat	38 g
Carbohydrate	96 g	Fiber	1.9 g
Protein	8 g	Cholesterol	113 mg

Pineapple Loaf Cake

◆

(6 SERVINGS)

1	lemon	1
1½ cups	all-purpose flour, sifted	375 mL
1 tsp	baking powder	5 mL
½ tsp	salt	2 mL
½ cup	soft butter	125 mL
1 cup	granulated sugar	250 mL
2	large eggs	2
½ cup	milk	125 mL
1 tbsp	kirsch	15 mL
¾ cup	canned crushed pineapple, well-drained	175 mL

■ Preheat oven to 350°F (180°C). Butter and flour 9 x 5-in (23 x 13-cm) loaf pan.

■ Finely grate lemon rind and squeeze out juice; set aside.

■ Mix flour, baking powder and salt together; set aside.

■ In electric mixer, cream butter with sugar. Add lemon rind and juice; mix well. Incorporate flour.

■ Add eggs, milk and kirsch to batter. Beat until well blended. Stir in crushed pineapple. Pour batter into loaf pan and bake 55 to 60 minutes or until tester inserted into center comes out clean.

■ Cool slightly before removing from pan. Finish cooling on wire rack.

1 SERVING			
Calories	429	Fat	16 g
Carbohydrate	64 g	Fiber	1.1 g
Protein	6 g	Cholesterol	113 mg

Apple Tartlets

◆

(4 SERVINGS)

APPLE FILLING:

4	cooking apples, unpeeled, cored and quartered	4
1 tbsp	cinnamon	15 mL
¼ cup	brown sugar	50 mL
	pinch of ground clove	

SWEET DOUGH:

2 cups	all-purpose flour	500 mL
3 tbsp	granulated sugar	45 mL
¾ cup	fat (half butter, half shortening), cut in pieces	175 mL
2	large eggs	2
	pinch of salt	
	beaten egg	

■ Place all apple filling ingredients in saucepan. Cover and cook 30 minutes over medium-low heat. Transfer mixture to food processor and purée. Set aside.

■ To make dough, place flour in bowl and make a well in center. Add sugar, fat and salt. Add eggs and incorporate thoroughly with pastry blender. Add just enough cold water to shape dough into ball. Wrap in clean cloth and refrigerate 2 hours. Then bring to room temperature.

■ Preheat oven to 400°F (200°C). Roll dough out on lightly floured work surface and line tartlet molds. Brush with beaten egg and bake 15 minutes. Remove and let cool.

■ Fill tartlets with reserved apple filling. Decorate with sliced caramelized apples if desired.

1 SERVING			
Calories	744	Fat	40 g
Carbohydrate	85 g	Fiber	4.6 g
Protein	11 g	Cholesterol	215 mg

Chocolate Marble Cake

◆

(16 SERVINGS)

2½ cups	granulated sugar	625 mL
2 cups	soft butter	500 mL
10	large eggs	10
1 tbsp	vanilla	15 mL
4 cups	all-purpose flour	1 L
5½ oz	bittersweet chocolate, melted	150 g

■ Preheat oven to 300°F (150°C). Butter 12-cup (3-L) bundt cake pan.

■ Place sugar and butter in electric mixer; beat until well creamed.

■ Incorporate eggs, one at a time, mixing well between additions.

■ Stir in vanilla. Incorporate flour, 1 cup (250 mL) at a time, mixing well between additions.

■ Pour half of batter into bundt pan. Drizzle melted chocolate over batter and use tip of knife blade to swirl chocolate. Pour in remaining cake batter carefully.

■ Bake 1½ hours or until tester inserted into center comes out clean. Let cool 10 to 12 minutes before removing from pan. Finish cooling on wire rack.

1 SERVING

Calories	498	Fat	30 g
Carbohydrate	50 g	Fiber	2.4 g
Protein	7 g	Cholesterol	194 mg

Flaky Dough

◆

1 lb	unsalted butter	450 g
1¼ lb	all-purpose flour	560 g
1 tsp	salt	5 mL
1 cup	water	250 mL

■ Place butter on lightly floured work surface. Flatten slightly with rolling pin. Set aside at room temperature.

■ Mound flour on work surface or in a bowl and make a well in center. Add salt and some of water to well. Use pastry cutter to combine mixture, scraping flour toward center. Add more water as needed to incorporate ingredients. Shape dough into ball and score a deep cross on top of dough with knife.

■ Roll out dough, making a large four-leafed clover shape. Be careful not to roll too thin.

■ Place block of butter in middle of dough. Wrap both ends and sides of dough over butter to cover completely*. Roll out dough into thick rectangle. Start rolling from the center towards the edges. Do not press too hard. Wrap dough in clean cloth and refrigerate 30 minutes.

■ Place dough on lightly floured work surface. Carefully roll out into long rectangle, about ½-in (1-cm) thick. Fold dough into thirds and mark dough with two fingertips. This indicates the completion of the second turn. Wrap dough and chill 30 minutes.

■ Complete 4 more turns following technique above. Always position dough on work surface with short side facing you. Do not overwork dough and dust away any excess flour before chilling. Mark each turn to keep track of the correct number.

■ Store dough in plastic wrap in refrigerator. Slice dough crosswise as needed. Bring piece of dough to room temperature before rolling.

The butter and dough should be of the same consistency. If the butter is too hard or too soft, incorporation will be difficult.

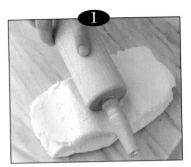

Place butter on lightly floured
work surface. Flatten slightly
with rolling pin.

Score a deep cross on top of
dough with knife.

Roll out dough into thick rectangle.
Start rolling from the center
towards the edges.

Mound flour on work surface or in
a bowl and make a well in center.
Add salt and some of water to well.

Shape dough into ball.

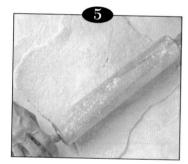

Roll out dough, making a large
four-leafed clover shape.
Be careful not to roll too thin.

Place block of butter in middle
of dough. Wrap both ends
and sides of dough over butter
to cover completely.

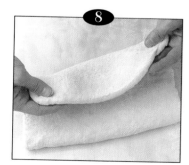

Fold dough into thirds.

Mark dough with two fingertips.

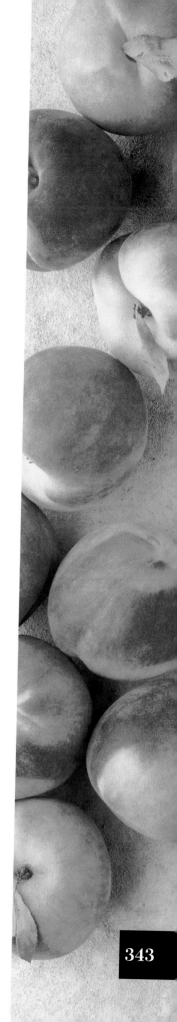

Chocolate Icing

◆

(2 CUPS – 500 ML)

8 tbsp	soft butter	120 mL
8 tbsp	cocoa	120 mL
3 cups	icing sugar	750 mL
1 tbsp	vanilla	15 mL
1 tbsp	Cointreau liqueur	15 mL
¼ cup	heavy cream (35% MF)	50 mL

■ Place butter in bowl and beat until completely softened.

■ Add cocoa and icing sugar; mix together until a batter forms.

■ Add vanilla and Cointreau; combine using a wooden spoon.

■ Whisk in cream until icing becomes smooth and creamy.

Orange Icing

◆

(¾ CUP – 175 ML)

1 cup	granulated sugar	250 mL
2 tbsp	cornstarch	30 mL
½ cup	orange juice	125 mL
	zest of 1 lemon or orange	
	pinch of salt	

■ Combine sugar and cornstarch in saucepan. Add orange juice, lemon or orange zest and salt. Mix well and cook 3 to 4 minutes over medium heat to thicken. Let cool on cake.

Pastry Cream

◆

(2½ CUPS – 625 ML)

1 cup	milk	250 mL
1 tbsp	water	15 mL
¼ cup	granulated sugar	50 mL
3	egg yolks	3
¼ cup	all-purpose flour, sifted	50 mL
1 tsp	vanilla	5 mL

- Heat milk and water in saucepan over medium heat; bring to a boil. Set aside.

- Place sugar and egg yolks in bowl. Beat with spatula 3 to 4 minutes or until mixture becomes white and fluffy. Incorporate flour using a spatula.

- Gradually incorporate vanilla to milk. Incorporate half of egg mixture, stirring constantly with a wooden spoon.

- Return saucepan to stove; cook over medium heat. Gradually incorporate last half of egg mixture, stirring constantly with a wooden spoon.

- Stir until cream becomes very thick. Pour into bowl, let cool and cover with sheet of buttered wax paper.

* Pastry cream will keep 48 hours in the refrigerator.

Index

A

APPETIZERS

Celeriac Rémoulade with Shrimp   56
Charred Garlic Peppers   37
Cold Julienne of Vegetables with Apples   35
Fresh Artichokes   39
Leeks Vinaigrette   49
Marinated Mushrooms   36
Shrimp and Artichoke Bottoms   52
Shrimp Cocktail   85
Tuna Spinach Paté   112

B

BEEF

Basic Beef Stock   9
Beef Bourguignon   188
Beef Stroganoff   174
Beef Tournedos with Poivre Vert Sauce   195
Braised Beef with Root Vegetables   170
Broiled Beef Tenderloin Shish Kebabs   190
Carbonnade of Beef   218
Easy Beef and Vegetable Stew   194
Hearty Sliced Beef and Rice Salad   48
Hungarian Goulash   199
Mushroom and Herb Stuffed Beef Flank   186
New York Strip Steaks with Mushroom Sauce   176
Old-Fashioned Beef Soup   27
Pot-au-Feu   208
Quick Beef Stir-Fry   207
Rib Roast – English Style   202
Rump Roast with Red Onion and Carrot   178
Short Ribs Braised in Red Wine   221

C

CAKES

Almond Cake with Cognac   326
Balthazar Cake   297
Banana-Nut Cake   322
Brownie Date Loaf   329
Chocolate Marble Cake   341
Chocolate Quatre Quart   312
Creamy Cheesecake   328
Harvest Carrot Cake   336
Lemon Bread Cake   310
Pineapple Loaf Cake   338
Spice Cake   318
Upside-Down Peach Cake   304

CHICKEN

Basic Chicken Stock   8
Brandy Braised Whole Chicken   147
Cashew Chicken with Grilled Peppers   140
Chicken and Vegetable Pot Pie   159
Chicken Chow-Mein   142
Chicken Cutlets   125
Chicken Dijonnaise   155
Chicken Fricassee   124
Chicken Gumbo and Rice   16
Chicken – Hunter Style   128
Chicken in White Wine with Ginger Root   132
Chicken Legs Paprika   134
Chicken Livers on Skewers   160
Chicken Livers with Bell Peppers   127
Chicken Livers with Mushrooms   153
Chicken Shish Kebabs   139
Chicken Wings with Curry   138
Chicken with Caramelized Apples   150
Chicken with Porcini Mushrooms   122
Chicken with Prunes   144
Chicken with Tomatoes and Olives   137
Hot Curry Chicken with Coconut   149
Key-Side Chicken   157
Marinade for Poultry   166
Pan-Fried Chicken with Peanut Sauce   148
Quick Soy Chicken and Cabbage   167
Rolled Chicken Schnitzel with Prosciutto   161
Sauté of Chicken with Eggplant   154
Sweet and Tangy Chicken Wings   126
Zesty Marinated Chicken   164

COOKIES AND SQUARES

Golden Raisin Boulders   325
Little Butter Wafers   314
Oatmeal Date Squares   303
Oatmeal Drop Cookies   299
Orange Cookies   307

CRÊPES

Basic Crêpes   300
Crêpes for Seafood   82
Crêpes with Chestnut Filling   300
Shrimp and White Sauce Crêpes   83
Viennese Crêpe Cake   332
Viennese Crêpes   332

D

DESSERTS

Almond Cake with Cognac   326
Apple Tartlets   339
Balthazar Cake   297
Banana-Nut Cake   322
Bananas with Rum over Ice Cream   298
Basic Crêpes   300
Bread Pudding   324
Brownie Date Loaf   329
Caramel Custard   331
Chocolate Marble Cake   341

Chocolate Quatre Quart   312
Chocolate Tart   335
Creamy Cheesecake   328
Crêpes with Chestnut Filling   300
Flaky Dough   342
Fresh Fruit Salad with Hot
    Sabayon   302
Fresh Strawberry Tart with Kirsch   317
Frozen Almond Soufflé   320
Golden Raisin Boulders   325
Harvest Carrot Cake   336
Lemon Bread Cake   310
Little Butter Wafers   314
Oatmeal Date Squares   303
Oatmeal Drop Cookies   299
Open-Faced Rhubarb Pie   309
Orange Cookies   307
Oranges in Caramel   315
Peach Salad with Candied Ginger   308
Pear and Kiwi Pie   319
Pears in Sabayon   334
Pears with Chocolate Sauce and
    Almonds   306
Peach Salad with Candied Ginger   308
Pineapple Loaf Cake   338
Quick Blueberry Pie   313
Spice Cake   318
Upside-Down Peach Cake   304
Viennese Crêpe Cake   332
Viennese Crêpes   332

DESSERT TOPPINGS

Chocolate Icing   344
Cream Cheese Icing   336
Flaky Dough   342
Hot Chocolate Sauce   306
Hot Sabayon   302
Orange Icing   344
Pastry Cream   345
Strawberry Glaze   317
Thick Custard Cream   323

DUCK

Duck in Red Wine   162
Orange Duck with Cranberries   131

F

FISH AND SEAFOOD

Baked Swordfish with Almonds   86
Celeriac Rémoulade with Shrimp   56
Cod with Mashed Potatoes and Swiss
    Cheese   91
Cold Lobster and Shrimp   110
Cold Shrimp with Curry Dressing and
    Fruit   100
Crab Patties   110
Crêpes for Seafood   82
Deep-Fried Smelts   76
Ginger Fried Shrimp   81
Grilled Whole Mackerel with Herb
    Butter Sauce   70
Halibut and Potato Casserole   119
Halibut Steaks with Bell Peppers
    and Red Onion   77
Hearty Cod Stew   113
Fish Stock   10
Fresh Clam Chowder   25
Fresh Cod with Tomato Curry   116
Fresh Fillet of Sole with
    Mushrooms   84
Fresh Mussels in Salad   59
Fresh Sea Scallops au Gratin   102
Lobster Newburg   88
Marinated Scallops and Vegetable
    Brochettes   87
Oysters au Gratin on the Half
    Shell   101
Pickerel with Fresh Herbs   116
Red Snapper Cooked in Foil   73
Salmon Steaks Poached in White
    Wine   94
Sautéed Pickerel Fillets with Anchovy
    Butter   80
Scallop and Mushroom Soup   24
Scampi au Gratin   92
Scampi with Julienne of Vegetables   96
Seafood and Rice   98
Seafood in Pastry   93
Seafood Salad with Roasted Bell
    Peppers   51
Shrimp and Artichoke Bottoms   52
Shrimp and White Sauce Crêpes   83
Shrimp Cocktail   85
Steamed Mussels with Cream Sauce   74

Steamed Mussels with Curry   79
Stuffed Egg Roll Skins   109
Stuffed Fresh Clams   90
Tomato Halibut Steaks   105
Tossed Vegetables with Sea
    Scallops   103
Tropical Scampi   75
Trout with Capers   94
Tuna Spinach Pâté   112
Turbot au Gratin   106
Turbot with Sun-Dried
    Tomatoes   114
Whole Snapper with Spring
    Vegetables   97
Whole Trout with Green
    Grapes   107

FRUIT

Apple Tartlets   339
Banana-Nut Cake   322
Bananas with Rum over Ice
    Cream   298
Brownie Date Loaf   329
Fresh Fruit Salad with Hot
    Sabayon   302
Fresh Strawberry Tart with
    Kirsch   317
Golden Raisin Boulders   325
Lemon Bread Cake   310
Marinated Apple Slaw   44
Oatmeal Date Squares   303
Open-Faced Rhubarb Pie   309
Orange Cookies   307
Orange Duck with Cranberries   131
Orange Icing   344
Oranges in Caramel   315
Peach Salad with Candied
    Ginger   308
Pear and Kiwi Pie   319
Pears in Sabayon   334
Pears with Chocolate Sauce and
    Almonds   306
Pineapple Loaf Cake   338
Pineapple Pork Tenderloin   183
Quick Blueberry Pie   313
Seasonal Fruit Salad   60
Strawberry Glaze   317
Upside-Down Peach Cake   304

L

LAMB

Lamb Chops with Fresh Tomatoes 173
Lamb Chops with Watercress 214
Lamb Shish Kebabs 211
Lamb Stew 181
Leg of Lamb with Potatoes 173
Stuffed Leg of Lamb 204

P

PASTA

Fettuccine à la Rouille 232
Linguine with Quick Fresh Tomato Sauce 243
Macaroni with Black Olives 239
Pasta Verdura 240
Roast Turkey Pasta Salad 55
Spaghettini with Zesty Anchovy Sauce 247
Spaghetti with Garlic-Basil Purée 241

PIES

Apple Tartlets 339
Chicken and Vegetable Pot Pie 160
Chocolate Tart 335
Fresh Strawberry Tart with Kirsch 317
Open-Faced Rhubarb Pie 309
Pear and Kiwi Pie 319
Quick Blueberry Pie 313
Turkey Pot Pie Suprême 152

PORK

Barbecued Pork Cutlets and Tomatoes 200
Barbecued Spareribs 185
Deep-Fried Pork Tenderloin 207
Pineapple Pork Tenderloin 183
Pork Chops with Honey and Apples 210
Pork Shoulder Stew 175

Pork Tenderloin with Bordelaise Sauce 215
Pork with Roasted Bell Peppers 184
Roast Loin of Pork with Garlic and Onions 213

POTATOES

Baked Potatoes Stuffed with Mushrooms 244
Garlic Potatoes with Rosemary 242
German-Style Potato Salad 44
Halibut and Potato Casserole 119
Pan-Fried Potato Cakes 230
Potage à la Crécy 13
Potatoes Anna 236
Potatoes in Cream au Gratin 228
Potatoes Lyonnaise 234
Potatoes Sautéed with Leeks 227
Potato Galette 235
Soup Savoyarde 15
Vichyssoise 23

POULTRY see also CHICKEN

Braised Rock Cornish Game Hens 143
Duck in Red Wine 162
Marinade for Poultry 166
Orange Duck with Cranberries 131
Roast Turkey Pasta Salad 55
Turkey Pot Pie Suprême 152
Turkey Vol-au-Vent Suprême 133

R

RICE

Basic Wild Rice 246
Chicken Gumbo and Rice 16
Hearty Sliced Beef and Rice Salad 48
Mushroom Rice Pilaf 249
Rice with Fresh Herbs 231
Risotto 226
Saffron Rice 237
Seafood and Rice 98

S

SALADS

Belgian Endive Salad 34
Caesar Asparagus 59
Celeriac Rémoulade with Shrimp 56
Charred Garlic Peppers 37
Cold Julienne of Vegetables with Apples 35
Curried Vegetable Salad 53
Fresh Artichokes 39
Fresh Beet Salad with Red Onion 56
Fresh Fruit Salad with Hot Sabayon 302
Fresh Mussels in Salad 59
German-Style Potato Salad 44
Hearty Sliced Beef and Rice Salad 48
Leeks Vinaigrette 49
Marinated Apple Slaw 44
Marinated Mushrooms 36
Mixed Greens with Avocado Dressing 43
Mixed Vegetable Salad 63
Peach Salad with Candied Ginger 308
Roast Turkey Pasta Salad 55
Roquefort Salad 63
Salade Drolet 47
Salade Niçoise 41
Seafood Salad with Roasted Bell Peppers 51
Seasonal Fruit Salad 60
Shrimp and Artichoke Bottoms 52
Tomato Bacon Salad 42
Warm Navy Bean Salad 289
Watercress and Radicchio Salad 46

SAUCES AND DRESSINGS

Anchovy Butter 80
Cheese Sauce 265
Curry Sauce 293
Garlic Butter 92
Herb Butter Sauce 70
Hollandaise Sauce 286
Homemade Herb Mayonnaise 66
Marinade for Poultry 166
Paprika Sauce 266
Suprême Sauce 166

SHRIMP

Celeriac Rémoulade with Shrimp   56
Cold Lobster and Shrimp   110
Cold Shrimp with Curry Dressing and Fruit   100
Ginger Fried Shrimp   81
Shrimp and Artichoke Bottoms   52
Shrimp and White Sauce Crêpes   83
Shrimp Cocktail   85

SOUPS

Basic Beef Stock   9
Basic Chicken Stock   8
Cabbage Soup   12
Chicken Gumbo and Rice   16
Cold Lettuce Soup   26
Cream of Fresh Asparagus   29
Fish Stock   10
Fresh Clam Chowder   25
Garden Bounty Soup   22
Gazpacho   31
Minestrone Soup   21
Napa Broth Soup   14
Old-Fashioned Beef Soup   27
Potage à la Crécy   13
Purée of Brussels Sprouts   18
Scallop and Mushroom Soup   24
Soup Savoyarde   15
Vegetable and Lentil Soup   19
Vichyssoise   23

T

TOMATOES

Barbecued Pork Cutlets and Tomatoes   200
Chicken with Tomatoes and Olives   137
Garlic Fried Tomatoes   259
Gazpacho   31
Grilled Tomato Halves   272
Flageolets in White Wine and Tomatoes   281
Fresh Cod with Tomato Curry   116
Lamb Chops with Fresh Tomatoes   173
Linguine with Quick Fresh Tomato Sauce   243

Tomato Bacon Salad   42
Tomato Halibut Steaks   105
Turbot with Sun-Dried Tomatoes   114
Veal Chops with Tomatoes and Onions   222
Vegetables with Sun-Dried Tomatoes   270

TURKEY

Roast Turkey Pasta Salad   55
Turkey Pot Pie Suprême   152
Turkey Vol-au-Vent Suprême   133

V

VEAL

Calf's Liver with Dijon   198
Country Veal Chops   201
Medallions of Veal Loin in Wine Sauce   182
Osso Buco   192
Veal Blanquette   217
Veal Chops with Fresh Tarragon   191
Veal Chops with Tomatoes and Onions   222
Veal Scaloppine Island Sauté   219
Veal Scaloppine with Fresh Lemon   177
Veal Scaloppine with Mixed Vegetables   197

VEGETABLES
see also POTATOES and TOMATOES

Artichokes with Hollandaise Sauce   286
Asparagus with Cheese Sauce   265
Baby Corn with Assorted Vegetables   257
Baked Eggplant with Ricotta Cheese   283
Braised Cabbage in Wine   271
Braised Fennel Bulbs   272
Broccoli with Paprika Sauce   266
Broiled Vegetables on Skewers   260
Brussels Sprouts with Bacon   258
Caesar Asparagus   59
Carrots and Onions in Foil   261

Carrots with Parsnips in Honey   268
Cauliflower with Jack Cheese   253
Charred Garlic Peppers   37
Cold Julienne of Vegetables with Apples   35
Creamed Onions and Peppers   278
Deep-Fried Eggplant   255
Easy Beef and Vegetable Stew   194
Flageolets in White Wine and Tomatoes   281
French Peas with Lettuce   256
Fresh Artichokes   39
Fresh Green Beans Niçoise   279
Fresh Snow Peas with Apple   288
Fresh Spinach with Julienne of Sweet Peppers   291
Garlic Fried Tomatoes   259
Grilled Tomato Halves   272
Leeks Vinaigrette   49
Marinated Fresh Vegetables   267
Marinated Mushrooms   36
Marinated Rapini with Garlic   255
Marinated Scallops and Vegetable Brochettes   87
Mashed Yellow Turnips   284
Mexican-Style Vegetables   262
Mixed Vegetables with Ginger   252
Mushroom Rice Pilaf   249
Mushrooms with Fresh Herbs   290
Ratatouille   285
Sauerkraut with Apples   276
Sautéed Zucchini   269
Stuffed Eggplant   275
Tossed Vegetables with Sea Scallops   103
Tuna Spinach Pâté   112
Vegetables with Curry   293
Vegetables with Sun-Dried Tomatoes   270
Warm Navy Bean Salad   289
Zucchini with Garlic and Parmesan   281

VINAIGRETTES

Basic Oil and Vinegar Vinaigrette   65
Garlic Vinaigrette   66
Lemon Vinaigrette   66
Yogurt Vinaigrette   65

Recipe Index

Almond Cake with Cognac 326

Anchovy Butter 80

Apple Tartlets 339

Artichokes with Hollandaise Sauce 286

Asparagus with Cheese Sauce 265

Baby Corn with Assorted Vegetables 257

Baked Eggplant with Ricotta Cheese 283

Baked Potatoes Stuffed with Mushrooms 244

Baked Swordfish with Almonds 86

Balthazar Cake 297

Banana-Nut Cake 322

Bananas with Rum over Ice Cream 298

Barbecued Pork Cutlets and Tomatoes 200

Barbecued Spareribs 185

Basic Beef Stock 9

Basic Chicken Stock 8

Basic Crêpes 300

Basic Oil and Vinegar Vinaigrette 65

Basic Wild Rice 246

Beef Bourguignon 188

Beef Stroganoff 174

Beef Tournedos with Poivre Vert Sauce 195

Belgian Endive Salad 34

Braised Beef with Root Vegetables 170

Braised Cabbage in Wine 271

Braised Fennel Bulbs 272

Braised Rock Cornish Game Hens 143

Brandy Braised Whole Chicken 147

Bread Pudding 324

Broccoli with Paprika Sauce 266

Broiled Beef Tenderloin Shish Kebabs 190

Broiled Vegetables on Skewers 260

Brownie Date Loaf 329

Brussels Sprouts with Bacon 258

Cabbage Soup 12

Caesar Asparagus 59

Calf's Liver with Dijon 198

Caramel Custard 331

Carbonnade of Beef 218

Carrots and Onions in Foil 261

Carrots with Parsnips in Honey 268

Cashew Chicken with Grilled Peppers 140

Cauliflower with Jack Cheese 253

Celeriac Rémoulade with Shrimp 56

Charred Garlic Peppers 37

Cheese Sauce 265

Chicken and Vegetable Pot Pie 159

Chicken Chow-Mein 142

Chicken Cutlets 125

Chicken Dijonnaise 155

Chicken Fricassee 124

Chicken Gumbo and Rice 16

Chicken - Hunter Style 128

Chicken in White Wine with Ginger Root 132

Chicken Legs Paprika 134

Chicken Livers on Skewers 160

Chicken Livers with Bell Peppers 127

Chicken Livers with Mushrooms 153

Chicken Shish Kebabs 139

Chicken Wings with Curry 138

Chicken with Caramelized Apples 150

Chicken with Porcini Mushrooms 122

Chicken with Prunes 144

Chicken with Tomatoes and Olives 137

Chocolate Icing 344

Chocolate Marble Cake 341

Chocolate Quatre Quart 312

Chocolate Tart 335

Cod with Mashed Potatoes and Swiss Cheese 91

Cold Julienne of Vegetables with Apples 35

Cold Lettuce Soup 26

Cold Lobster and Shrimp 110

Cold Shrimp with Curry Dressing and Fruit 100

Country Veal Chops 201

Crab Patties 110

Cream Cheese Icing 336

Creamed Onions and Peppers 278

Cream of Fresh Asparagus 29

Creamy Cheesecake 328

Crêpes for Seafood 82

Crêpes with Chestnut Filling 300

Curried Vegetable Salad 53

Curry Sauce 293

Deep-Fried Eggplant 255

Deep-Fried Pork Tenderloin 207

Deep-Fried Smelts 76

Duck in Red Wine 162

Easy Beef and Vegetable Stew 194

Fettuccine à la Rouille 232

Fish Stock 10

Flageolets in White Wine and Tomatoes 281

Flaky Dough 342

French Peas with Lettuce 256

Fresh Artichokes 39

Fresh Beet Salad with Red Onion 56

Fresh Clam Chowder 25

Fresh Cod with Tomato Curry 116

Fresh Fillet of Sole with Mushrooms 84

Fresh Fruit Salad with Hot Sabayon 302

Fresh Green Beans Niçoise 279

Fresh Mussels in Salad 59

Fresh Sea Scallops au Gratin 102

Fresh Snow Peas with Apple 288

Fresh Spinach with Julienne of Sweet Peppers 291

Fresh Strawberry Tart with Kirsch 317

Frozen Almond Soufflé 320

Garden Bounty Soup 22

Garlic Butter 92

Garlic Croûtons 65

Garlic Fried Tomatoes 259

Garlic Potatoes with Rosemary 242

Garlic Vinaigrette 66

Gazpacho 31

German-Style Potato Salad 44

Ginger Fried Shrimp 81

Golden Raisin Boulders 325

Grilled Tomato Halves 272

Grilled Whole Mackerel with Herb Butter Sauce 70

Halibut and Potato Casserole 119

Halibut Steaks with Bell Peppers and Red Onion 77

Harvest Carrot Cake 336

Hearty Cod Stew 113

Hearty Sliced Beef and Rice Salad 48

Herb Butter Sauce 70

Hollandaise Sauce 286

Homemade Herb Mayonnaise 66

Hot Chocolate Sauce 306

Hot Curry Chicken with Coconut 149

Hot Sabayon 302

Hungarian Goulash   199
Key-Side Chicken   157
Lamb Chops with Fresh Tomatoes   173
Lamb Chops with Watercress   214
Lamb Shish Kebabs   211
Lamb Stew   181
Leeks Vinaigrette   49
Leg of Lamb with Potatoes   173
Lemon Bread Cake   310
Lemon Vinaigrette   66
Linguine with Quick Fresh Tomato Sauce   243
Little Butter Wafers   314
Lobster Newburg   88
Macaroni with Black Olives   239
Marinated Apple Slaw   44
Marinated Fresh Vegetables   267
Marinated Mushrooms   36
Marinated Rapini with Garlic   255
Marinated Scallops and Vegetable Brochettes   87
Marinade for Poultry   166
Mashed Yellow Turnips   284
Medallions of Veal Loin in Wine Sauce   182
Mexican-Style Vegetables   262
Minestrone Soup   21
Mixed Greens with Avocado Dressing   43
Mixed Vegetable Salad   63
Mixed Vegetables with Ginger   252
Mushroom and Herb Stuffed Beef Flank   186
Mushroom Rice Pilaf   249
Mushrooms with Fresh Herbs   290
Napa Broth Soup   14
New York Strip Steaks with Mushroom Sauce   176
Oatmeal Date Squares   303
Oatmeal Drop Cookies   299
Old-Fashioned Beef Soup   27
Open-Faced Rhubarb Pie   309
Orange Cookies   307
Orange Duck with Cranberries   131
Orange Icing   344
Oranges in Caramel   315
Osso Buco   192
Oysters au Gratin on the Half Shell   101
Pan-Fried Chicken with Peanut Sauce   148
Pan-Fried Potato Cakes   230
Paprika Sauce   266
Pasta Verdura   240
Pastry Cream   345

Peach Salad with Candied Ginger   308
Pear and Kiwi Pie   319
Pears in Sabayon   334
Pears with Chocolate Sauce and Almonds   306
Pickerel with Fresh Herbs   116
Pineapple Loaf Cake   338
Pineapple Pork Tenderloin   183
Pork Chops with Honey and Apples   210
Pork Shoulder Stew   175
Pork Tenderloin with Bordelaise Sauce   215
Pork with Roasted Bell Peppers   184
Potage à la Crécy   13
Potatoes Anna   236
Potatoes in Cream au Gratin   228
Potatoes Lyonnaise   234
Potatoes Sautéed with Leeks   227
Potato Galette   235
Pot-au-Feu   208
Purée of Brussels Sprouts   18
Quick Beef Stir-Fry   207
Quick Blueberry Pie   313
Quick Soy Chicken and Cabbage   167
Ratatouille   285
Red Snapper Cooked in Foil   73
Rib Roast - English Style   202
Rice with Fresh Herbs   231
Risotto   226
Roast Loin of Pork with Garlic and Onions   213
Roast Turkey Pasta Salad   55
Rolled Chicken Schnitzel with Prosciutto   161
Roquefort Salad   63
Rump Roast with Red Onion and Carrot   178
Saffron Rice   237
Salade Drolet   47
Salade Niçoise   41
Salmon Steaks Poached in White Wine   94
Sauerkraut with Apples   276
Sautéed Pickerel Fillets with Anchovy Butter   80
Sautéed Zucchini   269
Sauté of Chicken with Eggplant   154
Scallop and Mushroom Soup   24
Scampi au Gratin   92
Scampi with Julienne of Vegetables   96
Seafood and Rice   98
Seafood in Pastry   93
Seafood Salad with Roasted Bell Peppers   51

Seasonal Fruit Salad   60
Short Ribs Braised in Red Wine   221
Shrimp and Artichoke Bottoms   52
Shrimp and White Sauce Crêpes   83
Shrimp Cocktail   85
Soup Savoyarde   15
Spaghettini with Zesty Anchovy Sauce   247
Spaghetti with Garlic-Basil Purée   241
Spice Cake   318
Steamed Mussels with Cream Sauce   74
Steamed Mussels with Curry   79
Strawberry Glaze   317
Stuffed Eggplant   275
Stuffed Egg Roll Skins   109
Stuffed Fresh Clams   90
Stuffed Leg of Lamb   204
Suprême Sauce   166
Sweet and Tangy Chicken Wings   126
Thick Custard Cream   323
Tomato Bacon Salad   42
Tomato Halibut Steaks   105
Tossed Vegetables with Sea Scallops   103
Tropical Scampi   75
Trout with Capers   94
Tuna Spinach Paté   112
Turbot au Gratin   106
Turbot with Sun-Dried Tomatoes   114
Turkey Pot Pie Suprême   152
Turkey Vol-au-Vent Suprême   133
Upside-Down Peach Cake   304
Veal Blanquette   217
Veal Chops with Fresh Tarragon   191
Veal Chops with Tomatoes and Onions   222
Veal Scaloppine Island Sauté   219
Veal Scaloppine with Fresh Lemon   177
Veal Scaloppine with Mixed Vegetables   197
Vegetable and Lentil Soup   19
Vegetables with Curry   293
Vegetables with Sun-Dried Tomatoes   270
Vichyssoise   23
Viennese Crêpe Cake   332
Viennese Crêpes   332
Warm Navy Bean Salad   289
Watercress and Radicchio Salad   46
Whole Snapper with Spring Vegetables   97
Whole Trout with Green Grapes   107
Yogurt Vinaigrette   65
Zesty Marinated Chicken   164
Zucchini with Garlic and Parmesan   281

351